GAY PARENTS/ STRAIGHT SCHOOLS

Building Communication and Trust

GAY PARENTS/ STRAIGHT SCHOOLS

Building Communication and Trust

VIRGINIA CASPER • STEVEN B. SCHULTZ

Foreword by Louise Derman-Sparks

Based on a collaborative study by
Virginia Casper, Steven B. Schultz, and Elaine Wickens

Teachers College, Columbia University
New York and London

Published by Teachers College Press, 1234 Amsterdam Avenue, New York, NY 10027

Copyright © 1999 by Teachers College, Columbia University

Library of Congress Cataloging-in-Publication Data

Casper, Virginia.
    Gay parents/straight schools : building communication and trust / Virginia Casper, Steven B. Schultz ; foreword by Louise Derman-Sparks ; based on a collaborative study by Virginia Casper, Steven B. Schultz, and Elaine Wickens.
        p.   cm.
    Includes bibliographical references and index.
    ISBN 0-8077-3825-5 (cloth : alk. paper). — ISBN 0-8077-3824-7 (paper : alk. paper)
    1. Children of gay parents—Education—United States.   2. Gay parents—United States.   3. Gay-straight alliances in schools—United States.   I. Schultz, Steven B.   II. Title.
    LC5159.7.U6C37   1991
    371.825'4—dc21   99-24052

ISBN 0-8077-3824-7 (paper)
ISBN 0-8077-3825-5 (cloth)

Printed on acid-free paper

Manufactured in the United States of America

06   05   04   03   02   01   00   99   8   7   6   5   4   3   2   1

**To
our children Evan and Max
with love**

Foreword

The Republic of South Africa's new Constitution includes the fol[l]ing article in its Bill of Rights chapter: "The state may not unfairly criminate directly or indirectly against anyone on one or more grou[ps] including race, gender, sex, pregnancy, marital status, ethnic or s[ocial] origin, colour, *sexual orientation*, age, disability, religion, consci[ence,] belief, culture, language and birth" (emphasis added).[1] However, i[n our] own country, the right to equal protection for people who are g[ay or] lesbian remains a pawn of our cultural/political wars—and, in 1[997,] still does not exist for the most part. It is not only adults who [suffer] because of this continuing injustice. So too do the children being [raised] by gay and lesbian parents.

Openly talking about the realities and specific needs of [the] children and parents in gay- and lesbian-headed families has bee[n taboo] in early childhood education at worst and difficult at best. For t[oo long,] most early childhood educators have defined tolerance as "not [discussing] the subject." In practice, this course of nonaction really has [meant] ignoring the growing reality of children being raised by gay [and les]bian parents, and, regardless of intent, is harmful. When the[re is si]lence, teachers cannot enter into true partnership with gay and [lesbian] parents. Young children are forced to face alone their peers' [misinfor]mation, prejudice, and rejection in what are supposed to be [caring] and learning environments. Moreover, other children are gi[ven] permission to engage in hurtful behaviors directed at child[ren in] gay- and lesbian-headed families.

Gay Parents/Straight Schools: Building Communication [and Trust] breaks through the silence and the subjective, emotional, o[ften un]informed controversy. Based on the best kind of research t[hat seeks] information and perspectives from all of the people who a[re]

---

1. Constitutional Assembly. (1966). *Constitution of the Republic of [South Africa.]* Article #9(3), pp. 7–8.

the educational relationship—the children, the families, the teachers, the school administrators—it provides educators and parents with solid information, wise insights, and useful strategies. It explores the complexities and challenges, while also making clear our professional mandate to create educational environments that nurture the education of *all* children.

The authors of this brave, pioneering book overcame obstacles that might have defeated less committed individuals. It took them several years to find a publisher. Then, shortly before word came that Teachers College Press had agreed to take their book, Steve Schultz tragically died. Virginia Casper was faced with revising the manuscript on her own, a task made even more difficult by her grief for her co-author's death. Steve was an extraordinary human being and a gentle warrior for children and families, beloved and now mourned by all who lived or worked with him. This book's existence is a tribute not only to its authors but also to the support of colleagues, friends, and family who believed in its importance—and to Teachers College Press for publishing it.

I look forward with all my heart to a time when everyone—children and adults alike—truly will be able to experience the respect, dignity, equality, and justice to which all humans are entitled. This book is an essential contribution to achieving that dream.

Louise Derman-Sparks
Pacific Oaks College

Contents

Preface

Life has a way of interfering with many admirable plans, and in the case of this book, both life and death had their way. Steve Schultz was a driving force behind this project right up to his death on December 7, 1996, two days before I was notified by Teachers College Press of their interest in publishing our manuscript. Most of our research was finished by 1992, and about half the book was completed at the time of Steve's death. During the subsequent year and a half, I continued the conversations Steve and I used to have, but in my mind. On walks or at the computer I could envision his smile, or his measured but impassioned gestures. Often, mired in an editorial dilemma, I heard him suggest that I should do what I think best. Thus, although I have finished this book alone, it is the result of a quintessential writing partnership that, for me, forever has redefined the term *collaboration*.

Margaret Mead was fond of saying that a smiling baby can keep a mother from her writing as much as a crying one. *Gay Parents/Straight Schools* arrives just a few months shy of 10 years from the time Steven Schultz, Elaine Wickens, and I began a 3-year ethnographic study of the educational interactions of gay parents and their young children's educators. The changes in the world during the past decade have been monumental, but nonetheless we believe the essence of this book to be more relevant than ever. There were, of course, many times during the intervening years when we wished we could speed up the tempo of our work. Yet it is not just in the service of rationalization to say that this time was also a generous gift. During these years gay, lesbian, bisexual, and transgender issues were brought into the light of public examination, heralding significant civil rights victories as well as multiple backlashes of repression. This time afforded us rich opportunities to reflect on the truly reciprocal effects at work vis-à-vis societal and personal change. These changes deeply affected our lives, the lives of our colleagues at Bank Street College of Education, our graduate students, and our extended family and friends. These remarkable transformations were like a baby's smile in keeping us from our writing.

For many of the lesbian and gay parents we interviewed, these historic events intersected with their own development as parents. Some, who had concealed their sexual orientation at work, for example, suddenly found themselves explaining that they needed parental leave to take care of their newly adopted baby. Others, who did not come out to their child's teacher during the first year of school, did so the following year, saying they could no longer live a secret, regardless of the risk. A decade later, a few of these same individuals can be counted among the leaders in the gay and lesbian rights movement, either regionally or nationally. In short, this is a book about change.

ON LANGUAGE

Because of the patchwork of participation in the research project, it will help the reader to recognize the different voices and their meaning. When the first person singular is used, one of the two authors' names will be indicated in parentheses. When "we" is used it refers to Steven Schultz and Virginia Casper. When the three researchers from our original study are referenced, they will be referred to either by their names (Steve, Virginia, and Elaine), or simply "the research team."

There is more to be said about language. Throughout the text, the terms *lesbian*, *gay*, and *gay/lesbian* are interspersed. We have not used the more inclusive term *GLBT* (gay, lesbian, bisexual, and transgender), because our research focused on the growing and increasingly visible parent population who, at the time, identified themselves as lesbians and gay men. As well, the use of acronyms to refer to human beings is not a convention we relish. And the image of a hybrid plant comes to mind in response to the term *lesbigay*. We use the word *queer* when this gender-neutral stance is to be communicated to the reader. Although "queerness" represents an increasingly important point of view, especially within gay scholarship, it also reflects a sense of "outsider" insurgency in ways that are probably less than helpful to our goal of increased communication with the early childhood community, or our stated goals of education as a path toward a more inclusive democratic world. More often, we use the umbrella term *gay* to refer to both lesbians and gay men, because consistently referring to "lesbian- and gay-headed families" is quite unwieldy. When we use the term *gay* in its more selective sense, we indicate that we are referring to gay men or gay fathers.

OUR GOALS

In our work as a research team, we listened to and supported the feelings, ideas, and beliefs of lesbian and gay parents, as well the ideas, practices, and questions of school staff. With the voices of our informants at our side, it became our goal to unwrap and then to examine the intersection between gay parents and educators with an eye toward helping others catch a glimpse into their thoughts. Thus we are presenting the points of view of some lesbian and gay parents and some teachers and administrators to tell what they know in a way that might be useful for all parents and educators. In reporting these data here, we have changed the names and, in some cases, other identifying characteristics of the adults with whom we spoke and the children we observed.

We had a clear vision to write a book for both teachers and parents. From the beginning, convincing others of the importance of this dual audience was not easy, and it certainly made the writing process more challenging. Nevertheless, I believe that the important content is accessible to both groups and that subtle frames of reference from both cultures require demystification. It is my hope that through exposing both educators and parents to a wider range of experiences and perspectives, this book will facilitate greater and more effective dialogue between them.

In the course of our work, we have been asked, "What is your real agenda here, anyway?" What we think is meant by "real agenda" is some kind of hidden agenda, the idea that even prior to entering our work, we had already arrived at a set of conclusions. This distinction between hidden and overt is important. All people carry a system of values, a history of experiences, and a framework for organizing their world that must at some level infiltrate their thinking. As authors of this book, we are not exempt. We don't think that our values should be sterilized into a bland objective view of the stories of the people we studied. Our own views are most valuable, most honest, and most overt when they can be seen as integral parts of these stories. This requires, as do ethnographic methods, that our perspectives be clearly identified, both to ourselves and to the reader (Wilcox, 1982).

We recognize the ideas the research team held in common. We all came to this work with a strong belief that schools should help to create more equitable relationships than those that exist in the larger society. We believe educators can make choices to either create a classroom that *reflects* the present social values and practices or that *pro-*

motes more equitable relationships and values. Our conviction that all family forms should be respected underlies our approach to identifying and addressing bias against gay-headed families both within and outside the schools. Our values are embedded in "anti-bias" work (Derman-Sparks, 1989).

Thus, the most important aspects of our lives in relation to this work have to do with schooling, parenthood, and sexual orientation. Among the three researchers of the study team, two of us are gay or lesbian parents and one of us is heterosexual and not a parent. We are all educators of teachers, and, in the past, all three of us have worked with young children and families. Our backgrounds include working- and middle-class upbringings, and we have attended a range of public and independent schools. That our experiences are not identical is important because, in the course of collecting and interpreting the diverse stories you will read in this book, our varied lives enabled us to see through the eyes of both parents and educators whose differences were never just sexual orientation. We view our obvious commonalties as well as our clear differences as important strengths in our work together. The commonalties allowed us to work together as a team. Our differences kept us honest.

WHAT COMES NEXT

Chapter 1, "A Tentative Trust," lays a broad foundation for understanding why homosexuality is perceived as such a threat to the inherent goals of early childhood education when, in fact, it has such potential to enrich the worldviews of both children and adults. Our research methods are described here, so the reader may develop a better sense of the overall approach as well as the mechanics that frame our study.

In Chapter 2 we look at the role of children's experience as a crucial aspect of how they come to understand families. Specifically, we suggest that children's learning will be better served by adults asking, "What do these children know?" rather than simply relying on experts to indicate what is "developmentally appropriate" for all children to learn at given ages. Some excerpts of young children's conversations about family are put forward and analyzed to help adults gain a better sense of how to help children think about families in a meaningful way.

Chapter 3, "Adult Points of View," is based on the questions we asked educators about their first experiences with people who were different from themselves. Their stories paint a picture of the complicated feelings behind their thinking across a range of differences, but about gay-headed families in particular. We follow the notion of "difference" as it connects with the aspirations of gay and lesbian parents raising their children in a heterosexual society.

Chapter 4, "Disclosure: The Dance," gets to the heart of the study's findings. In Chapter 4, we use the dance as a metaphor for a communication process and trace the various ways in which families became known to schools as lesbian or gay. The thrust of our findings confirms our notion that disclosure is an endeavor in which both educators and families must jointly participate.

Chapter 5 has a somewhat paradoxical title: "Finding Gender." The chapter's contents ultimately reveal that we never really do find our gendered selves in the complete way this phrase might suggest. Rather, through a review of the literature interwoven with our informants' stories, we put forth the idea that gender identity, roles, and sexual orientation are sharply different yet highly linked issues that require a frame of reference that moves us across the entire life-span. We enter into this tangled topic by remembering the many conscious and unconscious ways in which classical theoretical foundations about gender development frame a large proportion of our ideas and feelings on these gender-related topics. This chapter also contrasts observations and ideas of educators and gay parents regarding gender-nonconformist play in young children. This in turn leads us to to consider how each group's values about homosexuality and young children can influence the group's thinking about the relative importance of same- and opposite-gendered role models in children's growth and development.

Chapter 6, "Classroom Life," presents a range of factors affecting the curriculum and offers examples of the ways some teachers have thought about and constructed inclusive approaches with children. We proceed from the notion that curriculum is a negotiation among the classroom participants, yet clearly is influenced by outside factors as well. The continuum of what different gay parents advocate in order to treat their children and themselves fairly and with respect is considered. While there is no formula here, some suggestions are given regarding how teachers, parents, and administrators can begin to plan for inclusive educational approaches that make sense within their particular school and community setting.

Chapter 7, "Beyond Gossip and Silence: Next Steps," reiterates our basic findings but offers our perspectives more directly. Specifically, as educators, we have strong beliefs about changes that need to be made in education from preschool through graduate education and on-the-job training and professional development. We offer some ways to promote reflection on personal feelings and professional practice that we believe can effect positive growth and change.

The stories of the adults and children you will read about give a textured grasp to their expressed points of view. Once voiced, many informants confided that they understood the etiology of their own attitudes much better than they did prior to the initial interview. We allowed ourselves to interpret the stories we became privy to in a rigorous yet restrained fashion. We also recognize that these stories might be interpreted differently by different readers. By sharing a little of us with you, we hope that you will have a better sense of our findings. Ultimately, of course, we hope you will interpret this work for yourselves.

Virginia Casper

Acknowledgments

The story of a book, like a life history, may be told from a number of vantage points. One aspect of this book is that its story is a long one. Its origins can be traced back to the late 1980s in the form of a teacher's question about how to respond to a first grader with two mothers. It wasn't long before an animated conversation in a Bank Street hallway, between Steven Schultz, Elaine Wickens, and myself, reformulated the question into a research project on lesbian- and gay-headed family–teacher communication.

From another vantage point, this book was launched in 1992 when Steven Schultz and I extended our writing partnership. Between 1994 and 1996 a very rough draft of this manuscript remained an unopened file in our computers and in our lives, as family, work, and illness pulled us in various directions. During this time a few people were relentless in urging us to get back to work, reminding us that there were many people who were waiting for us to finish. I especially thank two California colleagues, Louise Derman-Sparks and Catherine Thomas, for their vigilance in this regard. On the east coast, Sara Blackburn and Harriet Cuffaro were equally persistent. Sara, my editorial sage, not only insisted that I finish, but had the temerity to suggest that I have fun at it. Deriving pleasure from writing seemed like a worthy goal, but after Steve's death from AIDS in December 1996, it was a struggle to achieve. Steve's expansive intelligence, deep humanity, and measured pace tempered with a quick wit are missed daily.

Many colleagues, advisors and friends, shared in partnering me through the manuscript, especially: Nancy Balaban, Andy Boxer, Ed Corrigan, Harriet Cuffaro, Carol Lippman, the Schultz family, Pat Sherman, Edna Shapiro, Jonathan Silin, Buffy Smith, and Karen Zabriskie. At different points, the manuscript was read critically, in its entirety, by Margie Brickley, Jim Clay, Marilyn Figueroa, Aimee Gelnaw, Jim King, Edna Shapiro, Jonathan Silin, and Elaine Wickens. Specific chapters were critiqued by Linda Levine, Harriet Cuffaro, Caitlyn Ryan, and students in three Bank Street graduate school classes over the spring and summer of 1998. At various points, the Family Group, the Lesbian and Gay Research Group, the Wednesday night reading group, and my friends and family have sustained and extended my thinking in significant ways. Over the years, I have come to depend on Donna Futterman's encouragement and enduring love. This was especially important during the months when there were two books gestating in our household.

In addition, many individuals went out of their way to provide specific resources that helped me move along in this extended process, especially Robin Abeshaus, Lisa Barish, Betsy Blatchly, Nora Gaines, Linda Greengrass, Kay Halle, Nancy Klein, Carla Poole, Pat Wasley, and David Wolkenberg. So while many people made invaluable contributions to the creation of this book, I, as author, accept full responsibility for its content. At Teachers College Press, Faye Zucker provided helpful support and advice in the initial stages, as did Susan Liddicoat in the latter stages, through her masterful editing and guidance. Elaine Wickens, always alert to important questions, was the lightning rod for the study that she, Steve, and I conducted. Without her ideas, spirit, and questions, this book would not exist.

A number of institutions also have been extremely supportive. During the 1997–98 academic year, I received a writer's grant from Bank Street College of Education, which enabled me to work on the manuscript in lieu of teaching a course. In 1990 and 1991, the Paul Rapoport Foundation generously granted funds to enable us to continue our research. And it was through Center Kids, in New York City, that we initially contacted a number of our informants.

Personally, I am extremely grateful for the opportunity to have been a part of this endeavor, in both its solitary and collective dimensions. Learning how to write alone provided me with the remarkable opportunity of "writing to learn" (Greene, 1995). Through our collaborative interplay, Steve, Elaine, and I were able to give each other what Vera John-Steiner (1998) refers to as the "gift of confidence" to move forward with our ideas.

The biggest thanks go to the parents, teachers, and administrators who allowed us to interview, probe, and record them. They generously opened their lives, and freely and sometimes unexpectedly shared their feelings, ideas, hopes, and concerns. They gave us their stories, and pieces of their lives and work. To the extent that this book will be found useful to parents and educators, we acknowledge that it was the rich information that these individuals entrusted to us that made it possible. We are grateful for their generosity.

GAY PARENTS/
STRAIGHT SCHOOLS

Building Communication and Trust

CHAPTER 1

A Tentative Trust

I think it's important as a teacher to trust all different kinds of families and to believe in the strength of family as people who live together, work together, to raise kids, in whatever sort of combination they happen to be. I don't think it's something I could just tell to a teacher. I think it's something they have to come to believe themselves.
—Cathy, public school kindergarten teacher

When parents send their young children to school, they entrust the children to their teachers' care. Trust between parents and teachers, as with any human alliance, takes time and commitment to cultivate, a truism that is underscored for children and adults alike, especially in the first few weeks of school.[1]

For gay parents, schools embody the socializing heterosexual world. This causes degrees of conflict and anxiety even among the most forthright parents who may appear bold as they advocate for their children. From the vantage point of educators, the increasing visibility of gay-headed families inserts homosexuality smack into the historically protected world of young children.

What about the children themselves? The experience of being part of a family is specific and personal and yet one to which almost everyone can relate. Thinking about family is an essential way for young children to express their identity and love relationships. Thus, learning about families is central to most early childhood curricula in this country. During the course of a day in school, young children share and play out evolving concepts of families from the world in which they live. All children beginning school suddenly find themselves in a

---

1. The use of the term *school* here is an inclusive one, referring to all and any programs of early care and education. Throughout the book, finer distinctions are made between elementary schools vs. child care, play group, nursery school, and Head Start programs, for example, each of which tend to engage children and parents in different ways.

structured, highly choreographed group setting with other children who are their developmental peers, but who bring a variety of personal and family characteristics that afford a wider and richer world experience. Children who have been raised from their first years by their gay and lesbian parents are now side by side in classrooms with children representing a range of other family constellations. For them, it is these more "traditional" families that represent difference. When we as adults talk about a "rapidly changing world," we must remember for whom this is more and less true. Many young children have never known a world without lesbian- and gay-headed families.

Yet for most adult Americans, gayness evokes thoughts of sexuality or pathology and thus provokes feelings in teachers and responses in children that most adults prefer not to address. Nevertheless, within this nest of converging ideas and values, most teachers want the parents of children in their classrooms to be able to trust them, as teachers, to make reasonable decisions about the curriculum for their children. Throughout this book, our voices join those of our informants to explore *why* the trust between lesbian and gay parents and their children's educators has been so tentative and, more important, what each of us can do to promote better communication and more truly inclusive formal learning environments for children.

Beyond the hospital nursery or the adoption agency, school is the first significant institution parents have a large stake in successfully negotiating. Of necessity, school and home are cut from different cloth, yet there must be common threads connecting them for children and families to grow and flourish. It is crucial that differences in socialization and teaching practices between school and home be recognized (Lightfoot, 1978). Negotiating school entry in a manner that serves the child's needs and helps parents work through their own feelings is a constant challenge. Teachers and parents must know something substantive about each other in order to really communicate, and they must communicate in order to know it. These important interactions evoke the image of a dance: the intricate nuanced coordination between the concerns and realities of homelife and the demands and values of the school in society. By definition, the issues and needs of young children require that infant/toddler and early childhood teachers be in more intimate and potentially complicated relationships with parents than the relationships required of teachers of older children. Trust and communication are the nuts and bolts of such partnerships, but not unlike arranged marriages (Scradnick, 1998), the strangers need some time to become aquainted and even then the long-term success of the relationship is uncertain.

In its function as a "normalizing community" (Carlson, 1997), the American educational system has long kept the gay world outside the schoolhouse gate. And while a movement has grown steadily around gay issues in education for teenagers—Project 10 in Los Angeles, the work of the Massachusetts Governor's Commission, and organizations such as the Gay Lesbian Straight Education Network (see resource list in Appendix A)—the field of early childhood remains a last stronghold against the inclusion of gay issues. Gay- and gender-based taunting can be heard from the mouths of first and second graders in schools across this country and is but a precursor to the queer-bashing and hate crimes that begin as early as junior high school. But as gay culture becomes more pervasive in the world, and the gay movement becomes increasingly visible and effective, heterosexual adults appear to be more concerned than ever about young children's exposure to gender-atypical ideas or anything perceived to be associated with homosexuality.

WHO ARE LESBIAN- AND GAY-HEADED FAMILIES?

Naturally, there cannot be a singular answer to this question. But characterizing lesbian- and gay-headed families as representing a rich diversity of family structures and beliefs is the best place to begin. The fact is, we are a sorting species (Minow, 1997). The problems lie, not so much in categorizing, but in doing so superficially and mechanistically. Our overlapping identities reflect the complex times in which we live, as do our attempts to sort through and make meaning of them. When we refer to ourselves or others within a single historical, social, or economic frame—as being *either* gay or Asian American or middle-class or elderly or male—we are dimly aware that one descriptor is always insufficient. In reality, of course, we have multiple aspects to our identities; all of us fit into a multitude of contexts, although we each might assign different weights to our gender, class, race, ethnicity, and sexual orientation.

Sources of Information

It is important to see these identity contexts as gay people themselves interact with them. In order to do so, we must ask ourselves, *"What are our sources of information about others?"* Does a teacher assume how a gay father weights his identities based on the straight media's portrayal of gay men, or does she attempt to discover what *he* most values for his child? Likewise, it is important to balance gay issues with those faced by other people who are variously perceived as "different," and not assume how they weight their overlapping identities. We view the experiences of the parents we interviewed as cogent examples of how "difference" distinguishes us from each other, while it holds the *potential* to link us all as human beings. *How* all adults and children understand and enact their identities profoundly affects what our shared humanity makes possible.

So much of our understanding of others is shaped by information and generalizations that are outside our immediate control. Who gay people and parents are is a prime example. Because the lesbian and gay population in this country is still at least partially hidden, it is difficult to even know exactly how many gay- and lesbian-headed families exist. Estimates range from 2 million to 8 million lesbian and gay parents who have between 4 million and 14 million children (Patterson, 1992, 1995a). In 1994 it was estimated that 10,000 children were being raised by lesbians who became pregnant through alternative insemination (Singer & Descamps, 1994), and that number continues to grow. Two separate studies have attempted to compare the *percentages* of lesbians and gay men raising children with the percentages of heterosexual men and women parents. One study conducted by Yankelovich Associates (Lukenbill, 1995) found the percentages to be comparable—with 31% of lesbians and 23% of gay men found to be parenting children, compared with 37% of heterosexual women and 33% of heterosexual men. Another sample, based on exit poll figures, was used by a labor economist to construct another set of comparison figures. She found 67% of lesbians and 72% of heterosexual women lived with children under the age of 18 (Badgett, 1994), although the figures comparing gay and straight fathers in this sample were not equivalent. Framing the data with percentages, not only absolute numbers, leads the consumer of these data to think about lesbian- and gay-headed families in a parallel relationship to heterosexual families.

In spite of these figures, it has taken a long time for gay families to be incorporated into the explosion of academic analyses of the American family. Only as recently as the mid-1990s were chapters on lesbian and gay parents included in edited books on family and parent development (Arendell, 1997; Gottfried & Gottfried, 1994; Lamb, 1997). Although some important work has examined the wide diversity within the North American gay and lesbian communities (Blumenfeld & Raymond, 1988; Carlson, 1997; D'Augelli & Patterson, 1995; Greene, 1997; Herdt & Boxer, 1993; Lewin, 1998; Savin-Williams & Cohen, 1996; Sears, 1991) and there are anthologies of lesbian family narratives (Arnup, 1995; Pollack & Vaughn, 1987), even the queer academic world has not taken the lead in documenting or describing the incredible diversity in lesbian- and gay-headed families.

Another example concerns myths about gay people and social class. The research on gay-headed families has focused almost exclusively on a middle-class population. When the "gayby boom" is presented in the media, there is a presumption that it is a new phenomenon that is a by-product of modern technology, along with a relaxing of adoption regulations that are utilized mostly by middle-class lesbians and gay men. Eager to invite gay-headed families to appear on talk shows and to feature them in mainstream popular magazines, the media tends to present lesbian- and gay-headed families as exclusively White, middle-class professionals. We know these premises to be incorrect but they are widely accepted as the truth. Labor economist Lee Badgett (1997) has shown that much of the data about gay-headed family incomes is derived from marketing research samples that are quite biased. According to Badgett's work, gay men actually make 11 to 27% less than heterosexual men in comparable jobs. Lesbians were cited as earning 5 to 14% less than heterosexual women.

Historically, people have had a range of sexual behaviors that today would be described as lesbian or gay. There is evidence that this has been so throughout Europe since at least the Early Middle Ages (Boswell, 1980), and, for example, in many Native American Indian communities (Schultz, 1993; Williams, 1986) certain men who engaged in homosexual relations—called the "berdache" by Western anthropologists—frequently raised children. Today, we, along with others (Clausen, 1999) hope that adult sexuality may be constructed in increasingly fluid ways. In parts of Europe, for example, there is less of a dichotomous pull to be *in* one identity or another; bisexuality is more of an accepted part of everyday life. Lesbians and gay men have always had children, even if the terms *gay* or *lesbian* may not have been in use. The suppression of these facts is but a chapter in a history of societal repression of behaviors that are seen to challenge the accepted norms. Gay parents have always represented a range of diverse social, ethnic, and economic class backgrounds, as do any other group of parents. What we believe *is* new is the gay political movement, which has created a fresh openness and visibility, and therefore a larger number of gay men and lesbians are having children with greater premeditation.

Community Issues: Diversity and Identity

As gay and lesbian adults come to parenting in conscious and varied ways, diversity is evidenced in their range of family structures: from nuclear, to extended and blended step-parent families, to communal living. A brother and sister being raised by two gay foster fathers in rural Oklahoma have a discrete experience being part of a gay-headed family; it is certainly different, in so many ways, from that of the son of an urban single lesbian mother who chose to become pregnant with the help of an unknown sperm donor. Adults who were married and raised children to various points of development before coming out, bring yet other experiences and frames of reference to their children's blended family experience.

And as a wave of "divorces" and separations have surfaced among lesbian-headed families across the country, these families must endure the wrenching pain experienced by straight families, but without the mediating influence of courts, which mandate the rights and responsibilities of most parenting adults. Inside the lesbian community, some argue that mediation within that community respects the integrity of lesbian and gay unions, while others insist that state-sanctioned involvement is the only way to achieve more secure resolutions, especially concerning the welfare of children (Benkov, 1994; Galst, 1998). Teachers already know how parental conflict and divorce affect young children in the classroom. The complications that can arise over parental conflicts about biological and nonbiological ties can be extremely threatening to young children, and teachers can play an important role if they have good working relationships with the family.

Regardless of the exact way in which gay people have children, some see an inherent pull away from traditional American notions of kinship in which, truly, "love makes a family" more than biological ties (Weston, 1991). Others emphasize that the experience of motherhood, for example, transcends any difference approach that lesbianism might hold (Lewin, 1993).

Within the lesbian and gay community, there is a series of debates about which behaviors/rights tend to assimilate gay individuals into heterosexual America and which move them in the direction of a sharper gay identity and greater freedoms. Formidable controversy has centered, for example, around the importance of legalizing gay marriage (Ettelbrick, 1993; Stoddard, 1993) and ways to consider gay men's sexual rights in the face of AIDS (Rotello, 1997; Smith, 1998a). Although quieter than these more public debates, discussions within the gay and lesbian parenting world focus on the ways in which raising children also function to assimilate gay adults into mainstream America and/or queer the heterosexual world of family. In fact, one doesn't have to look too deeply into any current issue in gay America without coming across this basic tension between assimilation and resistance (Vaid, 1995).

Akin to the institution of marriage, there is a built-in conservatizing effect of becoming a parent, and gay parents have a range of thoughts and feelings about this. In a 1992 *Boston Globe* interview (Jacobs, 1992), Edward Calderon-Melendez, a gay man with two children, reflects his views about assimilation.

> I don't have a white picket fence out there . . . but I have just about everything else. Aside from not being a heterosexual, there's nothing different from me and the married couple across [the] street. (p. 5)

Many of our parent informants reflected this desire to be viewed just like the family across the street. But beneath this vantage point was an awareness that by definition gay-headed families do challenge conventional family forms; that being a lesbian mother, for example, is in itself an act of resistance. Some felt a sense of unity with other "nontraditional" family structures that also challenge the norm. By their very existence, all these family configurations call into question certain fundamental givens about what can be considered "normal." The proliferations of families that include two mothers and a father, three fathers, or two fathers, a grandmother, and an uncle, for example, ask: "What do children need in a family?" "What are the myriad ways in which children can feel loved and attached to others, achieve a sense of self, and develop caring feelings toward others?"

WHAT DOES THE RESEARCH CONTRIBUTE?

There are a few bodies of research literature that can provide a background to our thinking about the education of young children with respect to gay-headed families. These data come from the independently situated fields of developmental psychology and education, each of which tends to have different methods of inquiry and assumptions about children and families. It is important to understand the different lenses of each discipline and approach before using the data to inform work with children.

To date, examinations from the field of education about the impact of gayness on young children, their education, and their families, have been limited to a few articles, with either a research (Casper, Cuffaro, Schultz, Silin, & Wickens, 1996; Casper, Schultz, & Wickens,

1992; Hornstein, 1996; Lipkin, in press) or a practical focus (Brickley, Gelnaw, Marsh, & Ryan, 1998; Clay, 1990; Corbett, 1993; Koerner & Hulsebosch, 1996; Wickens, 1993). The traditionally conservative field of child development (*developmental psychology*) has begun to include research on gay-headed families and the mental health of their children (Flaks, Ficher, Masterpasqua, & Joseph, 1995; Lamb, 1997; Patterson, 1992; Tasker & Golombok, 1997), providing data that have been instrumental in helping (especially) lesbian mothers maintain the custody of their children in the legal system.

The first wave of research reported in the child development literature was conducted on lesbian-headed families during the 1970s and early 1980s. This body of work demonstrated that children raised by lesbians are as mentally healthy as those raised by heterosexual single mothers (Flaks et al., 1995; Golombok, Spencer, & Rutter, 1983; Hoeffer, 1981; Kirkpatrick, Smith, & Roy, 1981). The research of the later 1980s and 1990s focused on the children of gay men and lesbians who came out *before* beginning families. Building on earlier research, this second wave of studies replicated the mental health findings but also began to investigate the subtle differences presented by children being raised by lesbian or gay parents, not just similarities with their heterosexually reared peers (Chan, Raboy, & Patterson, 1998; Patterson, 1992, 1995a, b; Patterson, Hurt, & Mason, 1998; Steckel, 1985; Tasker & Golombok, 1997).

The quantitative research methods used in the field of psychology and child development examine a *phenomenon* (lesbian and gay parenting) and its *sequelae* (mental health of the children) in a more distanced manner than does most educational research. Educational research that draws on anthropological and sociological methods tends to be more field-based and applied. Moreover, psychological research on gay parenting has focused solely on middle-class populations. Within the field of education there have not been any studies of lesbian- and gay-headed families, but there is a growing tradition of qualitative methods of inquiry about young children and families across socioeconomic backgrounds (Heath, 1983; Lubeck, 1985; Miller, 1982; Rogoff, 1990; Thorne, 1993).

BECOMING A PARENT AND FACING THE WORLD

The experience of becoming a parent is a powerfully evocative time of life, a moment that never really ends, but keeps changing, in its capacity to provide both exhilarating and exhausting moments. As it opens up new and renewed issues for growth and engagement, becoming a parent also carries tremendous responsibilities. Although the research of the past 30 years demonstrates that babies come into the world equipped with a variety of skills and abilities that allow them to be active organizers of and participants in their world (Brazelton, 1973; Stern, 1985), the survival of an infant is still in the hands of her parents. New parents must negotiate both their new role as parents—parent*hood*—as well as the intimacy and interpersonal relationships involved in parent*ing* (Michaels & Goldberg, 1988; Shanok, 1991).

Soon after the abrupt transition of birth or adoption, most parents find themselves searching for a "fit" among their new identity as parents and their values. As at any other time in our lives when a role changes, entering parenthood modifies the way we view other parts of ourselves. I (Steven) can offer a particular example of this process when I became a parent. A prided part of my self-identity prior to parenthood was my punctuality. But immediately after adopting Max, and for some time thereafter, the multiple demands of caring for an infant caused me to be chronically late to all my appointments and activities. To become known as—and to accept myself as—a "late person" was but one difficult new behavior to incorporate into my larger identity. This relatively mundane example opens the door to imagine the range of possible feelings experienced by new lesbian and gay parents, for whom there is little societal approval.

Theories about the general coming-out process (incorporating and communicating a gay or lesbian identity) now abound (Cohen & Savin-Williams, 1996; Herdt & Boxer, 1993; Ryan & Futterman, 1998; Troiden, 1989), but less thought has gone into the specific adjustments lesbians and gay men must go through in their transition to parenting in a heterosexual world, as Al explains.

> So there's a whole new way of life that opens up for you. My mother relates to me at a different level now. What do you talk about with your mother as a single gay male? Not really much, unless you talk about a couch for the living room, or gossipy things about family members. My mother is much more involved in our lives. She's a grandmother, and she really enjoys it. It's interesting, but . . . before I had the kids, I would go to them [family of origin] and all they would talk about was the kids. It was kind of lonely after a while, listening about their kids, their kids, their kids. I found out that after we had ours, all we did was talk about the kids. So we fit right in with them. And it wasn't the gay issue, it was the family issue. We had something in common. Our single friends had

very little in common with us now. So there has been a change. We were included in a whole other realm. Now we were with our family in terms of meeting new friends who also were gay and had children. Also, the disco days were over, and I haven't been to a movie for 2 years.

Al gives us a sense of the shifting alliances he and his partner experienced. As gay men with three young foster children, they were accepted with open arms into their families of origin. An exploratory study has found that such acceptance is more widespread than rejection (Patterson, Hurt, & Mason, 1998) but is usually not taken for granted, given the profound sense of loss experienced by those who have been "excommunicated" from their families of origin. And consider the highly charged nature of this time in the lives of new lesbian and gay parents, who face the majority opinion that they are not even fit to be parents, simply because of their sexual orientation. It makes sense that disclosure would be one of the aspects of identity formation shared by gay people regardless of their parenting status, but the consequences of disclosing one's sexual orientation to one's child's teacher or pediatrician clearly have an impact on a wider circle of people and are threatening in different ways from the consequences of coming out within a single adult's life perimeter.

Adult Development

Classical developmental theory supports the notion of parenthood as a key stage in adult life (Erikson, 1950). But unlike in Erik Erikson's time, becoming a parent is now defined less as a stage of development (adult maturation is not formative in the way it is for children) than as a marker process in which one changes through one's relations with others (Seligman & Shanok, 1995; Shanok, 1991). We appreciate how this revised definition of parenthood fits with a more open notion of adulthood, in which raising children can be seen as an option, not a requirement. As well, Erikson's work and the zeitgeist up until that period viewed homosexuality as evidence of unsatisfactory completion of early stages of development, and this notion persists in many psychological forms. Perhaps the most insidious attitude remains nested in thousands of parents' feelings about their gay adult children, whom they view as "perpetual adolescents" (McGoldrick, 1989a), even when the children hold responsible jobs, have committed relationships, and (may) have children of their own.

Even without children, gay and lesbian adults/families have a range of particularly difficult identity issues to process (Slater & Mencher, 1991), as they attempt to live a full life within their marginalized status in the world. Homophobia, from within and without, follows lesbians and gay men throughout life. People deal with these infringements and oppressions by creating various survival strategies for managing a "spoiled identity" (Goffman, 1963). The risks of coming out in the workplace or within one's family of origin remain high in all but a few enclaves, the viability and authenticity of same-gender relationship rarely is taken seriously, and social networks and supports don't just fall into place without significant and conscious efforts being made to create them.

The transition to parenthood opens the door to memories of one's own childhood. Increasingly, professional literature on families reflects a strong emphasis on the intergenerational aspects of our development. Understanding oneself in relation to past familial patterns of care and values creates a clear window for a self-aware outlook on one's present functioning and future endeavors. Recent psychological theory (Karen, 1994; Main, 1991; Stern, 1985) suggests that what actually occurred in our childhood is less likely to influence our interpersonal patterns than how we have reflected on those early experiences and what we have gleaned from such introspection. New parents often describe how these first years offer them a renewed empathy with their own parents, or at least some new insights. Others go through intense self-grilling, wondering whether it makes sense to tell elderly family members they are having a child as a gay-identified person, often erring on the side of overprotection (Pies, 1985). At the same time, it is important to consider that an intergenerational view pinpoints the seemingly obvious fact that lesbian- and gay-headed families experience their gay family as set apart, in at least this one dimension, from their heterosexual family of origin and the unknown future sexual orientation of their children. Reflecting on the family-specific implications of this simple point can lead to other questions, across a range of parenting issues, that may prove helpful for families to pursue.

For many parents of gay adult children, the news of forthcoming grandchildren makes them readdress their (adult) children's coming-out process anew (Martin, 1993). While for most the more basic desire for grandchildren usually wins out, there are a few who never sufficiently resolve their conflicts and fears to be able to take on the grandparenting role. Yet grandparents who are close (geographically and personally) often take on a role in the care of their grandchildren, if only on occasions. In such cases, grandparents are brought into the extended family life and have greater opportunities to demystify what gay family life is about. The findings from a small exploratory study (Patterson, Hurt, & Mason, 1998) on children's contact with grandparents and other adults, counter the stereotype that children of the lesbian baby boom are isolated from their parents' families of origin. The data also support anecdotal reports that these children have access to adult men in their lives as well as women with whom a parent had a previous romantic relationship. By going beyond research questions that look for similarities between children raised in straight and in gay- or lesbian-headed families, such studies are leading the way in helping us gain a better sense of what it truly is like to be raised by lesbian mothers or gay fathers.

Families Go Public

Aside from one's own changing adult identity, new parents are quickly sensitized to the extent to which even complete strangers feel authorized to comment on aspects of their parental behaviors, from how warm the baby is kept, to the best method employed to transport him, and the modes of feeding and clothing chosen. Aggravated by a general lack of parental preparedness in our society, the simplest of suggestions can fall on hypersensitive ears; direct criticism can feel like an assault. We believe that building confidence concerning one's parenting knowledge and abilities should be one of the primary goals of early childhood programs. This confidence-inspiring perspective is especially important for first-time parents who may look to educators for guidance either along with or instead of the advice of relatives and neighbors.

As infants, toddlers, and 2-year-olds become 3- and 4-year-olds, the parent–child relationship enters the spotlight of the public arena, especially for those children entering more formal learning environments. Even for children who previously attended child-care or infant/toddler socialization programs, the exclusiveness of the parent–child relationship is invaded by a whole new set of friends, teachers, and other school staff. The world of early education and care—child care, play groups, Head Start, nursery, pre-K, and elementary school programs—exposes the privacy of the family to a more public domain. At the same time, the child frequently displays strong feelings about being separated from his or her parents and placed in a group of new children and new adults. But it is not just the child who has strong feelings at this time. As Nancy Balaban (1985) describes in *Starting School: From*

Separation to Independence, "It is not possible to understand a child's feelings without simultaneously acknowledging the parent's feelings. School entry is a significant event for both" (p. 6).

Parents may sense a loss of control over which people and what situations their children will encounter. They, too, are at the threshold of new social networks that will affect their family's development. And teachers are not exempt from the September "willies." They also have expectations and anxieties about what the coming year may bring. Whatever the mix of confidence and anxiety about the prospects for the coming year, both teachers and parents have their own memories of school that contribute to their notions of what school is/should be, and therefore affect how they guide children through it. Some teachers and administrators have strong feelings about what for them may be an unfamiliar or even strange family constellation. They face tremendous obstacles as they begin to transcend these feelings, obstacles constructed by personal experience or political or religious convictions. Others have had experiences that place lesbian or gay parents in a natural light. And of course, some teachers and administrators are themselves lesbian, gay, or bisexual.

Parental Goals

Helping children understand all kinds of differences as an integral aspect of their learning enriches us as individual parents and teachers, and can positively shape classroom life. It is only when distinct values are placed on these different human characteristics that difficulties arise. Clearly, all parents want the "best" for their children, but their perceptions of what is "best" couldn't be more varied.

Anthropologist Robert LeVine (1974) describes the ways in which parents' goals for their children change depending on economic and environmental factors. Parents who must raise their children in hazardous environments work toward their offsprings' physical survival. There is little time or energy to spend on matters that press less persistently on their lives, and indeed these goals make little sense given the context in which they live. Parents who live in safer environments, where economic, physical, and social needs are met, expand the goals they have for their children to include such qualities as "fulfillment" and "happiness." They focus on issues of self-esteem and self-concept because they are not consumed with providing the simple basics of survival. So it is that issues of whether or not to disclose become more immediately relevant for parents who are not faced with a myriad of other mitigating factors in their lives (see Chapter 4).

First-time parents today can appear to have too many options, especially when compared with the parents of earlier times or more homogeneous communities, where everyone simply followed common childrearing patterns and advice. Because parents face so many possible choices today, many need help in formulating and articulating what their parenting values and goals really are. The endless number of guides to parenthood published over the past 50 years, which have expressed such wide and conflicting "expert" opinions, may be helpful at times, but also have weighed heavily on how parents view themselves and their parenting choices.

Yet exposure to some different values in ways that do not overwhelm can be transformative for parents. How many traditional nuclear family values have we endorsed simply because we have not considered the possibility that other values may exist, or given thoughtful consideration to what children derive from these values and ways of behaving? Examining other cultures helps us to see that the human condition does not prescribe a single best set of family practices. The Efe' people's custom of multiple mothering, for example, highlights the tremendous strengths promoted in children who receive the love and attention of a community of people from birth through adulthood (Tronick, Morelli, & Ivey, 1992). These practices make exquisite sense for the more community-minded Efe' culture. By contrast, along with other factors, the differently inspired, but parallel, multiple caregiving in American child-care centers has created a few decades of controversy because we, as a culture, place more value on dyadic relationships and nuclear families. Within America there are many variations of parental goals that can be distinguished by subculture, community, family, and individual parent, just as there are similar practices that parents share, but with different root goals. Taking the time to understand these roots helps both parents and educators move toward better communication with each other and the children in their lives.

Manuel, a single gay father, lives in the same neighborhood in which he grew up and attended the same public schools to which he initially sent his sons. As a child, he appears to have closely observed the relationships between parents and teachers. He has used some of this important information to recast his own ideas vis-à-vis his sons' education, insisting on full participation.

> There was "The teacher is God, we don't ask questions." Especially when you're dealing with a lot of single women, a lot of poor women, Latina and African American women . . . there's fear there. And I think a lot of the problem was the language barrier, and

parents who spoke English but were not comfortable with the language, . . . and I said, "That won't happen to me!" From the beginning my approach has been . . . I go in there when the child goes in there. When my son is in school, I'm also in school.

We may not be privy to Manuel's most basic parental goals, but we are aware that he strongly values education. His comment illuminates the multiple influences at work in the creation of just one parental objective: to take his child's education seriously and not be intimidated by teachers. Manuel also is a clear example of an adult who, through reflection, was able to alter a familiar parenting pattern from his own childhood.

Manuel is a prime example of a single gay man who would not be stymied. But many gay families are thwarted, made to feel invisible, or shut off, in subtle or obvious ways. We saw how this was operant among educators who expressed some version of a "mind your own business" point of view. In straight America, speaking up about who you are so people do acknowledge differences is, too often, called "flaunting it." But consider how any culturally different minority group of parents must feel when surrounded by a majority that tends to hold mainstream ideas of what is acceptable in a parent. Schools can and should more often be places where parents and educators can learn from each other. The intersection of home and school can offer parents help with formulating and articulating their parental goals. Teachers, too, have much to learn about the many different ways in which children are raised. Engaging in clear and open conversations is a good place to begin, but it also helps to understand the basic historical and political landscape.

EDUCATION FOR CHANGE

Schools, as microcosms of a society (Dewey, 1900/1956), can be created to promote fair relationships among people in the classroom setting. The challenge for educators is twofold here. It is to legitimize the lives of all children, regardless of race, gender, class, culture, and ability levels, and, certainly, even more challenging, to help children themselves become activists for this change. The point of view expressed throughout this book seeks to bring the education of children from lesbian- and gay-headed families within the scope of this larger educational project that seeks to change, not simply mirror, our society.

Given the ebbs and flows of school reform during the past 150 years, the functions of education have not maintained a single direction. Even within a single historical period, it is clear that there are multiple forces tugging at the influences of schooling on young children. Constructing a common value system and assimilating different values, practices, and customs into the dominant set have mingled with the goals of helping children and adults to attain power and freedom through knowledge and an understanding of the ways they can act in the world.

We are hoping for a world that defines lesbian and gay identity as one of a variety of ways to express close feelings and engage in intimate relationships with others. This world is far from the one we live in today. Our world is enveloped by an atmosphere of discrimination, with its attendant consequences of guilt, fear, and hatred. It shouts at parents and children to keep their lives secret. It often puts at severe risk the jobs of teachers who build inclusiveness of all kinds into their curriculum. Even when lesbian and gay parents are determined to lead open lives, and especially as children grow, becoming more aware of the consequences of discrimination, a few may sway, although not necessarily bend, to the weight of peer pressure.

An unjust world can never be an excuse for our own unjust practices, but it is a reality that illuminates the myriad levels of struggle that are required in order to effect change. Given the current realities of the world we live in, it is not the *fait accompli* that is most important, but the act of entering the process toward change. Within this process of change, both parents and teachers often can find pockets of acceptance, openings for inclusion; these vital spaces may be classrooms, a specific teacher, an entire school, or certain enclaves or networks established in concert with others.

For the last 2 decades of the twentieth century, emphasis on multicultural and inclusive education has been a significant part of this larger work in process. Some goals have arisen that are specific to the times, such as finding ways to provide a relevant quality education to the growing numbers of immigrant children, inclusive educational opportunities for children with special needs, and effective and inclusive methods of instruction for bilingual students, to name but a few. The overarching and integral goals of equity and social justice have their roots in earlier progressive movements (Banks, 1993; Sleeter, 1996). As we move into the twenty-first century, educators are working hard to reconstruct progressive education in ways that have meaning for American public education. A clear example can be seen in attempts to move beyond the "enrichment" approach built on a construct of deficit and disadvantage during the 1960s, to develop methods of assessment and instruction that are more equitable and responsive to individual needs.

It also has become clear during these past 20 years that curricula that are multicultural can be used in the service of either assimilation or plurality. We believe that educators and parents must take close looks at the aims of specific curricula in order to move beyond a simplistic assumption that all is well with the world as soon as the label "multicultural" is attached to their children's curriculum, as is sometimes reflected in whirlwind classroom tours of the food or dress of far-away cultures (Derman-Sparks, 1989).

Increasingly, too, educators seek to understand the vantage point from which they live and teach. At the same time, teachers are beginning to appreciate that they need to know more about children's lives outside of school in order to teach to children's strengths, rather than their deficits (Delpit, 1995). An anti-bias approach has introduced an atmosphere that asks teachers to question personal bias, inherent issues of power, and the tendency to generalize about "all children" (Shapiro & Nager, 1998). At an academic and political level, there is a move toward principles of anti-bias that do not distort or ignore differences through "benign pluralism," that is, the notion that "we are all the same because we are different" (McCarthy, 1988, p. 276). Our gay parental informants were in clear agreement that only *after* differences are acknowledged can we begin to find points of unity. This book will consistently take the view that educators should strengthen a democratic way of life, challenge bigotry and stereotypes, work for attitudes of inclusion and equity, and help to "build a new social order" (Counts, 1932/1978).

But whether one teaches to promote social change or not, schools are increasingly being held legally responsible for protecting the civil rights of their students, including preventing anti-gay violence toward youth. In 1996, a young man sued the superintendent of his junior and senior high school for not stopping the repeated gay-related attacks against him *(Nabozyne* v. *Podlesny,* 1996). The Wisconsin federal court ruled in favor of the student, Jamie Nabozyne, and held the schools accountable for the attacks inflicted on him. This legal decision has had far-reaching effects on principals and superintendents across the country, causing some to take anti-gay violence more seriously. Perhaps others are even thinking about ways to work with younger children to prevent such behavior as they become teenagers.

Other changes may be seen in and around the world of children and families. Today, books about gay-headed families are becoming more common (Arnup, 1995; Barret & Robinson, 1990; Benkov, 1994; Martin, 1993; Weston, 1991). There are increasing numbers of children's picture books related to being part of a gay-headed family, and annotated bibliographies for parents and educators in traditional text (Chapman, 1992) and on-line (Betts, 1998) formats. Educational organizations and related professional affiliations also are including presentations on this topic at their national conferences and in their journals (for example, American Psychological Association, National Association for the Education of Young Children, American Educational Research Association, and American Orthopsychiatric Association). Lesbian- and gay-headed families may not have been embraced by the world of early childhood, but their presence may be seen and heard, not just at circle time, but in print, on video, and, increasingly, as a part of public educational forums.

THE CULTURE WARS

Volatile debates over family values have become entrenched at the national level throughout the 1990s. Struggles have centered around a complex cross fire of values—religious, moral, political, and psychological. Skirmish-like debates and all-out battles about homosexuality have raged in the wider arenas of political conventions, military joint chiefs of staff, state amendments, ballot propositions, and presidential executive orders. Windows of opportunity for broad social change that embraces accepting a diversity of families co-exist with powerful social and political forces that attempt to normalize or marginalize gay people and anything perceived to be associated with them, like AIDS education or partnership rights. The religious and political Right is well organized and well funded and has made inroads into many aspects of society primarily through the mass media and religious organizations.

A conservative national mood as it affects anti-gay feelings is an important counterpoint to the progress made in other areas of civil rights, including gay rights. The onslaught of intolerance, prejudice, and fear directed toward gay people and supported by some religious, political, and media groups is large and powerful. Yet we have arrived at an important crossroads in the area of human rights and dignity precisely because of the dynamic provided by this counterpoint. For example, the 1995 Colorado State Supreme Court's striking down of Amendment 2, which prohibited anti-gay discriminatory laws, or President Clinton's 1993 military ban compromise "Don't ask, don't tell" solution have been imperfect, to say the least, but are also no small measures. The right for a gay man to lead a Boy Scout troop (Meers, 1998) is yet another unprecedented out-of-school ruling that keeps the ball rolling beyond any single event. In permitting an outspoken gay man a leadership role with young boys, a basic taboo has been broken that undoubtedly will have future significance for in-school, gay-related issues as well.

Surely the most emotional and deeply embedded sources of antagonism toward gay and lesbian people are the positions of some organized religions. Here, too, there are many variations on a theme, from religious groups that support gay rights, to outright hate groups at the other end of the spectrum. Perhaps the hardest to read are the more ambiguous "hate the sin, love the sinner" messages. The separation of church and state has led to more subtle practices than the removal of biblical readings and school prayer. Many educators continue to be reluctant to promote any issue condemned by religion. If a teacher wants to discuss lesbian and gay parents, and a child or parent says it is against his or her religion, to proceed is sometimes perilous. While we acknowledge the intense emotions it stirs, we cannot regard religious conviction as an acceptable rationale for anti-gay practice, just as the valuing of cultural differences cannot qualify as an acceptable defense for bigotry. Instead, religious conviction or cultural values should be perceived as other forms of "context," aspects of reality that must be taken into account and understood in order to best gauge how to move forward within the framework of a moral stance.

And those who hold strong religious convictions cannot themselves be considered as a monolith. The work of Elaine Wickens shows how some individuals—even in the heart of some of the most staunchly religious areas of the country—have employed their membership and commitment to the Catholic Church as support for lesbian and gay people in the move toward inclusion (personal communication, January 23, 1993). She found teachers and assistant teachers in the southwestern United States defending their positions in support of children who may be gay or lesbian by citing the teachings of Christianity and their own Native Navajo customs: to build an inclusive community, to see the *person* in all, to know your neighbor, and not to "shun" others for having a characteristic you don't share. But according to other more systematic nationwide research on the pulse of American attitudes toward "different" sexual orientation, Wickens's interviewees represent the exception more than the rule (Wolfe, 1998).

Survey researchers have begun to include more questions about gay issues in their public opinion polls. In trying to answer the question, "What do parents want?" a survey by Sylvia Hewlett and Cornel West (1998) found that only 29% thought banning homosexual marriage would be extremely helpful; and another national study demonstrated that voters reject the idea that the government should play a greater role in who can and cannot adopt children (Penn, Schoen & Berland Associates, 1997). These data are in keeping with a comprehensive 1998 study released by the National Gay and Lesbian Task Force, a Washington-based national advocacy group. Their data show a steady gain over the past 20 years in increasingly positive public attitudes toward gay men and lesbians in support for equality in employment, housing, and military service (Goldberg, 1998).

Lessons from the Rainbow Curriculum

A classic case study of competing values and goals was epitomized in the 1993 struggle between gay parents and their supporters on the one side, and conservative district superintendents and their adherents on the other, over the use of the New York City Board of Education's *Children of the Rainbow: First Grade* curriculum (1991). This was an early attempt to include gay-headed families in an early childhood citywide curriculum. The controversy erupted right after Community School Board 24 president, Mary A. Cummins, sent a letter to district parents asking for their participation in a protest against the curriculum. She argued that the curriculum was inappropriate, with "Orwellian thought control" overtones. She viewed any references to lesbians and/or gay men as an endorsement of homosexuality and sodomy, and was quoted as saying, "I will not demean our legitimate minorities, such as blacks, Hispanics and Asians, by lumping them together with homosexuals in that curriculum" (Myers, 1992, p. 134). Cummins banned the use of the entire guide, refusing even to discuss the issue with then-Chancellor Joseph Fernandez. The Chancellor suspended the district board, but it was subsequently reinstated by the Central School Board. The majority of New York City districts then altered, eliminated, or postponed until the upper grades the parts of the curriculum that mentioned lesbian and gay parents and people (Goldstick, 1993).

The storm over Fernandez's support of this curriculum guide, along with his support of an AIDS education guide and his publication of a frank book that expressed his opinions about some New York City Board of Education members (Fernandez, 1993), resulted in the Board's refusal to renew his contract. Its 3–4 vote removed Fernandez from the office of Chancellor in June 1993 and signaled the end of an administration of innovation and courage, but one that did not carefully pave the way in the community for curricular changes in the schools.

The 1993 controversy focused on two parts of the curriculum: one regarding the inclusion of several children's books about gay parents in a list of more than 600 books suggested to teachers, and the second, part of a section of the guide devoted to families, which urged teachers to include lesbians and gay men, and especially lesbian and gay parents, in their work with children. One of the rationales was the fact that many children knew gay people (relatives, neighbors, etc.). The second reason cited was that because at least 10% of the students in each class would grow up to be homosexual, teachers would have an opportunity to give young children a clear and healthy sense of identity early on.

That the curriculum itself was developed by the New York City Board of Education indicates the complex dynamics at work in current struggles over inclusiveness. Although *Children of the Rainbow: First Grade* had undergone evaluation by offices within the central board of education before its publication, when the controversy erupted, the board halted production of the original editions of these guides and stopped making them available to teachers, administrators, and the general public. A revised policy separated "multicultural" curricula from "anti-bias" curricula, and removed lesbian and gay topics from the latter. A new edition of the first-grade guide was compiled, but it did not mention the children's books about gay-headed families, and the words *lesbian* or *gay parents* were changed to *same-gender parents* (New York City Board of Education, 1992; Willen, 1992). While the majority of school districts altered this curriculum to exclude the lives of lesbian and gay people, the results of a 1993 poll reported in the *New York Times* found that "teaching about gay and lesbian families was supported by 72 percent" of adults in New York City (Barbanel, 1993).

Although the "Rainbow Curriculum" is the most well-known school board controversy, parallel confrontations have taken place in towns as small as as Provincetown, Massachusetts (Bedard, 1997; Sullivan, 1997); Boise, Idaho (Lesbian parents' school visit, 1993); and Surrey, British Columbia (*Chamberlain et al.* v. *Surrey School District #36*, 1998). And in at least one case, such community conflicts have grown into statewide referenda such as Oregon's anti-gay referendum (Egan, 1992), which used the well-publicized children's book, *Heather Has Two Mommies* (Newman & Souza, 1989), to launch its crusade.

Common themes emerge in these community-wide struggles when a group opposes the inclusion of gay and lesbian issues in the early grades. The most basic presumption equates gayness with sexuality. Religious and moral reasons as well as children's inability to comprehend the "far-off" concept of gayness may be used to help explain and extend this argument. More than any other, however, the "developmentally inappropriate" rubric is argued from both sides. Academics testify as "expert" witnesses by interpreting what Jean Piaget, Erik

Erikson, or Lawrence Kohlberg might have said about exposing young children to gay issues (*Chamberlain et al.* v. *Surrey School District #36*, 1998). The composition of a given community also influences the way in which queerness constitutes a threat. In Surrey, a small town in British Columbia, the relatively few gay-headed families in Canada is cited as one reason to keep gay issues out of the classroom. In Provincetown, Massachusetts, where the gay/lesbian population is about 50% during the school year and rises to at least 80% during the summer (W. Rokicki, personal communication, May 1, 1998), one can imagine a different twist to the quality of "homosexual panic." Here, over the course of at least 2 years, members of this small town showed tremendous persistence and continued to work at community education and staff development, taking the main lesson from the failure of the New York City Rainbow Curriculum to heart.

When Gay=Sex

Let's face it. For most people, thinking about sexual activity between two men or two women is at the core of a range of feelings, ranging from hostility to ambivalence. Of course, sexuality is an important aspect of gay relationships, but for many straight Americans, it is the defining one. Asked to imagine a gay-headed family on a Saturday morning, many Americans would not be likely to conjure up images of laundry and chores. In discussing this issue with each other, two gay fathers in our study, Matthew and his partner James, address the assumption of sexuality as a blatant form of homophobia.

> Matthew: Having people in bed is genital to [straight] parents. So it can't help but trigger the homophobia. I think generally people can keep it in check. [But] it's there. We have it in ourselves. Everyone's been taught it. It's how they deal with it that's the issue.
> James: When *I* think about parents in bed, I *don't* think about sex. But you're right. Many people would probably think of two men as, "it's all genital." . . . I think most heterosexuals would think of two men in bed in terms of sex.

If *gay* and *lesbian* could be decoupled even occasionally from such sexual connotations as James and Matthew discuss, would these words still be thought to be so inappropriate? Such discomfort is reflected in the refusal of most teachers to read the book, *Jenny Lives with Eric and Martin* (Bosche, 1983), or ones like it, in their classes. This children's book, a photo-essay of a week in the life of Jenny and her two fathers, depicts Jenny climbing into bed with her daddies, waking them up, and cuddling together. Yet if this book were titled, *A Week with Jenny and Her Mommy and Daddy,* and depicted Jenny climbing into bed with her parents one early morning, it would be hard to imagine similar resistance.

The first-grade public school teachers quoted below all had children with lesbian mothers in their classes. When asked whether he would include lesbian-headed families as part of his family curriculum, Sol said: "I'm afraid to use those words in a first-grade classroom." This response resonated with our interviews with other teachers, although some, unlike Sol, included sexuality as a concern. One first-grade teacher justified her exclusion of gay-headed parents from her family curriculum by stating that she wasn't about to do "sex education" with such young children because it could be "frightening" to the children. "I just don't know if this age is the appropriate time to discuss two women living together and making love." When we asked Theresa, a third teacher, if she would use the words *lesbian* and *gay* with her students, she responded with her own question: "Is it necessary in such a blatant way?" When we posed the same question about language to our parent informants, their responses were very different. Ricky, a lesbian mother, is crystal clear. She maintains, "You have to tell them that same-sex families do exist; that being gay or lesbian is one of the options. And then everyone gets the same message." Because the words *lesbian* and *gay* have become synonymous with sexuality makes it hard for many of us to use these words with young children. It *is* hard.

Even in more liberal settings, though, the use of "lesbian" or "gay" parents for "two mommies" or "two daddies" often is seen as inappropriate. But eventually, "two mommies" *are* recognized by children as lesbians. Unless we give them the correct words, by the second or third grade *lesbian* and *gay* are already basic vocabulary words, but have been distorted to *dyke* and *fag.*

Saying the words *lesbian* and *gay* in elementary school can automatically brand the teachers as lesbians or gay men themselves. And in some cases, it is professionally suicidal to speak even milder words in our own classrooms. The place of lesbians and gay men in our society's roster of perverse behaviors clearly affects teachers' willingness to use the words *lesbian* and *gay* with young children. Discomfort tends to increase for those of us who must consider our role as teachers of 6- or 7-year-old children. At this age children's interest in this topic, and their ability to make connections to lesbian or gay parenting, can cause explicit questions concerning the mechanics of conception for lesbian or gay adults. But this is all the more reason why it is important to take a stand. Teachers not only have to be prepared to discuss—or have discussed among their children—these culturally taboo topics, but they also will need to have some type of communication with the parents of the children in their class, before launching forward with such conversations.

"DEVELOPMENTAL APPROPRIATENESS" AND THE REAL WORLD

What meaning does identity politics have for children? In their own way, they live out the reality of first their parents, and then their culture, more broadly writ. While adults debate what words and concepts are "appropriate" for them, children imbibe the world around them. For many children, gay families are simply all they have ever known, in their own family, or the one next door. Sure, questions surface, especially as children's first experiences are framed against the larger world. Quintuplets want to know how a boy and a girl who do not have the same birthday could still be brother and sister ("A Team of Individuals," 1993). A child who calls his father "Papa" spends his days in a child-care center where the children all happen to call their fathers "Daddy," so he understands "Papa" to be his father's first name (Bernstein, 1994). Adults tell these stories with a chuckle, but are more likely to find their children's questions about lesbian- and gay-headed families to be extremely threatening.

"But how do you *know* what is developmentally appropriate?" is a question we have been asked repeatedly by parents and educators alike. The term *developmentally appropriate* is a well-worn phrase that has worked its way beyond its educational origins (Bredekamp, 1987; Bredekamp & Copple, 1997), where it gained the acronym DAP (developmentally appropriate practice), into the culture at large. In many ways, DAP has played a crucial role in helping teachers think about the needs of very young children, especially teachers whose only experience has been working with older children. Through a decade of practice, however, DAP has gone the way of other approaches, becoming a rubric and used, too often, in stale and rigid ways. Especially concerning controversial topics, we believe that simply determining appropriateness gets us off on the wrong track entirely. We resonate with the words of a colleague (Cuffaro, 1995) who asks, "Whose view of development? Who decides" what is appropriate? (p. 103).

The story behind developmental appropriateness goes beyond the judgments implicit in the word *appropriate*, such as the assumption that gay=sex. Consciously, or unconsciously, adults reify stages (transform the idea of a stage into a fact or concrete thing) to believe that there is a certain age/stage at which all children can comprehend a particular idea or issue. Of course, concepts should be somewhere within children's grasp. But children can stretch when given a rich learning environment full of encouragement. The emphasis on readiness has eclipsed other ways of thinking about learning that will be elaborated throughout this book. What helps us think about developing curriculum with children is the simple notion that children don't have to understand a concept in its entirety in order to wrestle with it. As Vygotsky has helped us understand, children tug at development; they don't just wait for it to happen.

Until the early 1990s it was the rare early childhood classroom in which challenging social topics entered unless by accident. As issues of homelessness, drugs, or biological origins were raised by children, some educators responded to the fact that it no longer seemed possible to them to bar such discussions. Documentation of children's personal experience with the effects of poverty and homelessness (Kozol, 1995), violence (Gabarino, 1992), and AIDS (Silin, 1995), or the stresses of growing up too fast (Elkind, 1981) or understanding one's high technology origins (Bernstein, 1994) gives powerful witness to the ways young children are indeed dealing with complex issues that previously were thought to be only within the domain of adults or teenagers. Slowly, educators are becoming more proactive than ever before. They are doing much more than just responding to crises; they are initiating activities and conversations that allow these ideas to be integrated into the curriculum over time in thoughtful ways.

Part of the tendency for DAP to become formulaic and narrow in use occurs because the ages/stages on which it is based do not, and in many cases cannot, include the complex variables that occur in particular children's lives. In addition, DAP has been criticized for its unilinear approach to all children and its failure to take diversity into account (Lubeck, 1994), as well as for its dry approach—notably, a conspicuous absence of the basic necessities of joy, pleasure, and desire in children's lives (Tobin, 1997). Teachers and parents seem to want guidelines, yet using DAP-based rationales for gay material can become a slippery slope with various "experts" arguing which age is "appropriate" for what content. Such debates erupted deep in the early childhood community in 1993 after the Governing Board of the National Association for the Education of Young Children circulated to its member affiliates a briefing paper concerning the children of gay and lesbian parents (NAEYC, 1993), and continue in the form of school board/community skirmishes around the country.

Obviously, we have deep respect for the ways in which young children's thinking, feeling, and moving differ from older children and adults. This book is based on the premise that children are different from adults, and that their worldview is dynamic. What often is missed is that these changes occur in complex interaction with the child's world, provoking individual differences that make children's age/stage but one of many curricular considerations. Beginning early in this century, the world of psychology created a false experimental and theoretical distance between adults and children and our ways of thinking about them (Silin, 1995). Reflecting on the theoretical gold rush that had its heyday in the 1970s, we can see the ways in which a study of children for purposes of education became subsumed by the field of psychology at the cost of remembering that children's real lives must form the basis of child study.

Finally, teaching is an art that must allow for the unpredictable. A narrow curriculum frame doesn't leave much room for unexpected moments in which great things can happen. If we proceed with a restrictive conception based only on what children ask or can easily grasp, we lose access to these moments of tremendous possibility. If we only wait for children to ask questions, we are, in effect, waiting for development to take the lead, when in reality learning tends to lead development (Vygotsky, 1930–35/1978a).

What about parents? Research has shown, for example, that parents believe they have more influence over their young children's emotional development than over their conceptual development (Melmed, 1997). It also has been documented (Novick, 1986), and it makes sense, that adults can have trouble appreciating the gap between young children's relatively greater receptive versus productive speech abilities (they can understand more than they can say). One need only observe parents (and teachers) briefly and informally to notice how often adults talk *about* children in front of them, concerning topics they need not hear (e.g., gossip about other children and adults), while at the same time often do not take the time to carefully explain simple and important aspects of their lives (e.g., that a beloved person is leaving their life or that a "bad" thing that happened is not their fault). Although the data refer to very young children, it has been our experience that these patterns are difficult for many adults to change. This tendency to both over- and underregulate what is said to children seems to derive from, yet also contribute to, the preference to steer away from having controversial conversations with young children. Most adults appear to be afraid of the content and unsure of the language to use with young children and thus resist helping children make meaning in their world by simply naming the obvious.

Taking a look at the scant research about how lesbian mothers talk to their children about conception affirms the anecdotal evidence that most lesbian mothers tell it like it is. In a study of middle-class lesbian mothers, Mitchell (1998) reports a composite narrative that represents the gist of most lesbian mothers' version of the birds and the bees. Throughout this book, this basic story can be recognized in various young children's responses to their peers' inquiries about how they came to be.

> A baby starts out very, very tiny, when an egg cell and a sperm cell join together. Women make egg cells inside a special part of their bodies, so Mom had one of those ready. Men make sperm cells in a special part of their bodies. [Either:] So your Dad gave sperm cells to Mom and they joined together in a special part of Mom's tummy where you started growing into a baby. [Or:] So we went to the sperm bank to get some sperm. Some men know that women like your Moms want to have babies, so they give some sperm to the sperm bank for us to use. When we were ready to make a baby, we went to the sperm bank and got some, and the sperm cell joined together with Mom's egg cell in a special part of Mom's tummy where you started to grow into a baby. (p. 403).

Using Piaget's basic theory as a guide, Gilby and Pederson (1982) conducted research on how children accepted or did not accept various family structures (see also Pederson & Gilby, 1986). Through this work, they showed how children's tendency to be inclusive in accepting various family structures forms a U-shaped curve, with younger children and older adolescents at the more progressive or accepting end of the scale, and middle-year children harboring the harshest critiques. In our study of children's conceptions of family, we too found this to be the case. This partially helps to explain a preschooler's runaway excitement with the idea of "two, three, many mommies!" compared with a fourth grader's measured realism. One common criticism of gay-inclusive curricula we've heard often sounds something like this, "Of course, young children think it's [gay parents] fine; they don't know any better." It is particularly interesting that in this case using Piaget's preoperational thought results in what seems to be more tolerant—and certainly more inclusive—ideas. That is not how most young children react to more elastic gender roles (Paley, 1984). Rather, they tend to defend gender conformity with a vengeance. And in their reaction to explanations of human conception (Bernstein, 1994), young children's concreteness is only heightened by their lack of experience. "Why would anyone want to do *that*?" children often are heard to respond when they have been told about sexual intercourse.

Perhaps the emotional draw that mommies and daddies have for young children holds sway over the budding conventions the children experience; hence we hear the message behind young children's words to be, "the more mommies the better." Here we again see how developmental theory may constrict us by drawing lines between various domains, in this case, cognitive and emotional development. That the tolerance young children demonstrate in this area may be due in part to "immature thinking processes" does not, in our minds, dwarf the meaning of their thoughts and feelings in any way. As we will show in Chapter 2, we take issue with the research findings that almost unanimously indicate that experience has little to do with children's conceptualizations of family.

BACKGROUND OF THE STUDY

Cathy's statement at the beginning of this chapter resonates deeply with us. No one can come to appreciate different kinds of families just by being told to do so. What is possible is to have educators and parents tell each other who they are, enlarging the possibilities for how each group considers the other. This was the primary goal of our study. We wanted to probe what we saw to be tremendous gaps in the communication process between teachers and parents, created primarily through avoidance. We also wanted to find the threads of unity, the avenues through which communication *could* occur. A large component of this was our interest in discovering and describing the curricular adjustments some of our teacher informants made, as well as finding out what kinds of curricular changes gay parents advocated. In this way, we hoped to bring teachers and parents closer, to narrow any gulf that might exist between them, and to increase the control parents have in their children's lives at school, without diminishing the important role that teachers play in the lives of children.

What Is Ethnography?

These days, just about everyone is a consumer of research of one form or another. When digesting various sets of data, it is important to do so with an awareness of the assumptions, the styles of gathering and interpreting data, and the professional uses of self characteristic of each approach. Some of us may be particularly skeptical as we read self-report data. Others delight in a straightforward graph. It is good to clarify one's expectations of any research approach, but especially those with an ethnographic base (Casper, 1996).

Ethnography entails sustained engagement with others in order to enrich our understanding and sensibilities of their lives as lived. Ethnography, the writing (graphy) of people (ethnos) and their culture, has grown to be used across many disciplines. The ethnographer uses multiple sources of data, including, but not limited to, consistent observations over time, collection of artifacts, and interviews with informants. Through a pooling of these, one comes closer to uncovering what matters more and less to those whom we seek to know better. What also differentiates ethnographic research from other interviewing or descriptive approaches is the foremost interest in context.

What we are describing is an ethnographic research method that does not produce percentage results, but rather describes "dramatic instances" of a broader social reality (Leavitt, 1994). As anthropologist Renato Rosaldo (1989) reminds us, in life human beings are temporally oriented "as if in midstream," between past experiences and future possibilities right in our midst. The more objective social sciences tend to describe human events as finished acts. In ethnography, human experience is addressed as an ongoing rather than a finished endeavor. The past and the future are not forgotten, and "objectivity" is not seen as a pure state. The researcher's subjectivity, of necessity, deeply affects the work. Ethnographers acknowledge their "positioned" stance (Rosaldo, 1989); voicing it becomes a responsibility.

Because our research team was made up of a lesbian, a gay man, and a heterosexual woman, we believed that together we offered both a "native" and a more distanced perspective. Embracing Geertz's (1973) criteria for a good ethnographic approach, we were able to blend "experience-near" and "experience-far" perspectives. Near experiences permitted a closer understanding and feeling for what it was like to be a lesbian or gay parent or a teacher or administrator of a child with lesbian or gay parents. Far experiences afforded a perspective sufficiently distant to label, categorize, and compare the information, to blend what was learned with knowledge gleaned from other research and theoretical writing (Casper & Schultz, 1994).

When Gay Is Not Enough

Gay research and queer theory about gay and lesbian lives are increasingly in the hands of gay and lesbian scholars (Herdt, 1992). Curiously, ethnography appears to have been underutilized in this body of research. The work that has been done, however, parallels ethnographic work in other fields in its tendency to explore less-researched topics such as gay youth (Herdt & Boxer, 1993) and lesbians' construction of motherhood (Lewin, 1993; Weston, 1991). Recently, feminist and gay anthropological scholarship has begun to delve into questions about "insider" and "outsider" perspectives in investigating a culture that one inhabits intimately (Lewin & Leap, 1996).

The first interview I (Virginia) conducted in this study taught me a lot about the complexity of the insider/outsider role. I quickly came to see how sharing one identity with an informant is not an automatic guarantee of shared values or experience. I came to reflect on this, in part, through Reissman's (1987) critique of women interviewing other women with different life assumptions and ways of expressing them. As stated, the research team believed that among the three of us, our combined gay, lesbian, and straight perspectives would serve us well. Before embarking on my first interview, however, I was especially aware that not all would share our view. Particularly suspect, I was afraid, would be the notion of a lesbian mother interviewing a lesbian mother. In 1990, there was not much writing or discussion from a feminist or lesbian/gay perspective on what it means to share or not share sexual orientation with one's informants.

Esperanza, a lesbian mother, had two children from a former heterosexual marriage. At the time of the interview she was raising them with her female partner. Esperanza came to our study through a contact in the Bronx, where she worked as a paraprofessional in a public elementary school. I experienced her as formal and distant in our first phone contact, and it took a while before we could arrange a time to meet at a coffee shop. During that phone conversation and at our first meeting Esperanza called me Mrs. Casper a number of times, despite my strong suggestion that she call me Virginia and the fact that we appeared to be roughly the same age. I decided to come out to her right away and let her know that I too was a lesbian mother. As soon as I did, her body movements loosened, she let out a smile, and we began to really talk. Evidently *her* concept of a research project did not allow for a lesbian interviewing a lesbian either.

During the interview, I tried to listen at multiple levels and found I could sense intuitively aspects of her story that simultaneously framed our commonalities and our differences. Esperanza, a Latina woman from a solidly working-class background, was not about to come out to her children's teachers for any reason, because the school in which Esperanza worked was in the same district as the school both her children attended. While a few years earlier I had shared a milder version of Esperanza's fear of coming out professionally, I knew my middle-class economic security was never really in jeopardy. After my talks with Esperanza, I was able to proceed with other interviews and observations with greater assurance that any aspect of identity I did share with an informant could serve as a tool through which, with great care, I might be able to hear the aspects of their lives that were less familiar to me.

What We Did: Methods

We began to plan our project during the 1989–90 school year. Building on our own interests, our past research, and the interests and questions of our graduate students, some of whom had children of gay parents in their classrooms, we started our interviews. Our pilot questions were open-ended, trying to discover, for example, what teachers thought was important to include or exclude in their curriculum and the ways that they found to make lesbian and gay parents and their children feel more included as a family in school. It was in our pilot interviews that we began to hear repeated messages about gender and disclosure from gay parents and educators, and used these data to craft our research questions. We came to appreciate the value of following up on responses in various ways depending on the person we were speaking with. This felt like a luxury, especially to me (Virginia), who had been trained in quantitative methodologies. The flexibility was important as it enabled us to gather a great deal of information in depth. It didn't lock us into a standard format that might have worked in an interview with one parent or administrator, but would have been a dismal failure in another.

Adult Interviews. As we saw the depth of the material the informants were raising, we began to construct a more formal study. Through a structured outreach process, utilizing our collaboration with Center Kids, an organization of lesbian and gay parents in New York City, and through personal and other organizational contacts (particularly organizations of lesbians and gay men of color), we put together a diverse group of parents to interview using "snowball" sampling techniques (see Table 1.1). Because lesbian and gay people are a hidden population with particularly sensitive issues of confidentiality (Morin, 1977), subject gathering in the gay and lesbian community uses informants to refer others to the study, a technique used even in some quantitative studies. We believe our population comes from a broad cross-section of gay and lesbian parents in the greater New York–Tri-State Area. But it is not, and could not be, a statistically representative sample because gay people are part of a hard-to-identify population.

A distinctive aspect of this study is the breadth of socioeconomic and ethnic diversity the participants represent. Our 17 lesbian and gay parent informants were of White, African American, and Latino/a origins. Their

Table 1.1. Descriptive Data of Informants

Informant Triads				School				
Parents & Children	**Teachers**	**Admin.**	**Years**	**Level**	**Type**	**Out?**	**Residence**	**Ethnicity**
Maritza & Sharon							Suburb of	Puerto Rican/
Alberto	Carla		1989-90	child care	private	no	Long Island	White
		Nilda	1990-91	K	private	yes		
	Linda	Lise	1991-92*	1st grade	private	yes		
James & Mathew							Manhattan	African
Jeffrey	Sasha		1989-90	preschool	private	no		American/
	Theresa	Emory	1990-91	K	public magnet	yes		White
			1991-92*	1st grade	public magnet	yes		
Paul			1991-92*	preschool	public magnet	yes		
Jacqueline & Nora							Suburb of	White
Dan	Fred		1990-91	K/1	public magnet	no/yes	Connecticut	
			1991-92		public magnet	yes		
June & Shelly							Manhattan	White
Jeremy	Penny	Enrico	1989-90	K	public	yes		
	Hazel	Enrico	1990-91	1st grade	public	yes		
Marcia	Penny	Enrico	1989-90	2nd grade	public	yes		
	Hazel	Enrico	1990-91	3rd grade	public	yes		
Shanique							Brooklyn	African
Ralph	Sol		1990-91	1st grade	public	no		American

Family / Child			Year	Level	Type		Location	Ethnicity
Ricky & Maggie							Manhattan	White
Elly	Cathy	Beverly	1990-91	K/1	public	yes		
Esperanza							Bronx	Puerto Rican
Nina			1990-91	1st grade	public	no		
Dominique			1990-91	4th grade	public	no		
Manuel							Manhattan	Puerto Rican
Clarence			1990-91	K	public-private	no		
Peter			1990-91	5th grade	public-private	no		
Al & Richard							Manhattan	Puerto Rican/ African American
Julio			1990-91	preschool	private	yes		
Lucas				preschool	private	yes		
Ernesto				1st grade	public	no		
Maureen & Naomi							Suburb of New Jersey	White
Derrick			1989-90	1st grade	public	yes		
Valerie & Diane (not interviewed)							Queens	White
Lonnie	Fran/ Leslie	Janet	1989	child care	private	yes		
			1990-92*	preschool	private	yes		

*Follow-up communication, not full interviews

socioeconomic backgrounds include middle-class and working-class and one lesbian mother living in poverty. The children, from 11 gay-headed families, were between the ages of 3 and 7, and attended child-care centers as well as independent and public schools up through second grade.

Our sample was triadic, whenever possible including the child's parent/s, teacher, and school administrator. Because a number of parents did not want the school personnel to know of their sexual orientation, we also have some parent-only interviews. In addition, of the 20 educators we interviewed, a few were individuals who could offer important information but did not have children with lesbian or gay parents in their schools at that time, or were unaware of such families (such as Eleanor, a guidance counselor, Father Stephen Moore, and a teacher in his school). Where follow-through was possible, some dyads or triads were followed up to 3 consecutive years. This enabled us to note developmental/educational and parental and teacher attitudinal changes.

Children's Voices. In our 3-year study, we observed in numerous classrooms but did not specifically go out of our way to interview children. In this book, most of the child observations and vignettes about children were made by teachers and parents and described to us in interviews. Still, a few children offered their thoughts to us directly and one sent us a message through one of her mothers. Most important, because of the perceived novelty of gay families in the era in which we began this work, messages from colleagues began to appear regularly on our voice mail, and little scraps of paper with intriguing anecdotes began to pile up in our mailboxes. We found that we had become a magnet for information gathered by a range of people in the schools, faculty from the Bank Street Graduate School of Education, and teachers of young children and parents who were not even in our study (all of whom had their antenna up for such moments). These unexpected contributions to our data enlarged the context for our study and seemed to confirm the direction of our findings.

These very compelling stories were also the impetus for me (Virginia) to initiate a small pilot study on Children's Conceptions of Family, which Steven Schultz and I carried out in conjunction with four teachers during the 1993–94 academic year. The children, whose class discussions are excerpted in Chapter 2, attended a small New York City private school, and are thus a different cohort of children from those discussed by adults in our original study.

What follows is the essence of what we learned from children, their teachers, administrators, and parents, as their lives intersected around the education of young children.

What Do Children Know?

"Are you pretending to be married?"

—Sam, age 5

In our own work with young children, we begin by observing them, then asking, "What do they know about?" and "What interests them?" Such questions are deceptively simple and moving toward answers entails no quick fix. Often, what children know is transformed in front of us, and that, of course, is the point. In this chapter we evaluate the traditional research on children's conceptions of family, counterposing it with children's everyday conversations about family, in and out of school. Through our observations of children we try to glean a sense of their worldview. Their conversations and behaviors become our pivot for their learning.[1]

CHILDREN DISCUSSING FAMILY MATTERS

If, in our everyday relationships with children, we maintain sharp observational skills, we stay in close contact with children's learning and growth, fostering a parallel evolution for ourselves. Asking what children know turns us toward children, not experts, and challenges us to watch, listen, and think with greater attunement. Of course, much escapes our grasp. Neither parents nor educators can or *should* be aware of a child's every turn. But precisely because missing pieces are inevitable, it becomes crucial to think about what children really mean through their actions and words. As adults, we often find humor in what appears to us as idiosyncratic interpretations of adult conventions.

---

1. Portions of "Getting at the Role of Experience" and "Thoughts on Research and Practice" from this chapter were published (in a section written by Virginia Casper) in a collaborative article (Casper, Cuffaro, Schultz, Silin, & Wickens, summer 1996, *Harvard Educational Review*, 66(2), 271–293).

If, after a chuckle, we then ponder the possible meanings in a child's comment or action, we begin a process that is both fascinating and productive for teachers and parents alike.

In my work I (Virginia) am continually amazed at the range of meanings and emphases different individuals may assign to behaviors, as well as the different ways people get to similar impressions. Below are two out-of-school conversations that occurred about a year apart, providing us with snippets of one child's thinking process over time. This particular vignette holds special poignancy because the adult in this story is an early childhood educator who is a lesbian. Contemplating the depth of her own internalized homophobia holds lessons for us all. Sam, age 3.11, and his aunt, Denise, are on a crowded New York City bus.

> Sam: Are you and Marie married?
>   (Silence. Denise does not respond.)
>   (Sam repeats the question even louder.)
> Sam: Are you and Marie married?
> Denise: Well, we live together.
>   (There is a pause in the conversation.)
> Sam: Well, then did you fall in love?
> Denise: Yes.

The topic was not mentioned by either one for over a year. In the next sequence, Sam is 5 years old and is spending the weekend with his aunts. He is jumping up and down on the couch as he shoots off another series of questions to Denise.

> Sam: Are you and Marie sisters?
> Denise: Sam, you know we're not.
> Sam: Are you married?
> Denise: Well, it's *like* we're married.
> Sam: Are you *pretending* to be married?
> Denise: No, we're not pretending.
> Sam: Do you kiss on the lips like mommy and daddy?
> Denise: Yes, we kiss on the lips.

How might one think about the treasure trove of ideas that surface in these two simple exchanges? It seems clear that by the second conversation Sam has become more sophisticated in his hypothetical thinking and his ability to distinguish between appearance and reality. He uses his experience with pretend play and some cognitive distancing to conceptualize his aunts *pretending* to be married. After all, Denise has defined her relationship with Marie in an "as if" mode that sounds just like what he does with his friends in play. One also might consider the different contexts and to what extent the "advanced" thought is supported by the comfortable environment.

But what is the subtext here? Something screams out at us in these conversations that is greater than the sum of its parts. Sam is begging for some way to put this all together. He is busy classifying every other aspect of his life and is missing language to understand what this special person in his life is up to. By holding back from giving children an explanation that qualitatively matches any other, we both make it harder for ourselves as adults and give coded messages to children that belie our true intents. The more lasting message for Sam is that some information is quite forthcoming from adults and other information requires pulling teeth.

The next installment of this saga was reported when Sam was 5-years-old. One day when Denise calls to speak to her sister, Sam overhears that she is on the phone and asks loudly, "How come Denise never got married?" Denise overhears the question and asks to speak to Sam. The following conversation ensues:

Denise: Usually people get married when they fall in love, and it
    took me a long time to fall in love. And then I met . . .
    (before she can finish her partner's name, Sam fills in her name
    gleefully, 'MARIE!')
Denise: Right, I met Marie.
Sam: But women can't love women and men can't love men.
Denise: Sure they can. Your friend Mitch has two dads.
Sam: But they're not in love!
Denise: I think they probably are.
Sam: So how come you and Marie never got married?
Denise: Because it is OK for women who love each other and men
    to love each other, but there's a law that says they can't get
    married.
Sam: But that's not fair.
Denise: No it's not. It's an unjust law.
Sam: What's unjust?
Denise: It's a law that isn't fair. Maybe you can ask your mom
    about it because she knows a lot about laws.

Even though much has changed in Sam's social-cognitive abilities, and new societal complexities have been introduced, he still grapples with the essential contradictions. Since the conversation prior to this one he has gained a new little brother which has only heightened awareness of the concept of fairness—one that is already on the minds of most 5-year-olds. It is also important to note that Denise's stance seems clearer. She seems freer to introduce concepts rather than just respond. This may be due to some combination of coming to grips with her own homophobia along with her awareness of Sam's abilities. Needless to say, Denise does not introduce concepts of law when Sam is 3 or 4. It is also important to note that in all 3 conversations Sam is the initiator and Denise concludes the interchanges. Finally, it needs to be stated that the word lesbian is never used.

Sam's little quandary is but one example of the ways children continually construct and reconstruct *all families*, not just their own. And although these two vignettes occurred out of school, they still serve as a good example of content for adult exploration. As stated above, there are always missing pieces for both teachers and parents. We don't know, for example, if Sam is in school with children from lesbian-headed families, or lives next door to two gay men. We don't know what conversations occur in Sam's home about Denise and Marie, and a host of other pieces of the puzzle. Teachers also would not have access to most of this information. But if teachers help children have group discussions about family, more of what they have experienced can emerge and provide a platform for deeper consideration and learning, with some adult guidance.

Children are famous for offering the most private information to family members on a crowded bus or posing the hardest questions to teachers during circle time. Because it is hard to gather one's wits on the spot, taking time beforehand to reflect on the ideas that are most challenging to us can help us have more courage to respond in a way that promotes learning in children and adults.

RESEARCH ON CHILDREN'S CONCEPTIONS OF FAMILY

As family forms and methods of conception are becoming more varied, complex, and visible, parents and educators find themselves in the position of playing catch-up with the children in their lives. While we are at times overcome with how long it takes for some things to change, we often do not pay enough attention to the ways in which the world has changed right before us. I (Virginia) have been struck by this awarenes in my personal and professional life. As a lesbian mother I became acculturated, over time, to the knowledgeable assumptions children have about personal aspects of each other's family structure, and the subtle comparative work going on, for example, as a group of first and second graders analyzed the differential meanings of "father," "daddy," and "papi" on a leisurely walk home from school. Such conversations are no longer rare, and are occurring much earlier than most parents (Bernstein, 1994) or teachers (Silin, 1995) expect. Hearing such conversations out of school as a mother, and in the classroom as a teacher educator, and because of my training as a developmental psychologist, I asked myself what the research had to say in response to the question, "What is the role experience plays in children's construction of family?" I was quite surprised to find that the research says that experience seems not to play much of a role at all.

Piaget's Gold Standard

Piaget's (1928/1965) specific investigations into children's thinking about kinship and family serve as an important initiation to the conceptual and empirical standards on which succeeding research on children's familial thinking is based. It is important to appreciate Piaget's method and intent. We know that he was most interested in the growth of the domains of conceptual thinking and logic. Piaget viewed these stages as each representing a deeply rooted way of approaching the world. He believed them to be universal and invariant, and, with few exceptions, to function consistently across different domains of a child's conceptual thinking. And although the field of developmental psychology has questioned the cohesiveness (Case, 1991; Flavell, 1985; Siegler, 1991; Turiel & Davidson, 1986) and universality of classical Piagetian stages (Case, 1991; Rogoff, 1990), years of research and thinking have been framed by these assumptions. And Piaget's clinical interview of individual children as his primary research tool also raises questions about his reliance on verbal performance as a true indicator of children's competence.

Piaget's ideas tell us that through a complex interaction of maturation and experience, children construct and reconstruct their ideas about how the world works: New information conflicts with their previous "schema" of an object, person, or idea, leading to new concepts. This is an important aspect of understanding how children construct knowledge. But Piaget's stages of children's thinking are the most widely circulated aspect of his work and are too easily simplified into discrete and mutually exclusive classifications.

In the first of Piaget's (1928/1965) two classic interview studies, he demonstrated that *having* a brother, for example, did not seem to help a young child more readily understand the reciprocal nature of the concept of *being* a brother. Until cognitive structures evolve that can support reciprocity of thought, the concept of brother was, in Piaget's (1928/1965) word, "unconscious".[2] According to Piaget, the increased socialization that school provides, contributes to egocentrism's eventual decline through a process of decentering. When children no longer view the world exclusively from the center, reciprocity of thought can develop. In terms of thinking about family, reciprocal thought means that the child can conceptualize that having a brother also means being a brother, a notion adults take quite for granted. For Piaget, reciprocal thinking, along with other significant abilities, marks the onset of the stage of concrete operations.

Piaget's second study looked at how a group of 30 boys, between 7 and 12 years of age, defined family and country. Piaget's interest here was the child's increasing ability to *reason* about these important concepts and his or her ability to *express a logical definition* of each. It was this work that produced the well-known path of familial understanding—that children first recognize the people around them as family (co-residence), then begin to include blood relations as a secondary and often confused criterion, then express the idea of relationship (blood relations), describing the more abstract notion of a family linked through generations.

As with other areas of developmental inquiry, Piaget's work from the earlier part of this century requires significant modification for application to our everyday work. Perhaps the greatest discord between Piaget's assumptions and ours was his interest in a purer form of knowledge that did not take school or group learning into account in the ways in which we have become accustomed over the last few decades of the century. In thinking about how Piaget's original work applies to today's families, some observers of child development put it quite bluntly: "Piaget's studies about family were as much about family as his studies of conservation of liquid were about volume" (Margie Brickley, personal communication, September 8, 1998). Interestingly, Piaget and his associates (Piaget & Inhelder, 1969) considered themselves attuned to the intertwined relationship of affective-cognitive aspects of development, in which emotion provides the "energetics" to the more structural aspects of cognitive development. Yet such discussions are rare in Piaget's

---

2. Piaget's use of the term *unconscious* is confusing. The term *nonconscious* is used following Vygotsky's (1934/1962) distinction between the relatively sophisticated Freudian concept, which suggests repression, and the notion of what has not yet come to be conscious thought (Vygotsky, 1934/1962, p.19).

work. And, as Bernstein points out (1988), Piaget's view, akin to some psychoanalytic thinkers, is one in which affectivity may be seen as an intrusion, or impediment to cognitive progress in a given domain. In short, it can be stated that Piaget was more interested in tracking the growth of knowledge than in the child's overall development.

The diversity of family configurations in today's world offers a range of difference with which children must contend in order to identify their own family situation. In other areas of development, engagement with "just-the-right amount" of complexity is acknowledged to lead to greater cognitive differentiation and an optimal learning environment (Selman, 1980). In Switzerland, in the 1920s and 1930s, children had more homogeneous family structures that required grasping the basic kin relationships. The complexity and range of today's family structures simply was not part of Piaget's world. Finally, research that draws from children's everyday interactions with others rather than assessments of individual child knowledge, tells us more about *how* children come to understand what they do. Likewise, inquiry that derives its inspiration from theories about the practice of education rather than more abstract theories of learning (Bruner, 1992) also more closely approximates children's learning under real-life conditions.

What do other theorists and researchers tell us about children's abilities? One significant change in the developmental psychology landscape has to do with new ideas and data that contradict Piaget's thoughts about young children's perspective-taking abilities (egocentrism). Margaret Donaldson (1978) has argued that young children are able to use the perspectives of others when these endeavors make what she calls "human sense," and neo-Piagetians have presented evidence for nonegocentric thinking in young children in a number of different realms (Borke, 1975; Hart & Goldin-Meadow, 1984; Shatz & Gelman, 1973). If at times young children are capable of some perspective taking, one can see more easily how they can think about the family structures of others and begin to integrate that information in ways that are meaningful for themselves.

For his epistemological purposes, Piaget made a distinction between the child's verbal intelligence and his or her concrete or practical intelligence. According to Piaget (1928/1965), the child becomes increasingly conscious of a concept as he or she struggles with definition, a process he sees as being "occasioned by adult thought and not by direct or spontaneous experience" (p.114). He believed that a child's understanding of the concept of family evolves less from a child's experience with family and more from exposure to the word and the adult transmission of the concept, along with the child's conceptual readiness. Through this adaptation to the formal concept/word, the child's nonconscious experience becomes more conscious and verbal. Logic and verbal expression is what counts for Piaget.

But if we think about children's lived experiences, their thinking abilities and their emotional grasp can't be seen separately. When we take children into a room and ask them a series of questions, we get one version of their thinking. When we listen to their conversations and watch their play, we often observe other variations. In thinking about a 4-year-old's idea of brother, for example, one can reflect on how the emotionally charged yet vague classification, "brother," referring to the little guy in the bottom bunk bed, is of tremendous personal as well as cognitive importance in a child's life. These are some of the theoretical assumptions integral to Piaget's theories and data that have eclipsed the role of children's family experiences. These assumptions serve as a foundation for the 20 or so related empirical studies that have followed Piaget's work over the past 25 years and continue to influence how we pose research questions about children's family-related thinking.

Vygotsky: What Children Know But Can't Yet Express

Meanwhile, from our classroom observations of children exploring family, we saw, simply, that children *do* bring their various experiences of family to discussions, play, artwork, and even off-hand remarks that demonstrate their ongoing thoughts about what constitutes a family. The depth and simplicity of the children's expression were powerful. We became much more interested in how these affect-laden experiences *interacted* with children's developing relational thinking, and beyond this, about the teacher's role in creating opportunities for children to develop such concepts (Gash & Morgan, 1993; Rogoff, 1990). Vygotsky's (1934/1962) theoretical approach to spontaneous (everyday) versus formal (scientific) concepts provided a strong foundation from which to build. However, these two processes are very different—"the child's spontaneous concepts proceed upward, and the development of his scientific concepts downward" (p. 108). Vygotsky stressed the importance of their connection and mutuality. *There is an interaction between what we know intuitively (spontaneous/everyday), but cannot yet express, and concepts we have learned (formal/scientific) but for which we do not yet have significant experience to bring richness of meaning.* If we continue with the example of a young child having a brother, we can see how Vygotsky's everyday experience of "that little guy in the bottom bunk bed" moves upward, and mingles with the formal/scientific kinship term over time, as the child's more abstract and relational thinking develops.

More recent works that build on Vygotsky's (1934/1962) ideas reflect a renewed appreciation of situated learning (Lave & Wenger, 1991), degrees of contextual support (Rogoff, 1990), and the role of individual differences (Scarr, 1992) in how a child links meaning with experience.

Getting at the Role of Experience

A review of research on children's conceptions of family from the 1970s through the 1990s (Gilby & Pederson, 1982; Newman, Roberts, & Syre, 1993; Pederson & Gilby, 1986) shows a trend in which experiences with family have a minimal impact on two key areas: how children *define* a family (intention) and which groupings of people they determine to be examples (extension) of a family. What sifting through this data reveals, is newsworthy. Time spent with various family members (Pederson & Gilby, 1986), family-related curricula (Watson & Amgott-Kwan, 1984), and, most important, living in a particular family form (Brodzinsky, Schecter, & Brodzinsky, 1986; Newman et al., 1993; Pederson & Gilby, 1986; Powell, Wilcher, Wedemeyer, & Claypool, 1981) seemed to have no effect on children's comprehension or validation of those living situations as family, at least when evaluated through individual child assessments.

The essence and the strength of these data seemed counterintuitive to us. While almost all these researchers used increased family diversity as a rationale for their work and some called for more diverse samples in future research (McGoldrick, 1989b; Newman et al., 1993), only a handful included samples of divorced/single-parent-headed households. It is these few studies that point toward the finding that children living in such families *are* more likely to accept a single-parent-headed family as an example of family (Camara, 1979; Moore, 1977; Wedemeyer, Bickhard, & Cooper, 1989); that children with primary parenting by heterosexual married fathers, *do* appreciate the nurturing potential of fathers in significantly different ways from their mother-parented peers (Pruett, 1992); and that children's experience with divorcing parents *is* instrumental in their ability to think about both marriage and divorce with greater complexity (Mazur, 1993). No studies to date include samples of children from lesbian- and/or gay-headed families as a form of family experience.

Where does all this theory and research lead us? We believe it is important to be aware of the historical context of the theoretical approaches in our midst and think about the ways in which they have influenced the research questions asked and the methods used in studies about children's lives. And while some of us may use various aspects of theory and research that others discard, what seems most important is to consider what the particular children in our lives are actually thinking, feeling, and saying. Teachers and parents are then in a better position to support and extend their learning, not just answer their questions.

CLASSROOM CONVERSATIONS

To test out our theories, we listened to discussions about family that were held in first- and second-grade classrooms in an urban, independent, progressive school for children ages 3 to 13. In this school, teachers often open daily classroom meetings with questions to prompt a discussion as an ongoing part of the curriculum. Each class already included family study as a part of its naturally evolving curriculum. While perhaps not "typical," we view this school environment as rich in family-related experiences. From these discussions we can see how children's ideas about human conception, gay parents, and their strong emotions about their own families are inextricably linked. In short, it seems clear that young children do learn about a variety of family structures from the families and children around them.

First Graders

As part of an ongoing focus on families, 5- and 6-year-olds in this first-grade class had wondered about exactly who could marry. During the course of their play a question had arisen about boys marrying boys, or girls marrying girls. The children arrived one morning to see that their teacher, Paul, had put these questions on the chart to discuss in their morning group meeting: "Can a man marry a man? Can a woman marry a woman?" A child with two gay fathers was a member of this group but did not participate in this particular discussion nor, on this occasion, was that family raised as a specific example by any other child. Also of interest is the fact that Nell gets the conversation off the ground by relating a story about her lesbian aunts. Clearly, it is heard by members of the group, but no one comments on it directly. As adults, we don't really know what effect this story has on the other children. This subtle moment highlights a case in point about individual differences as well. Consider how the following conversations affect these two children who have experiences with gay-headed families but do not play a central role in the discussion. The meeting begins with Robert responding to the question on the chart.

> Robert: They don't really marry. But they can live together if both agree. It's called roommates. It's not when a woman and man live together, but it is when a man and a man or a woman and a woman live together.
>
> Nell: My cousin has two moms. They got divorced from their husbands. They started to love each other and asked each other, "Do you want to live together?" They said yes.
>
> Jacob: A man can marry a man and a woman can marry a woman. Two people could adopt a child and take care of it for a couple if they're too sick.
>
> *Paul*: Would they have to adopt a child for it to be like marrying?
>
> Mark: I'm not sure.
>
> Jeff: It means "gay." It means if a man and a man get married.
>
> Sarah: Is gay for a woman marrying a woman or a man marrying a man or both?
>
> Jeff: Both.
>
> Ned: We're not talking about gay or adopting a child. We're talking about a man marrying a man and a woman marrying a woman.
>
> Kwana: What are you saying?
>
> Ned: When you get old enough, the child who's adopted goes off on his own and is on his own.

Parts of this discussion reflect dialogue that is classically Piagetian in its pre-operational nature, or, more exactly, an example of the egocentric thinking of children. The juxtapositioning of thoughts that results in such striking use of non sequitor is punctuated with occasional moments of clarity (what adults recognize as logical thought), as spontaneous and formal concepts work toward a common ground in the manner Vygotsky outlines. Yet underneath the apparent chaos, big ideas are in motion. Individual differences shine here as well. Children's experiences of family are sufficiently varied as are their abilities and motivations to express them.

As the discussion proceeds, children connect the question of marriage to rules of the state in a manner not unlike Piaget found children to do in his twin studies of family and country. The children slide back and forth with great fluidity, moving with apparent ease from rules to laws, cities to the universe (Casper et al., 1996). Children's main source of evidence tends to be what they see and what they've been told. Gross generalizations mingle with specificities. There are occasional attempts at making connections, which Paul, their teacher, helps to orchestrate with clear questions. Soon their conversation drifts back to who can marry. The reader can see that Paul is gently nudging them back to consider the difference between getting married and "living together."

Ned: My friend has two mothers, and they told me they were married, and they aren't breaking any laws. I'm not sure, but maybe.

Dan: They probably got married in another place and came here.

Ned: You might be right about that.

Paul: What's the difference between living together and getting married?

Rachel: When you get married, it's a wedding and you have lots of people.

Sarah: In New York when someone falls in love they want to live together and get married.

Paul: Can you talk about falling in love?

Sarah: They meet somebody. They like each other a lot and fall in love.

Leah: My brother is getting married. He's only inviting a few people.

Kwana: You don't have to have a lot of people to get married. My mom didn't.

Ned: When my uncle got married, he didn't go to a building or church. He stayed in his house and got married there. You can do it in a synagogue.

Paul: What's getting married?

Sam: You don't have to like . . . you have to love to get married. Loving means more than liking.

Rachel: You have to wear fancy clothes. There's something called a wedding dress.

In the above, the children become embroiled again in issues of states and laws. Only Sam is able to rise above the fray and distinguish loving from liking someone. And it is clear that the children have a burgeoning comprehension that rules, laws, love, and marriage are connected, but they get bogged down in the details. Again, Paul helps redirect. He uses his professional self in an uncommonly bold manner as he tells them, "*I* more than like you. In certain ways you could say I love you. What does that have to do with getting married?" The chil-

dren take him quite literally, almost chiding him with a feigned con-
descension, saying, "Grownups can't marry a kid. They are too young
to get married." Paul takes another tack. He summarizes the essence of
what the children have said so far about marriage and asks, "What else
is there about marriage?" This too gets derailed with a long and involved
discussion about conception and birth. Paul follows up on their lead,
asking, "Can a man and a man have a baby? Can a woman and a woman
have a baby?

> Mark: A girl, woman, can have a baby without getting married.
>   Like my mom.
> Ned: You don't have to have a baby to get married. Men can't
>   have a baby.
> *Paul*: Can two men living together have children?
> Ned: They'd have to adopt.

In this part of the discussion it is Mark who identifies his own family configuration as an exception to the rule that adults usually get
married before having a child. Aside from Nell's remark about her aunts,
he is the first child to use his own family in such a self-revealing manner. The class discussion has covered quite a bit of ground and it is time
to bring the meeting to a close.
   The next week, these first graders continue their discussion, focus-
ing more closely on the question, "What is a family?" By the middle
of the meeting, Paul summarizes the various family structures that have
been mentioned so far.

> *Paul*: Listen, we've been talking about what is a family. And many
>   of you folks have said a family is a mother and a father and a
>   baby, a mother and a father and more than one child, and
>   some of you said there can be a mother and a child, and some
>   of you said that there can be a father and a child, and Jeff said
>   that it could be two.
> Jeff: Two mothers *or* two fathers.
> *Paul*: Two fathers and you called that gay. Is there anything else
>   (than in the above list)? And how about Jeff's idea about two
>   men.
> Jeff: Two *fathers*.
> *Paul*: Not two men, two fathers, you called them two fathers and
>   two mothers. Let's talk about that a bit.
> Sarah: There could be a grandfather and a grandma and some-
>   times there's an uncle or an aunt.

Kwana: I don't think a woman and a woman or a man and a man can make a baby together.

Paul: Why don't you think a woman and a woman or a man and a man can make a baby together?

Kwana: Because the man has to help the woman make a baby.

Maggie: A man and a man can't have a baby because a man can't have a baby, and a woman and a woman can't have a baby because the man has to help the woman have a baby.

Paul: Can a woman and a woman be a family without having a baby?

Kwana: Yes.

Fred: When a man and a man live together, I think I know what it's called.

Paul: What?

Fred: When they just live together, they're roommates.

Paul: So anytime a man and a man are living together, then it's called roommates?

Fred: I don't know.

Paul: You don't know. (Pause) Last week, Jeff said that a man and a man together is gay, and you are saying that a man and a man living together, that's roommates. Are gay and roommates the same thing or is it different? Does anybody have an idea about that?

Leah: Well, I don't really know, but I'm going to take a guess. I think it's sort of the same thing.

Kwana: It doesn't mean the same thing because gay is a little older and roommates are a little younger.

Maggie: Sort of gay is where you kind of like aren't really married, but kind of roommates don't sleep together they just live together.

Paul: Well what would be the difference between being kind of like married and being roommates. How would they be different?

Maggie: It's hard to explain.

Paul: It's hard to explain or it makes you uncomfortable?

Maggie: Hard to explain.

In this section, Jeff begins by insisting on specificity. He is clear that the topic is two fathers, not just two men, and this appears to make a difference to him. The group eventually gets down to basic biological issues when Fred sidetracks them again. He makes the same pronouncement Robert made at the beginning of the original discussion the week before, only to have Kwana offer the insight that age is the distinguishing factor between being roommates and being gay. Finally, Maggie gets very close to the center of the issue by offering her understanding that roommates don't sleep together. She takes this notion as far as she is able. Paul is a bit frustrated, and a spectator might wonder if this discrepant discourse is really worth the effort.

Yet listening to just these two discussions serves as an introduction to how and why children may be thinking what they are thinking. Paul achieves a fine balance of letting them explore the issues while guiding them to help them name what it is they know. These children were not being *taught* about gay and lesbian families, they were being encouraged to struggle with definition, using both their everyday/spontaneous experiences with family and more formal language that some children had already begun to integrate into their everyday life.

Second Graders

In discussions held in 2 second-grade classrooms, we saw children bring their own experiences into the service of more fully developed ideas in which they were increasingly invested. The conversations wandered less.

A year-long study of the city had culminated with each of the classes building a "crate city" (they used wine crates to create individual buildings—such as apartments, a library, and an auto shop). The crate project became central in both rooms, with excitement mounting as the cities began to take shape. In this study, children worked as a community to make decisions about who would live in the city (using scaled figures created by the children), what relationships they would have, what buildings should look like, and what jobs were necessary to make the city function well. Parallel to this study, both groups had spent a good part of the year discussing families, their own and others', and what was important to them about family.

In mid-spring, Pat, one of the teachers, expressed her surprise and dismay to us at the conventional nature of the families her children created for their city. The children's actual families represented great diversity, and they had had such rich discussions about family all year. When she then presented her puzzlement to the children, their response was "it's the usual" (i.e., "it's normal"); there was "no room"; "they wouldn't fit." Toward the end of the discussion, Pat asked the children to think about a child with two mothers who was in the other group. She asked them to consider what it might be like for him. Most of them had more than just an awareness of his family—they had experienced his parents at school, seen the family in the neighborhood, or played with him in his home—all experiences Pat asked them to bring to consciousness.

The group in the other second-grade classroom were a bit behind Pat's group in the construction of their city. After our research group and both second-grade teachers watched a videotape of the discussion in Pat's room, Lia, the other teacher, held a meeting with her class in which she reminded the children that they previously had talked about the different kinds of families represented in the room and that she was asking them again to think about "the people you live with—what you think of as your family . . . [or] maybe you don't live with them and you consider them to be your family." A few children named those in their family, and the discussion then went to some of their feelings about family, including how children feel when grownups argue. Lia facilitated the expression of these important childhood emotions and then encouraged others to talk, noting specifically, "Or, if what other people are saying is making you think about ways in which your family may be different, we'd like to hear about that."

After various children described what their divorced, blended, and single-parent families look like, eventually the one child in the class with two lesbian mothers described his family as ". . . two moms and a dad. My two moms live with me, and my dad lives in Philadelphia, and it's confusing." A discussion ensued about just what the confusing part was, a discussion that was no different in tone from a preceding conversation about how another child figures out which parent's apartment he will be at on the weekend. Lia concluded the discussion by telling them that there probably were even a greater number of kinds of families that weren't mentioned because not everyone spoke and some children were absent. She continued, "But you know what, folks? In the next couple of days I'm going to ask you to be thinking about what kind of family would you like to make. I'd like you to be thinking about how many people you'll be creating—who they might be."

When the city was finished, one could see that this discussion did more than just remind the children that they all come from a wide variety of family structures. In the process of drawing and constructing people for their families in the crate city, the children experimented, commented, asked questions, and sometimes changed their family planning. When, during the course of their discussions, the idea of a family headed by two men came up, one 7-year-old said emphatically, "A man and a man *can't* make a baby . . . because an egg and an egg . . . what can *they do*? You need a sperm and an egg." Whereupon, a classmate responded, "I wasn't talking about making a baby, I was talking about sex!" This part of the discussion directly parallels the content of the first graders' conversations about two women needing a man to make a baby. The last words we were privy to in that conversation open the door to the concepts these youngsters enter into with more clarity. One first grader let us know that roommates don't sleep together and gay men living together do. This second grader is able to distinguish between making a baby and sex.

Three girls initially expressed the desire to create a lesbian-headed family with a female child. One also included two gay men. When the families actually were created and the city finished, there was one lesbian-headed family (not created by the child with lesbian mothers) and numerous other constellations that broadly represented the family diversity of the children in the class. And, by a unanimous vote it was decreed: No babysitters allowed in this crate city!

What was the role of experience for these second graders? In itself, the creation of a city with families served as a grounding experience. Yet without conscious framing, children automatically leaned toward a more prototypic model for their families. After their families were completed, Pat took quite an active role when she asked children to consider a child they knew well whose parents were two mothers. Children in Lia's group had an opportunity to reflect on their own and each other's families and some particular feelings and thoughts about family *before* creating families for themselves. Once again, a group discussion made their experiences and knowledge more consciously available for them to use in their work and play.

THOUGHTS ON RESEARCH AND PRACTICE

These discussions are but moments in the long year that a class of children spend together. What transpired there cannot be directly compared with the many quantitatively based studies that preceded it. Yet in these moments multiple issues were raised. What these three classrooms had in common was the creation of an environment that made lesbian- and gay-headed families salient, but as a natural part of the spectrum of family possibilities. In different ways, each learning environment was transformed into a place in which assumptions about what constitutes a family were unhinged, creating a different standard from the one from which children usually take their cues. This allowed children to venture forth with their thoughts, questions, fantasies, and feelings about family, which clearly were based on their experiences with their own families and those of children around them. Their conversations also make us question how such basic topics can ever be considered finished in a curriculum module, never to be revisited again.

The research literature on family appears to be based on samples that do not fully reflect today's families and methods that do not evoke all we need to know. In order to learn more, research methods must give children greater room to describe what they know across the range of contexts in which they learn and know about families. It's clear, for example, that children's thoughts about family are deeply informed by their emotional responses to family, and a way must be found to look at these interconnections. Children's questions, too, seem very important to understand, especially at a time when there is so much adult conflict over what constitutes a family. Much of the foundational theory we use seems rooted in a past that promotes family form over function.

Do young children really just copy the prototypic view of family, regardless of the form their own family takes? Do these traditional molds really provide security for all children? Are they truly the "Ideal" against which the realities of difference compete (Newman et al., 1993; Pederson & Gilby, 1986)? Our practice helps children name the known and the obvious, sure, but it must do more. Evocative questions help children reach into their own experience and pull out what they know and want to know. In the next chapters we explore some of the paths adults must take in order to develop the courage and master the skills required to have such conversations with children.

CHAPTER 3

Adult Points of View

The biggest thing about being gay and interacting in the straight world. . . . Among those people whose hearts are basically in the right place, but whose consciousnesses have not had a lot of exposure, the biggest problem is that they just don't want to discuss it.

—June, lesbian mother

I think a lot of times people will know someone who is lesbian or gay, but it's not really discussed and they don't really know if the person is lesbian or gay.

—Cathy, kindergarten teacher

We each grow up with different experiences that shape us. For parents, educators, and children, one's age, background, and the historical period and geographical area in which one has lived all shape one's developing lens. While most of our stories differ, even the ones that appear similar in nature or theme are not experienced in the same way by the individuals who figure in them. Who we are—our temperaments—and the cultural, economic, and social contexts in which we find ourselves are all influential in shaping the way we read life experiences, our own and the stories others tell.

EDUCATORS' OUTLOOKS

We wanted to discover what teachers and administrators think about gayness—what they bring to their interactions with children and gay families. The educators we interviewed represent a breadth of points of view about gay and lesbian issues based on their own childhood experiences and their past and current interactions with gay people. None of their stories are out of the ordinary. Their typicality is their strength. We glean from the interviews the ways in which prior experiences have influenced them, and how they have used their experiences to think about the lesbian- and gay-headed families with whom they work. We heard stories from people whose points of view changed greatly, and from others whose personal thoughts on these issues remained consistent.

Another of our intents was to explore if and how teachers' ongoing work with lesbian- and gay-headed families changed them. We wondered if and how these experiences may have helped them further develop their own values and philosophies about child development and pedagogy. Where discomfort with the topic persisted, some educators clearly articulated the origins of their own biases and tried to stay aware of them. This process is crucial in making distinctions between one's personal belief system and how one approaches a family that one encounters in a professional capacity.

Prior Experiences

When we asked educators about their first experiences with gay people, they shared their thoughts and memories quite openly. In the following, Sasha, a young preschool teacher, reflects on how she came to discover that a little boy in her class had two fathers:

> I can't say I've always been comfortable with it [gay and lesbian issues]. It's hard for me to look back on it and remember. But I remember thinking, when Jeffrey said, "I slept with my two daddies," "OK, now what do I do with that?"

The next recollections are from a teacher, Penny, who got to know gay men and lesbians during her college years, a time that for many presents a first opportunity to meet young people who may be different from themselves.

> I have gay friends . . . men. I guess when I was in college, some classmates were lesbians. I don't remember a time not being comfortable talking about it. I went to college when I was 16, and then I became aware of it. . . . I don't remember discussing it with my family until recently, and it is totally unacceptable. The Bible says so. My father would never see it as a normal situation. My mother is more open to it. I don't remember when I first became aware. But when I came to America the first person I met was a gay male who is now a very good friend . . . someone I have felt very comfortable with.

While personally knowing gay and lesbian people outside of the world of education is not a prerequisite for interacting with gay and lesbian parents in the schools, for some teachers it seems to have made a difference in their own comfort level. It allowed them to ask questions and become more knowledgeable about gay issues and concerns. The next teacher we quote, Cathy, who also met gay and lesbian people for the first time at college, makes an important distinction about the explicit or implicit manner in which a person's gay identity is revealed to a "straight" person.

> I think [I first became comfortable with lesbians and gay men] as an undergraduate at college. There were a whole lot of people who were very open about it. I think a lot of times people will know someone who is lesbian or gay, but it's not *really* discussed and they don't *really* know if the person is lesbian or gay. Whereas at college, people were out in no uncertain terms. They were very clear about it. I've heard this many times, that one of the biggest ways of breaking down stereotypes is actually spending time with someone who is whatever it is you have a stereotype about. So I guess if I had a lot of stereotypes, and I'm not really sure at this point what I did think . . . but knowing people and working with people who I knew were gay, definitely encouraged me not to have them anymore.

In this last excerpt, Cathy not only reflects on her first experiences getting to know gay people, but realizes that what was particularly important was their clear acknowledgment about their sexual orientation. It wasn't just quietly assumed and forgotten, but openly discussed. Cathy identifies a well-worn notion that not only getting to know gay people, but being engaged in their issues, can help chip away at one's stereotypes of others. Research reviews on attitudes toward homosexuality demonstrate that people with negative attitudes tend to report less contact or knowledge of gay people (Herek, 1984), as well as the converse (Schmalz, 1993). Measuring attitudes is sticky business, however. Much of the literature is conflicting and difficult to untangle (Sears, 1992), and the relationship between attitudes and behaviors has never been a clean one. It is also worthy of note that each of these three teachers state that they just don't remember very well what they used to think. Often we screen out memories that are painful or irreconcilable with current thinking.

What about experiences later in life? In the next excerpt, Emory, a public school principal, is asked what has helped him to develop an inclusive philosophy in his school. By his account, inclusiveness is based on a "live and let live" point of view. For him, first contact with gay men and lesbians came through the neighborhood in which he lives, long after his college years were over.

> As a matter of a fact, I grew up in an area that was very White, middle-class, looked like everyone was cut from the same mold. I think what has affected me the most is living here [in Greenwich Village, New York City] where so many—I don't think you can function here unless you become a person who is very acceptable, understanding of difference. . . . As far as I'm concerned, everybody has the right to do whatever they want to do, as long as it doesn't infringe on my rights. I can do whatever I want to do, they can do whatever they want to do. People can live the way they want to live. I'll live the way I want to live—doesn't bother me.

Emory repeats his points enough times to make them border on the defensive. While emphasizing that Greenwich Village requires an openness to diversity, he juxtaposes his life with the lives of his gay neighbors by distancing himself from a way of life that is separate from his. There is no overlap. According to a study of American beliefs (Wolfe, 1998), Emory's distanced viewpoint is representative of a large proportion of Americans. A commonly found precept seems to be that as long as you keep your judgments to yourself, you are engaged in a form of "Thou shalt not judge." It's also noteworthy that compared with the rich descriptions of the personal contacts with gay people described by the three women teachers above, Emory's description is more objective and cerebral. In the following, Enrico, another public school administrator of the same generation as Emory, recalls that it was his sister, a lawyer doing civil rights work for gay people, who started him thinking about the issue. Until then, he hadn't given the matter much thought.

> I don't even remember thinking about it, to be quite honest with you. No . . . I don't think I ever really thought about it. I'm laughing because I have a sister who's a lawyer, who at one point was representing gay people. She had a very strong point of view with respect to their needs being incorporated into all aspects of our society and had a very strong opinion about what was going on. I remember teasing her, kidding her about that.

For some, their attitudes and feelings about being gay derive from broader associations with diversity and their own parallel experiences of bias in other areas such as race, gender, and class. Here Nilda, an Afro-American early childhood administrator, articulates this in simple and clear terms.

> I have biases, but that's not one of them. I don't know. What makes me open to some things and not open to others? . . . This may not be all of it, but it's a link I can think about right now. I don't like bias or prejudice, I'm very intolerant of bias or prejudice in whatever form. And I see too much of it, I have to live with too much of it, I see the implications, I see the effect it has on people. I don't know if the worst thing you could be in the world is a homosexual. I don't know *what* it is, but I detest bias.

Lise, another early childhood administrator, has had experiences in which she felt different. Such moments, whatever their duration, serve as a pivot to help her identify with what gay parents might be feeling in a heterosexual school culture. Growing up as a child of Polish immigrants who felt different and isolated contributed to Lise's sensitivity to differences.

> Very shortly after I was born, they [my parents] moved to Long Island, which was at that time a very White, monolingual middle-class culture. Differences weren't tolerated very easily. I just remember being very sensitive to that, and I've always felt I had one foot in the American culture and one foot in the Polish culture. And that's how it is, and that's how it will always be. And that's fine, but I think about other people who have other diverse styles that are just an integral part of their identity that really isn't part of the mainstream, that you have an area of yourself that in many ways is very different from what other people have experienced.

For Beverly, a guidance counselor, it was her own politicization through family members that affected her thinking about difference. She believes one has to work backward from one's current philosophy to construct the roots of one's consciousness. She sees that in her own case; her political upbringing made a difference in how she then raised her children, confirming for her the importance of inclusive policies in schools.

> It seems to me that all my adult life I've been involved in areas where that is exactly what we were trying to do, be inclusive. I think the civil rights movement had a very big impact on me—its

successes and its failures. I think probably my childhood, which included very strong feeling about unions, and also a pair of aunts who were Communists in the 1930s and who were closer to my age than to my mother's age, and whom I spent a great deal of time with. They taught me a lot about people being different, that that's the way life was, and that everybody deserved a break. That certainly influenced me politically, and that carries over into an educational philosophy.

The connections made by these two educators, connections between early experiences and present-day attitudes, point to both the importance and complexity of the development and investigation of one's perspective. The common feature in both of these stories is the importance of personally feeling different for some reason, and the concurrent emphasis on diversity. Lise describes a set of experiences that were linked by theme and that affected her on a deep, unspoken, almost visceral level. She can recall and connect these experiences to her own sense of present-day identity, and identify how they help her to be respectful of a variety of other differences in people. The explicit communications to Beverly by her family about the sanctity of human diversity are highlighted—made more personal and therefore more powerful—by the human connection that is evident in her description of her two aunts. In both stories, the recognition of diversity raises the unexpected; it challenges assumptions and prevents the establishment of human blandness inherent in the false idea that all of us are (or should be) the same in every way.

Sometimes diverse ways of experiencing and of expressing occur within the same person over a period of time. For me (Steven), how I received the world, and what I expressed in it, was changed the moment I became a parent, just as it did after I became ill, when my companion died from AIDS, and also by the children in each of my classes starting at the beginning of each school year. All of these people and events affected me deeply. They seemed to be more than what they were. Like the experiences cited by Lise and Beverly, they created shifts, they let the kaleidoscope through which I received the world be twisted; and they altered the range, pitch, or tone of my voice as they suggested new vocabulary to describe my new sets of experiences. Just as these same events must affect the lives of other individuals who experience them, they changed my perspective; they changed my world. Because perspectives are so personal, so idiosyncratic, and at the same time are shaped by cultural and social dynamics, they conspire to make the deconstruction of one's view anything but a simple matter. But certainly autobiography—remembering and connecting the stories of the people and events that make up one's life—makes us take a step forward.

Sometimes our own stories—although maintaining their potent effects—become elusive as they are lost to our conscious selves. And sometimes we get them back by talking about an experience. Philip Jackson in his book *Untaught Lessons* (1992) writes of the mysterious ways that our early experiences and our memories of them affect our present-day selves. They are mysterious because it is so difficult, and sometimes impossible, to put our finger on the particular event or interaction that was so influential to our current ways of understanding (Schultz, 1994). It is interesting that, when events or interactions are inaccessible, the *person* usually is not, for Philip Jackson or for our informants. The person, the values, and the relationship form the essence of those memories that are especially meaningful, but we may not know in exactly what way.

Jackson, for instance, remembers his high school math teacher with affection and with the distinct impression that although he cannot identify why or how, "Mrs. Henzi, standing at the side of the room opposite the windows, her glasses flashing with reflected light," had a definite and powerful influence on him (pp. 1–2). Given this complexity, the deeply rooted ways we have of seeing and interpreting our experiences, and, at the same time, the always-present possibilities for changes within ourselves, we wanted to explore the snippets of stories teachers shared with us, but with caution. We wondered which stories from their own childhood come forth without effort. What did they recall? And how did they use these recollections to connect with the children they teach?

Teachers' Childhoods Recalled

Numerous educators spoke about a dichotomy between the ways in which they were raised and the ways in which they wished to make changes in their own attitudes toward difference. Carla, a young preschool teacher, works in a child-care center just outside the NYC metropolitan area where there has been no discussion about gay and lesbian issues, although a child in her group has two mothers. Carla did not, at first, recognize that Alberto's parents were lesbians, even though they altered the application so they could write their names in as "co-parents" rather than use the "mother/father" slots originally on the application. Carla tried to fit the fact that a just-3-year-old child has two female parents into her existing worldview. Maybe one of the

women is Alberto's aunt, she thought, or his mother's friend or room-
mate. When the realization hit that this child's parents were lesbians,
Carla struggled with the knowledge and the way that it made her feel.
She was not immediately comfortable with this family arrangement.
In an interview, she searched for reasons, from her past, that could help
her understand her own reactions.

> I'm not always the most liberal person in the world, so when I meet
> somebody who is in some way different I know that I have my
> prejudices. You can't help that. I grew up in middle-class America
> with White people all around. So all of those things are still there as
> much as you can eventually get rid of them—however you get rid
> of things like that. It's hard because you don't know what questions
> to ask. How do you approach someone and ask them something
> personal? Where do you begin? . . . What if somebody says to me,
> "It's none of your damn business"?

This same teacher begins to answer her own question about how
"you get rid of things like that," by citing a childhood memory from
fourth grade in a Catholic school. She recalls the confusion she felt
concerning the origin of her name as an empathetic link with Alberto,
who was being asked by other children in the class if he had a father.
Carla describes the child as "a very sensitive boy. . . . Who knows, he
might feel that he can't ask or . . . I don't know, maybe kids build up
huge stories." Carla then describes how unbeknownst to her, her name
had been changed at age 1. When it was time to be confirmed in school,
she brought in her baptismal certificate, and the nun told her it was
the wrong name. Carla clearly has access to the emotions that were
unleashed for her at the time.

> You know you don't need much time as a child to think up things,
> your mind just goes crazy and I started thinking I must have had a
> twin sister and she died or maybe they gave her away or maybe
> there was something wrong, maybe she's still alive. So you start to
> think these things. And I think that even at 3 you certainly have a
> vivid enough imagination to begin to think, "Well, where is this
> father of mine?"

Even more personal memories were spontaneously raised by our
informants as handles with which to get a better perspective on theoretical child development questions related to the children they were
teaching. Of the teacher informants represented in our study, there were

only two male teachers, reflecting the scarcity of men in the early child-hood teaching profession (Lee & Wolinsky, 1973). The following ex-changes compare the experiences of these two men who, by chance, both lost their fathers in childhood and both are teachers of 5-year-old boys being raised by lesbian mothers without a father living in the home. Fred's story is recounted first.

> My father died when I was 15. . . . You go through everything then. About 5 years ago I started to be objective about it. . . . [I had a] chip on my shoulder. But now I'm starting to look at how I acted then. It's only been in the last 5 years that I can sort it out, that it's become clear. That reflection, I think, comes with time. The same thing with the situation with Dan [the child in his class]. They [the child's parents] can set up as much as he can handle, but there are some things that you're just not going to be able to foresee . . . with the father gone, the fact that he doesn't see his father any-more. . . . It's a big break. I went through that. It causes a lot of pain, and you have to deal with it, because it's not going to change.
>
> Say in the case of Jacqueline and Nora they logically can say, "Even though we're not XYZ family, we are a functioning family and he doesn't have his father but we have this and it is important that he has us and he knows he can come to us bla bla bla," . . . and logically that's right on mark. But, the more I think about it, the more I think there's some unconscious . . . you know . . . that may play a part at some time, as in a need or even, like I say, something that's not even voiced. He is a bright boy, but he knows he's different.

Fred compares his own father's death with Dan's father's absence through divorce. We see a conflation here between the meaning and causes of father absence in childhood. It is clear, however, from this statement alone, that his concerns about this child's long-term devel-opment come from a place of caring, influenced by his own personal experience. During another point in the interview, Fred talks about trying to identify with any child in a situation of need. He offers other anecdotes emphasizing the lack of a father figure in Dan's life, which he thinks makes Dan feel different.

Also drawing from personal experience, Sol brings up his father's death to make a different point concerning the effects of father absence. Sol questions the assumption that a boy growing up with two mothers must, of necessity, have a male figure in his life. His experience with father loss has a very different meaning for him. He is clear about this, and it has become part of his viewpoint about what children need to develop.

> Where I'm coming from is that my father died when I was 9 and a lot of the adult men really moved in to fill the gap. I appreciated it, and even then I understood that my mother was alone and a lot of people were supporting us and it was important. [But] without being able to verbalize it, I understood from that age that this was really offensive. The assumption wasn't that I had lost a specific human being who could not be replaced, but that I had lost the man that has to be in a boy's life, and I was offended by the whole idea of big brothers. So whether I was gay or straight, I would have this perspective that it is absurd to say you need a male or a female role model. You need at least one caring adult caretaker, period.

These two teachers most clearly demonstrate how similar experiences, when framed against their own worldview, make it possible to come up with diametrically opposed conclusions. Many of the points of view expressed in these vignettes pull from deep personal experiences. Just as we know the power they have to influence an individual's present understandings of lesbian and gay people, we want to interject a note of caution. Without stepping back and looking at any charged issue with a more objective lens, the closeness of personal memories also *can* have the potential to cloud one's vision. We would not want to encourage educators to allow these raw materials to unreflectively direct their practice.

These are such personal stories. We know the interview process plays a role in bringing these experiences into the foreground of an informant's consciousness. To what degree, and how, such recollections intermingle with theory and training in a given teacher, however, is never fully known. Personal experience as a basis of teacher knowledge is a double-edged sword (Bowman & Stott, 1994). It is exactly this kind of personal examination, especially when extended through dialogue, and reflective examination with others, that can help educators make distinctions and connections between their own experiences and how they understand other families. Here then, are just a few of the myriad ways in which one's prior exposure to similar and different experiences doesn't by definition, but can, with varying degrees of self-conscious examination, help educators open themselves up to the needs of others.

At the same time, it was not always clear either at what level connections were made to one's personal life or whether those connections were consistent with one's work in the schools. For example, one administrator said that after the series of interviews and having given this topic more thought, he no longer let his older son say the word *faggot* without having a discussion about the disrespect inherent in the word. This same administrator talked to one teacher before a child with two same-sex parents entered her class, but neglected to do so the following year for the next teacher. We don't know what his reasons were, and never will. But if it was not an oversight, his lack of communication the second time around makes us wonder why an administrator would think some teachers should be informed while others need not have that information. Change is complex. There is no way to predict how a new sensitivity displayed in one context may match a person's behavior in another context.

These interviews speak to the dearth of earnest dialogue on the general topic of homosexuality in our society, specifically as it surrounds issues in early childhood education. We believe educators have few chances to think about their own experiences with any kind of diversity. Such moments can open up pathways for reflection, which in turn may help teachers think about new ways to approach parents who are or are perceived as being different from themselves. As more people in education incorporate principles of anti-bias (Derman-Sparks, 1989), multiculturalism, and inclusion, we strongly encourage educators to take some time to reflect on their prior experiences with homosexuality. This will help prepare them to really be able to respond to the needs of gay and lesbian parents and their children.

PARENTS' PERCEPTIONS

Like educators, parents we interviewed also represent a wide range of experience, in terms of both their family structures and the degrees to which they are open about their sexual orientation. In spite of these differences, they also share some similar thoughts and feelings about being gay or lesbian parents in a heterosexual school culture. Like the teachers of their children, gay and lesbian parents' prior experiences affect them too. Given that these experiences occur in a heterosexist world, they frequently can contain an internalized form of oppression (Friere, 1986) that can be difficult to locate and name.

Nevertheless, parents have similar aspirations and educational goals for their children, regardless of whether they are out to their children's schools. A commonly expressed sentiment was that their first school or child-care experience (the point of entry into an educational system) was the hardest, but was also one that had great meaning for them in their development as parents.

Experiences in Schools

The most crucial point has to do with parents appreciating a proactive stance by educators. This was a resounding message expressed primarily by those who were out to the school as being gay or lesbian, such as June.

> We have tried to make ourselves available to our kids' teachers from the time we first put them in nursery school. One of the biggest problems for us is getting the teacher to ask the questions. It doesn't matter how many engraved invitations we send or how much information we volunteer, we get the lowered eyes . . . and you know, yes, they're all just fine about it, as long as we don't really talk about it much. And Penny's really the first person who's said, "What can I read, what should I tell children about it?"

Open discussion is central to our findings and comes up repeatedly in a multitude of our informants' statements. The idea that gay families can become like other families only once a difference has been acknowledged was inherently understood by lesbian and gay families and even, implicitly, by many of their children. Many gay parents related that heterosexual parents of children in their children's classes also don't acknowledge their different family structure. The following story is told by two lesbian mothers who spent the first year in their son's new school going to many parent meetings and events.

> Maureen: And we went to a family meeting this fall where all the parents sat around with the teacher and we went around and said who we were.
> Naomi: You went first. You said, "I'm Derrick's mom." And I said, "I'm Derrick's other mom."
> Maureen: And we didn't know at that point if the other parents knew what was what. Nobody raised their hand and said, "I don't understand!" . . . Nobody said, "How disgusting." People are very, "Did I hear that right?" They let it go. And unless you want to be very dogmatic, that kind of strategy is OK 'cause they will get clearer and they need to take it in slowly. Anyway, we went to a Christmas thing, and by this time we knew a number of parents, and we really talked to people about

school stuff, but no one had brought up the issue. No one
said, "Gee, this is interesting what you're doing. Can you tell
me about it?"

Naomi: But Paul, the class *yenta*, the father . . .

Maureen: Oh yeah [Maureen chortles], Paul, he asked, "So how
long have you two been together?" But nobody else has ever
acknowledged it. So, I don't know if we'll ever get to that
stage, because we're not the kind of people who push it, you
know.

Here, Naomi and Maureen are discussing a strategy concerning
how best to "acculturate" straight parents to a view of lesbian and/or
gay life. From this story, one can begin to appreciate the complexity
of such public encounters. Clearly, this couple wants to be acknowledged as such, yet Maureen's tolerant assessment that a slow approach
is needed doesn't articulate this need explicitly. What she describes
is a kind of process that many lesbian and gay parents think about
and implement more or less consciously with both teachers and other
parents. In other words, this couple did not say to the other parents,
"We're a lesbian-headed family." They were aware, however, that they
were perceived as such. Their feelings about the class *yenta*'s forward
questions are also mixed, as can be detected in Maureen's chortle. And
while straight people might imagine being taken aback if Paul's question were posed to them at a first school social event, nevertheless,
with his upfront style, Paul found a way to acknowledge them, which
allowed them to move on. According to our interviews, it was more
common for parents to directly come out in a one-on-one or small-
group setting than in a large group of parents or teachers. Even in
small-group situations, some of the statements our informants have
made sound clear and forthright, but they have let it be known to us
that the feelings and thoughts behind such statements are anything
but simple.

Many gay and lesbian parents spoke candidly about how they think
they are perceived by parents of other children in their children's classes.
As interviewers, we became aware of a sophisticated level of micro-
analysis of what usually are considered everyday parent-to-parent
interactions. Simple encounters such as saying hello, or families responding to playdates or birthday party invitations, are reviewed and
scrutinized in the minds of gay parents, especially at the beginning of
the school year. Below, Maritza shares her anxiety but, again, reveals
an implicit understanding or description of the processes through
which other parents become acclimated to their family makeup.

I get nervous about parents, what their reactions will be once they know the situation. How will they feel about their kids being with Alberto, being with us. . . . It's those kinds of things I worry about. Meeting the parents and what their reactions will be. Last year, one of us would pick him up, and the other would bring him to school. They thought we were the same person in a different dress (laughter). This year a few parents have been very open. It is nice. I guess the word has spread.

Another lesbian couple felt less anxiety, although their perceptions were similar to those of Maritza and her partner, Sharon. Maggie and Ricky said they really had no idea what people said about them behind their backs, but thought it was important to establish a presence with parents as well as teachers and work on helping them to develop a sensitivity and consciousness around gay issues. Ricky tells a story about a conversation at a birthday party.

We find ourselves in a struggle. I remember one birthday party we went to. Maggie had pointed Elly out as her daughter to a mother, and a half hour later I told the mother that Elly was my daughter. She was a single mother, but she certainly did not think that her child should have two mothers. . . . She gave us all her political views on how it is wrong to have two mothers . . . [that it's] quite confusing [to a child].

Growing up and living in a heterosexual society makes self-advocacy a hard-won attribute. What we want to emphasize here is what it feels like to the parents themselves. Below, a lesbian mother, Nora, in a post-divorce blended family explains why she thinks their daughter's teacher takes the biological mother [Jacqueline] more seriously than her.

From my point of view, I've always felt uncomfortable with [the teacher]. I think there are probably a lot of factors in that. When he first met [the family], Jacqueline was like everyone else. She was married and acceptable and so that was his impression of [Jacqueline]. And then I appeared on the scene. Next thing he hears is [that] Mark [Jacqueline's husband] is leaving—so I'm sure that had an impact. Also just in terms of style, I look more like a lesbian than Jacqueline does and I don't ever try to hide that so I'm just kind of there with it. . . . Every Monday I pick Dan up. Usually as parents come in, he says, "Oh, how are you?" And I just don't get that. I get, "Dan . . . Nora's here."

It may occur to some readers that Dan might have behaved similarly to a male who appeared on the caregiving horizon, if *he* was perceived as attracting Jacqueline away from Mark. But that possibility does
not take away from Nora's assessment that heterosexism is at work here.
She believes that the teacher perceives her role to be one of converting
Jacqueline to lesbianism. But more clearly, Nora is aware of being treated
differently than other parents in the class, that a social judgment is
made because she dresses and acts in masculine ways. Only a few parents could be so specific in identifying homophobia with such clear
linkages, but everyone did reveal the various ways in which they are
constantly aware that teachers, principals, and other parents may view
them differently. While they may in fact be very comfortable with their
sexual orientation, that doesn't mean they don't have to work very hard
at communicating and at simply trying to figure out what people think
and why they think it. Lesbian and gay parents spend a lot of mental
energy reading and analyzing fine social cues, which they might not
be as concerned about, except for their children's welfare.

Gay families resemble other modern families in many ways, including that many are "blended" or "reconstituted" families moving
out of either heterosexual or other gay or lesbian unions. In this
respect, too, it behooves educators to make no assumptions about
exactly who is in a given family. In the following story, Jacqueline, the
biological mother, describes in exquisite detail how her 5-year-old son
is making his transition to kindergarten as he checks out his developing feelings for his mother's new partner, Nora.

> Jacqueline: It's interesting. Part of that transformation was him
> saying things to me when we were alone, like, "Do you mind
> when Nora wasn't feeling well, that I went and got sherbert for
> her? Is that OK with you, mom?" He's kind of saying, "I might
> act to her like I might act to you, and is it OK?" So that he can
> begin to incorporate Nora . . . and has begun to express that
> verbally over a period of time in asking those kinds of questions.
> Nora: So I think in terms of school, as that evolution took place it
> seemed to him normal . . . that it would just be the way that it
> would be at school as well. And he has made a . . . connection
> between his private life and his public life.

Through the awareness of the everyday sensitivities just noted, parents must advocate for themselves and their children; and race, ethnicity,
age, and gender are but some of the aspects of a parent's identity that
interact with the experience of being gay or lesbian adults. Our infor-

mants were generous in providing the textured aspects of their lives that contribute to feeling "different," and the ways they worked to put their families forward, regardless of whether they were "out" to the schools. The following excerpts present the reflections by gay fathers who all voiced the double-edged bias they felt as a result of being gay parents and being male. Below, Manuel, a single Latino father of two sons, uses some sarcasm to express how he feels he is perceived.

> Even though we're . . . doing a relatively good job at it. (laughter) You know . . . they [the children] seem happy, content, and everything's cool and—"He manages the household and a job!" You know, it's like it's this big mystery. It's like, "Wow." Women have been doing it for, how long? There's a lot of sexism that gets tied up in all of that.

Al, a Puerto Rican man co-parenting with his African American partner, makes an even more specific link, in this case to his roots in Hispanic culture.

> One of the things that bothers me about school, and about society, is that everything has a mother and a father. And in education systems, especially in minority education systems—Puerto Rican and Hispanic—the mother is much more involved than the father. So we're the oddity. First of all, there is no mother, and secondly, two daddies. . . . So I'm battling how I'm going to deal with those questions that Luca asks later on about two daddies. "Why aren't you married?" "Why don't you have a wife?" And later on when he starts dealing with the sexuality issue of it. These are the things . . . that I don't know how to answer. And the school doesn't do anything to get people ready for that. They don't even deal with the issue of single parents, much less gay or lesbian parents.

In sum, the challenge is walking the fine line between being an advocate for your child and living in a system that may not understand your culture. As a parent you must simultaneously advocate for yourself and your child, yet stay in tune with the dominant culture. In a very powerful statement, Manuel digs back into his own educational experience, well aware that he has no choice about advocating for his children's best interests.

> I always thought, and growing up in this community and having gone to public schools here and finally getting out to go to a high

school [in another borough] which is very different . . . the one thing that I always saw was the lack of parent involvement. And I said, "If I ever have children, I'm not going to be afraid to come talk to the teacher. They're a person."

Whether or not they are out to the school, for the parents, their first priority is to get *into* the school, find out what is going on, and let the teachers know they are concerned parents. Al, for example, feels that he has to become involved in his oldest son's classroom in order to ensure that he is treated properly. But he feels that this is necessary only because the public schools are not doing their job. It's also important to remember that Al's family is not out to the public school his son attends, although he is out to his other two children's child-care center teachers.

> I go to school every day to talk to the teacher. I make sure I know what's going on in the children's classes and what's happening. And if I don't like it, I'll go in and sit in on a class. They know me in school, but I make an effort to do it. That shouldn't have to be. I shouldn't have to go to work late every day because I have to watch out for his education. That should be a part of what's being taken care of.

For parents who are out, the idea of school monitoring can be extended in other ways. James, a gay father who is out to his children's public school, told us that he and his partner make sure to interview their child's potential teachers for the following year and ask them if the gay issues will present problems for them, hoping, he said, that if they did think it would be hard for them, they would at least say so. At the same time, he speaks, as an Afro-American, about the limits of what he is willing to let his child go through to get a good education.

> I'm not going to let my child be a test case. I have so much respect and admiration for Black people who did that in the 1960s and sent their kids to those schools and were tortured. But I have no intentions. I'm sure Matthew feels the same. . . . So that's why we talk to the school and to a teacher. And we'll do the same thing next year . . . and see which one feels comfortable.

Like other parents, gay parents want the best for their children's educational experience. From these excerpts we are in touch with the ways a few parents, strongly committed individuals, have found ways to advocate for a good education for their children. It is also clear that this is not always a simple desire, but reflects many of the pressures and fears they experience as gay people who must look out for their own rights.

DILEMMAS OF DIFFERENCE

The parents we spoke with discussed their children as they interact with the heterosexual world. Embedded in this discussion were some of their hopes for their children; some of the ways in which they saw their children as similar to or different from other children as a result of living in a gay-headed household. Overall, however, gay and lesbian parents have a sense that ultimately their children will not be different from other children, although many acknowledge that there will be aspects of society that will be less than supportive. Ricky, a lesbian mother, said, "It's important to strengthen your own child so she can help herself to understand." Their daughter made her own book about her family with two moms. That book "has been a Godsend," says one of her mothers, referring to the child's ability to see her family form represented in print. James feels similarly. He fills in the details specific to *his* family traditions with the raw materials of everyday life that empower children to respond to any possible critique or hostility about their family form.

> The kids know we sleep in the bed together, and many times they end up sleeping in the bed with us, all four of us climb in the bed as families do all the time. I remember as a kid we used to climb into our parents' bed. We get kicked all the time by the kids. But that's part of being a family, and doing family projects together. So I don't see any difference. And through all that, through the comfort of who we are, and also through preparing our children to be part of a family unit, comes that strength and empowerment for them to deal with the outside world.

Dilemmas of difference come up in terms of what parents believe their children represent to others. Parents seem aware of the fact that their children's teachers may (consciously or unconsciously) be on the lookout for some unstated effects of being raised by gay or lesbian parents. In this respect, parents are unilaterally clear that their children are not different.

> June: Yeah, I think that there's a tendency for people to look at the kids, and for every characteristic about them that they find

> questionable, to wonder, are they that way because of who their parents are, instead of really respecting the child's individuality?
>
> Shelly: Right, and they would never look that closely at a kid from a regular, you know . . .
>
> June: Or they might, and they might not be looking at it in the same way. They would say, "Oh she's a tomboy, and she's very athletic." From our family, they say, "I wonder if she's that way because her moms are lesbians." Well, truthfully, she's that way because she was born with a powerhouse body and she likes to use it, you know, she's wall-to-wall muscle and you know, she was that active in the womb before she ever knew who her moms were. But that kind of stuff changes with familiarity.

Manuel thought that there is at least one important sense in which children with gay and lesbian parents *could* be different from children with heterosexual parents. Here he identifies what he sees as special qualities that develop from being aware of differences.

> I think the children in our families, our special families, come out ahead. There's a lot more for them to deal with. But I think it brings them to a level of social sophistication that these other children don't have. They're more tolerant and more sensitive, putting them in the teaching position, in a sensitizing position.

In a different but related vein, the idea has been put forward that children with gay parents need to develop special coping abilities, and comments by educators seemed to hold this implicit assumption. But the idea of coping mechanisms goes beyond the idea of special sensitivity or sophistication. A commonly accepted definition of a coping mechanism is "any conscious or unconscious adaptation that lowers tension in a stressful experience or situation" (Goldenson, 1984, p. 181).

When we brought up the issue of coping in our conversations with June and Shelly, we received an emphatic response. June thinks particular coping skills may be utilized by gay and lesbian *adults* in dealing with society, but doesn't see young children as being in that position.

> There is something that disturbs me [about the idea] that a kid in a gay or lesbian family is going to have to develop some special coping strategies, because I don't think there is any special task of coping for the kid. I think there is a certain bias built into the assumption. I think my child is going to have to develop more

coping skills to deal with the fact that she has some mild learning disabilities. I think that is going to be a bigger factor in her life in learning how to value herself . . . learning how to present herself to other people . . . than in her feelings about, or other people's reaction to, the fact she has two moms.

As outlined in Chapter 1, defining a "difference" depends on one's vantage point. Based on classroom observations of children from lesbian- and gay-headed households, we saw and heard stories of instances in which children explained their families with pride. In our interviews with parents, there were only two occasions in which the children themselves added to the discussion, directly or indirectly. Interestingly enough, Marcia, June and Shelly's daughter, echoed the thought expressed above by June, although she was not actually present for their discussion with us. Shelly thought it was important to convey Marcia's message to us.

I told her that you were coming over and are interested in children who have two moms, and two dads, and different kinds of families . . . and I asked if there was anything she wanted to say about it, and she thought that I should tell you that children aren't that different, that, in her class, you could never pick out the children that have two moms or two dads, or come from one kind of family or another kind of family. So, that's what's important to her.

This was a moment for us, as educators, in which we saw a life example of what Ricky previously described as gay parents strengthening their own child so she can "help herself to understand." When we view the world from Marcia's eyes, coping is not a word that comes to mind.

As researchers and authors, we have some thoughts about what might be considered sophistication in specific areas of development on the one hand and "coping skills" on the other. Often lumped together, these two principles reflect very different individual aspects of development. By *coping skills*, some people really are referring to a sensitivity and knowledge about gayness and disclosure. For others, there is an implicit deficit model driving the idea. The former can hold an assumption that some children sense that there are certain times and places to be quiet or hold back, akin to a silence that saves. In the latter, *coping* implies that children adapt to their yearning for a parent of the gender they do not have in their family and compensate in some way for this *lack*. This is not simply a question of semantics. It raises the familiar question of whether the deficit is within the individual, or within society's view of an entire group of people or an individual.

It is our impression from parents' reports, our own observations, and anecdotes like the one above by Marcia, that young children who are raised by gay and lesbian parents who are open and explain who they are to their children in age-appropriate ways *do* seem to be more open to *other* differences, especially, but not limited to, differences of family structure. That many children seem able to generalize about "difference" in significant ways has little to do with coping. Our sense about this is strong, and there are also some initial maternal reports that children develop increased tolerance for diversity as a result of their *queer* upbringing (Rafkin, 1990; Riddle, 1978). Young adults, who as children were raised by lesbians in the 1970s, also concur that they feel and think more openly than their peers about differences (Center Kids, 1992), although the sample size is small.

Yet, open, consistent discussions and awareness of one's different position in society vis-à-vis family may indeed make some children more alert to differences of many kinds. Some children do grow up in hostile communities. In these situations, coping may become an important asset or even a mechanism for survival. Here, the need to cope does not originate in the child and therefore is not a reflection of a deficit within her, but within the environment. We believe this is a very important use of the term *coping*.

No conclusive study of these social skills has been undertaken to date, much less how they may change over time. It does appear, however, that when family values are made explicit, children know where to go with their perceptions. Open, consistent discussions and awareness of one's different position in society vis-à-vis family can make some children alert to a more sophisticated understanding of how people are both different and the same. Both sides of the question of the effects of peer or community prejudice are well expressed by Martha Minow (1991), who refers to *any* child who is subject to such pressure.

> Experience with community hostility may injure the child's sense of self, yet such experience could also itself be the best educator and strengthen the child to deal with a world where her difference has been made to matter. (p. 40)

We also know that individual factors come into play here to a large extent and that peer pressure beginning in middle childhood often can offset such developing strengths, at least temporarily. Closer examination of how children in middle childhood understand different family constellations should help us learn about a host of intervening variables. A study of children growing up in heterosexual primary caregiving father households (Pruett, 1992), for example, supports the idea that varied parenting configurations do create a feeling of being, as a child in the study called it, "specialer" while promoting an awareness of difference being interesting and okay.

And there is other evidence supporting the idea that children raised with two mothers *are* different in some aspects of their development. Alsa Steckel (1985) did a very thoughtful study of children raised by lesbian mothers and compared their separation-individuation with other 3-year-olds raised in heterosexual families. She found that the children with lesbian mothers were less aggressive, saw themselves as somewhat more helpless, and were seen as stronger in their verbal skills than the comparison group. Yet this is only one small piece of the puzzle. We know that resilience (Werner & Smith, 1992), individual differences (Scarr, 1992), cultural context (Rogoff, 1990), and the "goodness-of-fit" (Carey & McDevitt, 1995; Thomas & Chess, 1977) between the environment and the individual child all work together as just a few of the variables that are in constant movement as children develop.

CONCLUDING THOUGHTS

Just about every parent and many of the educators we interviewed stated that the process of simply discussing their innermost concerns and questions out loud helped them clarify their thoughts and feelings. Parents had an opportunity to reflect on the process they went through in portraying, and advocating for, their family. They also had an opportunity to examine how their own internalized homophobia may have interfaced with heterosexist assumptions within the school culture to make communicating with teachers more difficult than they wanted it to be.

All this speaks to the dearth of earnest dialogue on the topic of homosexuality in our society, but specifically as it surrounds issues in early childhood education. We believe educators have few chances to think out loud and with others about their own experiences with diversity of any kind. Such moments can open up pathways for reflection, which in turn may help teachers think about new ways to approach parents who are or are perceived as being different from themselves. As more people in education incorporate principles of anti-bias, multiculturalism, and inclusion, we strongly encourage educators to take some time to reflect on their prior experiences. If this can be done with others, in the context of common educational goals, even greater possibilities unfold.

CHAPTER 4

Disclosure: The Dance

I have so many friends who are gay, but I had never known a gay couple before who had a child. And I thought, "Wow, this is really happening." When [a child in my class] told me he had two mothers, my radar went up, and I said this is probably what is going on. In a way I wish that I was consulted with it, only because I never saw the other parent. It was sort of like these people were operating behind closed doors, and for what reason? I think that made me feel a little bad. I wish they could have trusted me on that. But they don't know, they were probably protecting themselves, which is perfectly understandable. It's nice to be who you want to be, rather than fighting it all the time.

—Theresa, kindergarten teacher

We would like to think that there are close connections between parents and teachers, and many teachers and school administrators aspire to make this so. To illustrate the sometimes aborted yet frequently successful interactions between gay parents and educators, we use the metaphor of a dance. In the most extreme situations, we visualize a solitary dance, with the teacher, parent, or administrator dancing alone. At other times, parents and educators engage in intricate tangos, sometimes formal and elegant waltzes, sometimes intimate dances, and at times wild modern dancing that is beautifully choreographed but in which the dancers never touch one another. Although we use this metaphor to describe communication between gay parents and educators, it can be used to describe school communication with any parents and, indeed, any kind of communication at all. Given the particular stories we collected from educators and gay parents, however, and given the specific feature of disclosure, we find the dance to be a particularly relevant image here.

In Theresa's statement we hear a regret that these parents did not join her in the dance of parent–teacher communication. Although she says she understands their protective stance, she also wished they could have been more trusting of her. But we are all familiar with situations in which not only parents seek to protect their privacy, but teachers also hesitate to share certain information about children with their parents. Topics that many parents find difficult to discuss with "outsiders"—a term that includes those of us who work in schools—might be divorce or separation, adoption, or a family member with AIDS. And the difficult-to-share information teachers are reluctant to discuss includes a problem they may see in a child, or a child's having divulged sensitive information about the family or parents, which the parents themselves are keeping private. Information as socially sensitive as homosexuality—especially when it involves children—is particularly difficult to share.

THE ANXIETY/OPENNESS DYNAMIC

Although the parents we interviewed took many different approaches in disclosing their family makeup, all grappled with two opposing factors in order to come up with how and whether they would take the initiative—and risk—of coming out to the school. The first factor was anxiety. Almost every parent expressed levels of anxiety, stress, and fear when describing how they brought out their family configuration to the school, or in explaining why they had not done so, and this factor crossed all economic and cultural boundaries among the people we interviewed. One lesbian mother describes the experience of first talking about her family as "scary." A gay man who has not yet informed the school about his sexual orientation describes the imagined reaction of his child's teacher: "Oh my God. He's raising the child in sin!" These feelings are echoed by a lesbian mother who discussed her family's advantages of living in a "tolerant area." She describes herself and her partner as having good interpersonal skills and as "resolved internally about [our] choices about being gay . . . [and] comfortable with [ourselves] about it." Even with these advantages, she reported that coming out to school personnel was difficult. She and her partner are skilled dancers; nevertheless, when they dance with a member of the school community, they suddenly become anxious about stumbling, or even falling.

> I mean, with all our practice and skills and whatever, I'd say that every time we have to do it you feel your blood pressure go up, you feel your heart pound, your palms sweat. It isn't easy. . . . We

get the lowered eyes, and the muffled clearing of throat and the back-turn.

The fact that this anxiety was so pervasive among our informants is vital knowledge for both parents and teachers. Parents can find solace in knowing that they are not alone in their feelings, and they should remember that there is good reason for this anxiety: Revealing one's family configuration in the "official" school setting is risky. In doing so, families are providing information that may be used against them.

Several of the parents expressed the fear that teachers could "take it out on the children." Manuel, who is not out to the school his older son attends, describes this fear, a situation in which the teacher moves to one rhythm and he to a very different one.

> But if the need arose, you know, . . . [that would] be the occasion for me to say, well, "Look, I'm gay. Peter is living in a gay household. All right. I'm not with anybody, but I'm gay and he knows it and understands it." But of course . . . another fear that you have is how they're going to treat your children . . . after you say that, and with that you have to be real careful. Very careful. I mean there's a lot that goes on.

The second strain running through our interviews with parents provides an important balance to the first. It is the desire to live their lives openly as lesbians or gay men who have children, and this includes disclosure to the school. So while anxiety is clearly present, so is a wish for openness.

James and Matthew, parents who were closeted for almost 2 years before they disclosed their sexual orientation to their first child's teacher, discussed the hazards of *not* coming out.

> Matthew: It's wrong. I think it's really wrong. What message are you giving to grow up with, how you feel about yourself and your relationship.
> James: It's also giving a very negative message that what you're doing is wrong. So how can [your children] have a clear positive concept and understanding about what this relationship is about if someone's telling them not to tell anybody?

Needless to say, when they adopted their second child, they came out to his teachers right away.

Nora and Jacqueline, lesbian parents living a modest lifestyle in an affluent New York suburb, affirm this desire to be open and, in a nonbiased world, to reap its rewards. Asked what they would like from their son's school in "the best of all possible worlds," they respond:

> Nora: Anything! More than three words [from the teacher] at a time would be fine. . . . So in the best of all possible worlds I feel like I should be welcomed in [the classroom] as he would welcome anyone else. . . . I guess basically I want to be treated like anyone else is treated.
> Jacqueline: Any other parent.

A CONTINUUM OF CONTEXTS

The diverse personal characteristics of the lives of families and differences in the ethos of the schools affected the outcome of the anxiety/openness dynamic. But we found contextual differences as well. Some of the parents we spoke with live in heavily gay-populated neighborhoods. Some live in suburbs or in urban neighborhoods where gay people are not visible. Some of the parents are middle-class, some White and working-class or people of color. These variables *do* appear to affect the levels of constraint parents felt about their relative comfort or power to communicate openly with the school. Clearly, the resources parents have to bring to the dance, their cultural history that affects the music and steps parents know, and *where* they dance are powerful in affecting the grace, comfort, and intimacy of such a complex interaction as disclosure.

Esperanza, a lesbian mother of two and a paraprofessional in a Bronx school near the one her children attend, epitomizes the power of these variables. She says, "[If I could be sure there would be no repercussions in disclosing my true family structure] I would shout it at the top of my lungs, from the highest mountain. But that's not real."

Shanique, raising her 6-year-old son in a poor section of Brooklyn, also expresses her unwillingness to come out, but no sense of the pleasure she would like to take in coming out tempers her fearful obstinance. Rather, as Shanique explains how she believes this information will be used against her, it leads her to challenge school personnel to figure it out on their own. "No, there's no way I would come out. If you tell them, they might . . . change their attitude against you, and you gonna feel, like rejected. So let them find out on their own."

Manuel is also single, raising two children (only one of whom was legally adopted at the time of this remark), and he also has not yet come out to the school. He describes the constraints he feels as a pre-adoptive father.

> And it's really sad that we can't . . . because of the repercussions. It's very unfair. It's sad and unfair. . . . Because people make parents, not gay or straight. That doesn't make a parent. People. And you have some lousy heterosexual parents that I see on the street, you know. I mean, so it has nothing to do with the sexuality issue. But especially when you're dealing with city agencies. All of the nonsense. All of the bureaucracy. You're not really sure of the person you're dealing with. It's not wise. It's not wise at all.

When we look carefully at these statements, we find two important principles concerning the issue of disclosure. Shanique frames her rationale for *not* coming out around the theme of personal rejection. For her, the experience of rejection is heightened when she is the one who makes clear reference to her sexual orientation. She believes that volunteering the information opens her up to ridicule, to a vulnerability. By assigning responsibility to the other, perhaps Shanique experiences herself in a more powerful interactional position.

Manuel realizes the power of the official social agencies that have direct links to his family. He says it is not *wise* to come out to city agencies. It isn't wise because these agencies have the power to literally take his family away from him. The removal of two foster children from the home of two gay men in Boston in 1985 is a real-life case-in-point, even though the Massachusetts Supreme Judicial Court declared this policy unconstitutional in 1990 (Vaid, 1995). Given the extreme consequences of disclosure falling into the "wrong hands," Manuel's reservations are not only understandable, they are eminently rational. Manuel reminds us that not all dances are created by two; some dances are done in groups, where each dancer must watch out for the ways in which the subtle moves of others affect their own moves, and for the potential harm of the others' movements.

Cultural reasons also weigh for and against disclosure, but certain social realities can virtually dictate keeping one's family configuration hidden from the school. In Manuel's case, this meant hiding his sexual identity from his own son until the boy was 11 years old in order to be sure that neither the school or the adoption agency could find out potentially damaging truth through him. Before contrasting the previous points of view with those of other parents, it is helpful to return to Theresa's comments at the beginning of this chapter. Although Theresa did not teach any of the children of Esperanza, Shanique, or Manuel, she reflects on how it feels to be in the dark about the family structure of a child she teaches, forcing her to construct possible scenarios, ultimately saying, "I wish that I was consulted." Even more to the point, Theresa wonders why on earth a family would not simply come forth with this information. Then, we witness the power of a professional finding her center of empathetic feeling. As Theresa puts herself in the shoes of these particular parents, she is open to the possibility of the profound and differently wrenching answers Esperanza, Shanique, and Manuel could give to her question, "and for what reason?"

How do these feelings and ideas contrast with those of some of the other parents? June and Shelly, White middle-class professionals, are raising their children in Greenwich Village and are open about their family with both school and community. June was forthright and spoke with great clarity and conviction.

> Our kids are growing up with an expectation of acceptance by friends, straight parents. If they run across nonacceptance, that is going to look to them as an aberration. I think they expect that there will be peers there and they aren't going to have any problem with them. . . . Our kids have the experience of a gay-positive culture that they get from us . . . that shapes their expectations, and shapes how much trouble they are going to have. . . . You don't know what people know about. I want to make sure they [other people in general and parents and school staff] know and they can talk about it if they are interested. We don't like the experience of not being seen. . . . there is a certain invisibility in being a lesbian mom. I find [that if] you are a mom, people will assume you are heterosexual and there either is or isn't a man. And I don't like that assumption being made.

James and Matthew, who also live in a rather accepting New York City community, describe some of the factors in their being open. James is Afro-American and makes a clear parallel between racial bias and gay bias.

> And I still think the issue is . . . that you have to be comfortable yourself. And you should be out. It's easy for us to say because we live in New York City. We live in Manhattan. But if we lived in Queens, or if we lived in New Jersey, or one of the suburbs, I'm sure

it would be a lot more difficult to be out. I guess we would have to think that through. But the other part of all that is why we live here. We accept the fact that we want to be in a community where our family is accepted. Just like, for example, I wouldn't raise my children in some totally White area, because I don't think that's part of who they are. And being here in Manhattan, in a metropolitan area, they can be all that. They can be Black; they can also live in a gay family, because of other gay families that live here. So I would say you should select an area where your family will be comfortable. Not do it where you are going to be comfortable, but where your family will be comfortable.

For some families, freedom of mobility is constrained by financial or other family resources, or by racial or cultural discrimination that restricts their abilities to gain easy access to housing in "comfortable" areas. But just as important is some parents' consideration of the ways in which they would be viewed by the school or community if they were open about their sexual orientation. The combination of being a person of color *and* a lesbian or gay man is felt as a double form of oppression. And, as we have seen, even such factors as place of residence or parental occupation can press more heavily on the anxious side of the anxiety/openness dynamic. Given how various New York City school districts, for instance, supported, rejected, or altered the *Children of the Rainbow* curriculum, one can see how school district residence alone can affect this dynamic.

In Chapter 1 we outlined the survival aspects of parental goals (LeVine, 1974). Only when the basics are in place can parents allow room for enhanced parenting. So it is that issues of disclosure become more immediately relevant for parents who are not faced with a myriad of oppressing factors in their lives. And, indeed, we have found that it is precisely those parents who are dealing with multiple oppressions who have *not* come out.

Disclosure was not easy for any of the parents we interviewed, and, in fact, not all of them had come out to the schools in their children's lives. But in considering the differences between parents who did disclose and those who did not, several factors become important. Parents who clearly and purposefully disclosed their family makeup were generally middle-class parents. This is not to say that all middle-class parents came out to the school, but those parents who did lived in middle-class neighborhoods or sent their children to schools with a more accepting staff and parent body; they were independent private schools more often than not, or liberal magnet schools. As one parent who moved her son from a public to a private school told us, "We were not going to be paying money to hide the whole thing." By framing her statement in the extreme, this mother creates great irony in an already strong statement. This belief, that sending your child to a private school entitles you to be open about—and to demand respect for—your family, is worth examining. There is an implication that only when parents pay for private schooling do they have the right to expect respect for their family structure. Further is the implication that public schools are not expected to provide this respect. While reality may follow such lines of logic, the ideal should not. All parents have the right to expect that their family—lesbian- or gay-headed, single-parent, or divorced—will be accepted and respected by the school, whether it is a private or a public institution.

DISCLOSING: WHO DOES IT AND HOW IS IT DONE?

Parents find various ways to come out to the school. Sometimes this coming out is simply the process of parents making themselves visible to teachers and administrators. Obviously, this is easier for two-parent families than for single parents, who are usually assumed to be heterosexual.

Disclosing brings up the question of who initiates the dance. For some, circumstances or simple appearances are the initiators, bringing with them their own set of intricacies. For others, more active, purposeful initiation is required, carrying with it the risk of rejection expressed with more or less explicitness. Maureen and Naomi spoke about how they became visible to the teacher and the parents of their son's kindergarten class.

> Naomi: On the emergency forms and stuff, we put both our names. There was an open school night for all the parents to see what was going on in the classroom. We both went to that.
> Maureen: We both signed the list of who attended.
> Naomi: Right, without specifying.

This visibility was not announced and, like Shanique, these parents seemed to feel that it was not their responsibility to announce their sexual orientation to the teacher or the other parents. At the same time, if the other parents or school staff could put two and two together, Maureen and Naomi were telling them it was fine for them to find out on their own. In single-parent families, this option is not generally available; coming out to the school *requires* a more explicit, sometimes rehearsed approach. In all cases, however, disclosure is not so much a decision made by parents or school staff alone as much as it is a *process of communication,* an activity requiring interaction.

The willingness of each parent and educator to engage in their dance affects its tone, its elegance, its coordination. In real life, however, the dance may involve more than these two parties. For example, in addition to becoming visible to the teacher, the fact of both parents' participation in the school frequently results in an acknowledgment of their family makeup by some children in the classroom. Our informants reported that sometimes this acknowledgment is communicated to the child with gay parents and not to the parents themselves. Children as young as 3 have asked their peer, "Who's your *real* mother?" In one instance, these questions caused a 6-year-old child with two mothers to ask the teacher for a class meeting to discuss his family with the other children (see Chapter 6, "Classroom Life").

Coming Out on Paper

Closely associated with deploying one's presence to make oneself visible, many of the parents used the school application forms as a vehicle either to hint about their family structure or to make their family form explicit. Many crossed out "mother" or "father" on these applications and wrote in "co-parent." Again, this vehicle is not so available to single parents, although some, like Manuel, found ways to be a bit more explicit through the use of these forms.

> You know what I've done on mine? I X-out "mother." I don't leave it blank. I X-out "mother," and then when it goes "mother/father; work," I X-out "mother." And then when I go [there], they say, "Why did you . . . ?"—'cause they don't know by the application till you get to the interview. . . . Or I put a big "N/A" N-slash-A, not applicable, you know. And they say, "Wait, what's this?" Or it was funny because I took Clarence to a psychologist [who was putting] the information in a computer. And he says, "Father?" and I tell him. And he says, "Mother?" and I tell him, "There is none." And I didn't even go into details. And he's waiting for me to say something [laughter]. A suspicion . . .

Problems with this approach center precisely around the ambiguity about which Manuel speaks. Considering that he has already told us he doesn't believe it is safe to be out to his son's school, this approach does have some puzzling, almost taunting qualities. And while some teachers have the experience necessary to pick up on the meaning of an altered application form, others do not. Carla, a nursery school teacher in New Jersey, describes her own difficulty with deciphering this information.

> All you have is this piece of paper [the application with "father" crossed out and "co-mother" written in], and you're going to have a little boy in your class, and you're looking at it and you're saying, "Well, what is this? What does this mean?" And you go to the director [and ask] "Well, when [they] filled it out, what did they mean?" [She says] "Well, I don't know." There's a lot of mystery there that could be cleared up right away.

On the other side, Cathy, a kindergarten teacher in a public school in New York City, describes what happened when she assumed that Elly's parents were lesbians.

> I got Elly's records, and I saw on the records that they had crossed out "father" and written in "co-parent." It [Ricky] was sort of a name who could be a man or a woman. So I wasn't exactly sure what all that meant, although the first thing that I thought of was that they were probably lesbian parents. . . . So that was the first thing I thought of, and I mentioned it to another teacher. I said if someone has crossed it out and put "co-parent," [but] that was not at all what she thought. She thought, "Oh, how weird, why would someone do that?" She thought it was very pretentious or something. And then I said, "Well, maybe they are lesbian parents." And she said, "Oh, I didn't even think of that. That would make more sense."

Coming Out Through Spontaneous Interactions

Our interviewees found that there were also times when the child's teacher or other classroom staff simply knew or guessed the family configuration. Al's 3- and 4-year-old sons attend a child-care center that surmised that he was gay.

> They knew about it, because they're sensitive. They're open to these kinds of things. There's a reality there. Gerry [the teacher] is gay. You pick up that I'm gay. . . . There's a reality there, because

this is how our staff is made up. There are different kinds of people and we talk about it. Gerry . . . is extremely flamboyant and very gay. . . . He's not there saying, "I'm gay, and everybody should be gay," but it's just that freedom you have to go in there and that openness to be able to say I disagree with you. . . . You're able to get a human response from people. You see them as human beings in a place that's very reflective of society. . . . The day-care center is Black, White, Hispanic. It's a mixture of people.

Nora and Jacqueline describe a different kind of situation. The assistant teacher in their son Dan's public school kindergarten classroom approached Jacqueline.

And she ultimately just said to me point blank one morning when I dropped him off when we were just sitting around chatting, "Well, you didn't tell me about you and Nora." [I said] "Noooo." . . . And from there, that kind of discussion opened up and I fished around for what exactly it was she was looking for. Apparently, though, she put some of it together, and also because of Dan's discussion at school in circle about who lived at his house and who didn't. . . . It was not something I didn't intend to bring up and to raise. I would have set a meeting, I wanted to do it. She did it in the morning when there were parents behind me, children all around who had needs, and it was inappropriate for her to bring it up at that point and it's not as if it's something I wouldn't have discussed in all detail, in all detail within limits, that any questions that she had to ask about I would have been thrilled to talk about it. But the setting really limited the focus, and then it's hard to get back to it.

There are many possible interpretations about the role the assistant teacher played. We might hypothesize that she was encouraged to speak to Jacqueline by the head teacher, who believed that an informal approach would be best. Or we might perceive it as a purposeful cutting off of further discussion after eliciting acknowledgment of the family configuration. Or perhaps the assistant teacher liked these parents and simply spoke in a spontaneous and friendly way. In any case, this kind of "forced" disclosure—the dance of the unexpected—clearly met with ambivalent feelings by the parents. On one hand, Jacqueline and Nora describe how they were relieved that their family makeup was out in the open. At the same time, they expressed resentment, because they were foreclosed from choosing the time and setting to come out to the school. They would have preferred to discuss their family in the privacy of a parent conference with the head teacher. Instead, it was quickly—and unexpectedly—brought up by the assistant teacher during a time that the parents felt was both uncomfortable and inappropriate.

Al gives us another perspective as he describes the staff of the child-care center figuring out his family structure. He sees the center as embracing comfortable real-world qualities and a sensitivity that accounts for the ease with which his family situation is simply *known*. In Al's eyes, there was nothing inappropriate about the center staff figuring out his family makeup and his own sexual orientation. In many ways his perspective is compatible with the feelings expressed by Shanique: that the responsibility to know is the school's; the parent should not shoulder the full responsibility to tell. But there are some crucial and unusual qualities to Al's sons' school. The day-care center staff reflects the makeup of the surrounding community. Teachers and the director are African American, Latino, White, and lesbian and gay. The children reflect the diversity of the community as well. This enriched atmosphere—a reflection in every way of the diversity of the community—has an important impact on the ease of disclosure and communication for Al. At the same time, it is a powerful case-in-point for the inclusion of a diverse staff and student body in promoting an atmosphere that is genuinely multicultural. Being a member of a gay-headed family becomes simply one aspect of many parts that make up the individual in this community setting.

Children Outing Parents

Sometimes parents have no choice about disclosure. Several described how the process of coming out was done for them by their children—sometimes dragging them out before they were ready. When James and Matthew's son Jeffrey was 3, he told Sasha, his preschool teacher, that "he had a good weekend because he got to sleep in the bed with Daddy and Matthew." And this was a full year before Jeffrey's parents made the decision to inform her about the family themselves! Certainly, then, especially when children are younger, the telling becomes more complicated. A young child who has information and the language to communicate it, will not always be bound by the constraints of social intolerance against this lifestyle.

These disclosures by children, sometimes unknown to their parents, are described in the stories of several of the parents we spoke with. Maureen, who had never spoken to her 5-year-old son's teacher about her family structure, told us:

> For the parent conference, I just went and the teacher said to me,
> "Derrick tells me that he has two moms." She said, "I assumed he
> meant that he was referring to the other woman that he lived
> with." . . . Derrick did tell the other kids in the after-school program
> and in his class that he had two moms; he never hesitates. And
> sometimes the kids would say to one of us, "Derrick says he has
> two moms, who are you?" And we'd just say, "The other mom."

These disclosures can put all parties in difficult situations. The
parents don't know that the teacher knows, and they sometimes continue to behave as if they are single parents or a heterosexual couple.
Teachers most frequently find it difficult to do anything with this
information because they don't want to overstep their roles. They experience discomfort in possessing information that the parents are not
yet ready to divulge themselves. Jeffrey's teacher, Sasha, elaborates on
this feeling.

> I didn't know how comfortable his father was in talking to me
> about it. I wasn't even sure it was necessary to bring it up. But it
> was this very awkward position, because I knew this about them
> and I didn't know what they thought I knew, or what they thought
> I thought. . . . But I remember feeling—like when Jeffrey said, "I
> slept with my two daddies"—"Okay, now what do I do with that?"
> Should I tell them that I know? Should I go to them and tell them
> the anecdote and just sort of laugh? Or will that push them and
> make them feel like I'm intruding into something that they're not
> ready to talk about? And I did just sort of let it go and sort of
> referred to them as a family. I wasn't the one to initiate it—the
> words, the vocabulary, "Are you gay?" anything like that—and I let
> them do it. Looking back on it, I think that was all fine, because
> they ended up telling me. But I guess I also feel like I could have
> said, "What are the rules here? How does [your son] Jeffrey see
> [your partner] Matthew?"

Besides her own feelings of discomfort, Sasha describes a way in
which teachers can open a dialogue that can lead parents toward disclosure. Without making a direct reference to the nature of the family
structure, or making accusations, Sasha reflects that she simply might
have asked how Jeffrey sees Matthew, or his understanding of the family "rules" or structure. This shift from "What is your family?" or "Who
is Matthew anyway?" to a dialogue about the child's perspective pro-

vides the space for parents to discuss this question, whether they come out in the process or not. It allows James and Matthew to know that, if they decide to ask Sasha to dance, they will not be rejected.

Intentional Communication

Several of the parents we interviewed believed that it was important to take control early on by approaching one or more schools before their child had even entered the classroom. Some parents described how they interviewed the teacher and/or the school's principal before deciding to send their child there. Other parents approached the school to *inform* rather than to inspect as a candidate for their child's attendance there. Some parents found that the responses they elicited from members of the school staff were not always either clear or open. June and Shelly describe their feelings about having discussed their family with members of the school staff, a good example of an *informing* approach.

Shelly: Oh no, we've talked to a lot of teachers!
June: We've gone to all of them and said, "You know, our family structure is different from the other kids', and it may not be familiar to you and there's lots that we can tell you about it if you have questions. When discussions of family come up, we'd be happy to offer another perspective, and it's something that I speak on." And we get downcast eyes and they change the subject. When we first went to the schools, we felt very strongly that we weren't going to go to a school unless we had some assurance ahead of time. . . . We spoke to the principal, and he couldn't have walked up those steps ahead of me faster.
Shelly: . . . I remember that we had gone on a tour of the school and we stopped to speak to him and we said, "Are you comfortable with a lesbian family?"
June: I think he felt assaulted by the question.
Shelly: I think he wasn't so comfortable at the time; he just wanted to say "Yes." But he's been fine, he really has been.
June: We were not belligerent; we were really gentle with him. We are fairly practiced in doing this now, and he clearly felt backed up like he was being either criticized or asked to deal with something. It was like, "Why are you discussing this with me? I don't have a problem with this, so we shouldn't talk about this 'cause there isn't any problem."

Shelly: Yeah, like, "I don't have a problem with them, and none of
    my teachers are going to have a problem with it."
June: As long as it isn't mentioned it's okay.

June and Shelly received another kind of response from other school
staff. Penny, their son's kindergarten teacher, told us she responded to
their disclosure in the following way:

The parents have been very open to me, and [said] if I had any
questions and if I had any problems or questions in my family
curriculum [they would be glad to help], and I am sure they
extended the same to any other teacher. Or maybe because I was
very open to them they talked to me. I don't know. Last year the
little boy came to visit me because he doesn't like new situations.
She wanted him to know me. . . . When there was a family night, I
met his other mom, who was introduced to me as "his other
mom." . . . [It is important to] communicate with parents and find
out how they explain [things] to their children so you are passing
on the same message. They can help you.

As with any reciprocal relationship, it is a challenge to define its
origins. This is exemplified when Penny says, "or maybe because I was
very open to them they talked to me." This teacher underlines the key
point that communicating enables the teacher to "find out how they
explain it to their children so you are passing on the same message."
And while communication requires an initial disclosure, it must evolve
into a more complex dance if the teacher is to most effectively vali-
date the families and the lives of children who have lesbian or gay
parents. Since the parents described real differences in the level of detail they shared with their children about their family and its origins,
it is crucial that teachers and parents develop and expand their avenues
of communication so that these important details can be brought to
the surface. For example, some parents want alternative insemination
discussed with their children and others expressly do not. Some parents have prepped their children to respond to the questions of their
peers concerning their family structure, while other parents want the
teacher to take the initiative in any explanations or discussions with
other children. These are the issues that each family must ponder, discuss, and decide for themselves.

The second school experience of James and Matthew, an interra-
cial couple living in Manhattan, offers another approach. After hav-

ing been outed by their child in preschool, they took a decidedly different tack when it was time to enroll him in a public school at age 5. Rather than simply informing the school about their family configuration and their sexual orientation, this couple discussed their desire to determine whether the school would be an appropriate place to send him *before* deciding to enroll him there.

> Matthew: In general people can avoid what they want to avoid.
> James: True. That was part of our reason why we went and spoke to the teacher and principal about it. [We asked,] "Would you have any problems?" And if they did have any problems, I was hoping they would tell me. Not say, "Oh no, [we aren't] going to have any problems," when in fact, they certainly knew they were going to have problems. And the issue is that I wasn't ready to slap a lawsuit on their hands, it's just that I didn't want to deal with it. Right now I'm not interested in moving to Bensonhurst or any of those areas where they didn't want Black people. If they want to live and think that way, that's fine, I just don't want to be subjected to it. Let them live there; I won't send my child to that school.

James and Matthew discussed their family makeup with the school's principal and the kindergarten teacher. Early in the school year, they invited every child in their son's class to his birthday party, where their family configuration was clear to everyone. The following year, they worked with their son's first-grade teacher to help her to incorporate aspects of lesbian and gay families into the ongoing curriculum.

INTRASCHOOL COMMUNICATION PRACTICES

But these initial disclosures sometimes offer another problem for the school and the family. Parents often experience confusion about whether this disclosed information is passed on to other staff members (for example, gym teachers or other specialists), and whether it is passed on to the child's teacher as the child moves to a new grade the following year. In addition, different parents we interviewed had different ideas about the appropriateness of such intraschool sharing of this information. Some parents believed that the information should be shared within the school, so that the burden of disclosure would not again be placed upon themselves. Others were concerned that information about their familiy makeup be kept confidential, and still others were ambivalent.

For example, Maritza and Sharon described how surprised they were to find that their son's first-grade teacher did not know that he had two mothers. Since they had already gone through the uncomfortable process of coming out to the school the previous year, they had expected that they would not have to do so again, and that the information would be internally passed on among the staff. Interestingly enough, this situation occurred in a school in which the staff communication process is both intricate and comprehensive. A variety of meetings were routine there, as well as other means for staff communication where this information could have been shared. It is unclear whether administrators and teachers allowed this information to "fall through the cracks," or thought it to be private, letting the information unfold naturally again each year between Maritza, Sharon, and Alberto's teacher. The school's policy appears to have been either unknown or unclear to these parents, and this situation is instructive for all. Equally instructive is Maritza's ultimate response about what we viewed as an apparent glitch in the school's communication process. She says, "I'm glad that Mary [the new teacher] got to know Alberto first before she found out that he has lesbian parents." In retrospect, not having known what the biases of Alberto's new teacher might be, Maritza realized she didn't want this information to color the teacher's thinking about her son before the teacher had an opportunity to form an independent opinion. Here is an example where we as researchers became aware of an unexamined bias about routes of communication in schools. It became clear to us how important is it for both parents and school personnel to consider how they feel about these issues of intraschool communication in a clear and self-conscious manner.

Another incident further demonstrates the pitfalls of inconsistent communication policies within a school. The principal in Jeremy's school spoke very candidly and sensitively to his kindergarten teacher prior to Jeremy's arrival in September. In turn, the teacher employed this information in interacting with Jeremy and his parents as well as in planning her curriculum. The next year, however, the principal did not inform Hazel, Jeremy's first-grade teacher, about Jeremy's family. His parents assumed that Hazel knew their situation, and in fact, through *unofficial* channels, she ultimately did. Although Hazel discussed her knowledge of Jeremy's lesbian parents without having been "officially" informed by school staff or parents, she refused to act upon this information herself, either on a curricular level or by talking about it to Jeremy or his mothers. Without explicit invitation, Hazel will not meet her partner on the dance floor. She defends this approach.

> I think I have known setups where women for economic reasons have shared. . . . You see it on television where they had Kate and Ally. They certainly were not lesbians, going out and having their own social life, sharing the children. . . . There are a lot of setups like that.

And to further complicate the question of what the routes of intraschool communication should be, we have to take into consideration the parents who *don't* want information about their family structure routinely passed on to every member of the school community. Given the anxiety and fear of retribution against themselves or their children associated with coming out to a member of the school staff, some parents may want the information restricted to the individual whom they trusted enough to tell. Emory, the principal of a well-regarded public elementary school, told us that a number of lesbian or gay parents initiate communication about their families with him. His careful response concerning the sharing of this information is instructive.

> I would ask the parents if the teacher was aware of it. In some cases they would assure me they were. In other cases [they] would say they would rather the teacher not be aware of it. [I handled this situation] whatever way the parents chose to . . . whatever way they decided to handle it.

Emory's experience provides a roadmap of sorts, indicating that what the internal routes of school communication should be—and whether it even should occur at all—depends on the wishes and needs of the family. This understanding has direct implications for both parents and teachers. Teachers who have been approached initially by lesbian or gay parents must discuss possible routes of information about the family among school staff. And parents can help to clarify this process, for themselves and the school. Taking the initiative to discuss whether they would like the information to remain confidential or to become public within the school, would be extremely helpful in furthering the communication process.

What about other parents? Again, open and direct dialogue can lead to a partnership between the school and gay parents. This connection can lead to holding educational meetings for all parents concerning lesbian- and gay-headed families.

COMMUNICATION: WHOSE RESPONSIBILITY IS IT?

Where does the responsibility lie for coming out? Our findings tell us that school personnel frequently see the onus lying squarely in the parents' laps, while parents see setting the stage for disclosure as part of the schools' charge. If these two may seem to go hand-in-hand, Esperanza, mother of two and an educator herself, reminds us of real-life difficulties. She says,

> That's a hard one. As an educator I'd say it's the family's responsibility to tell the school the family's lifestyle, especially as a way to show the child that that lifestyle is okay. As a parent, I would love that to be true, but you have to think twice.

Fran, a teacher of infants and toddlers, emphatically describes the responsibility as belonging to the parent.

> I think . . . that you have to have an open line of communication. . . . I mean if people chose to do this, they chose to have a child, then they have to be open about it. . . . I would want that . . . because I feel that if you're not open about it and you're not going to be open to questions, you're going to have a lot of questions. You really are. I would just assume that that's the way these families are and I would want them to be that way too. . . . I would think that if you have a gay family that comes in and they're trying to hide the fact that this is the kind of family they are, or not address it at all, then I think that this needs to be addressed to the family first of all. I guess that's not really the teacher's position to do this, but maybe—if it is—saying, "Gosh, you know, we have a school psychologist," because I think [nondisclosure] would be detrimental to the child and the family as a whole because I think that's too key to the family's well-being if someone's saying, "Oh my God, I'm embarrassed that we're a gay family."

Fran's statement is rich in the beliefs she expresses and the assumptions it contains. She places the task of coming out to the school right on the shoulders of the parents. She expresses a certainty about the location of responsibility and the degree of harm that she believes will fall upon the children if the parents are not open about their family structure. She wants parents to be open about their family and assumes that all families would want that as well. She is also clear that, if asked to dance, she will do so. But the risk of asking is left entirely up to the parents. Fran is not alone. Evidently a slow shift of values has taken place within some areas of the psychology and social service professions (and even parts of the gay community itself), and the result has been to frame coming out by gay men (at least) as the healthy norm (Cain, 1991). There is also an implicit assumption in such advocacy, and throughout Fran's remarks, that any teacher will be able to identify families as being gay-headed. Fran's belief that a parent who opts for privacy requires psychological intervention (her statement that nondisclosure will be detrimental) seems particularly ironic when we consider it from the perspective of Al's complex parenting situation.

Al shares the fathering of three boys, two of whom have been diagnosed with AIDS. He sheds a different light on this issue as he talks about the underlying beliefs and contextual constraints that determine his actions as a gay parent regarding communication with his children's schools. He has not yet informed his oldest son's school (a public, neighborhood school) about his family structure, even though, as we have seen earlier, he appreciated the discovery of his sexual orientation by his younger son's child-care teacher.

> I never volunteered anything. It makes it very difficult, because homosexuality is not accepted per se, but in the Spanish culture it is even worse. I don't want to advertise, and I don't think it is my responsibility to sit on a soap box and tell everybody that we're gay and we have three children. Because it doesn't make any difference. If you're going to ask me, I'm going to say it. So I don't volunteer the information. I make it known in other ways. If you're smart enough, you're going to put it together. If you have a problem with it, it's your problem, it's not my problem. It's you that has to tell me, not I to tell you.

Al's version of the world is more complicated than Fran's. While he takes into account cultural attitudes toward homosexuality, he also reveals different ideas concerning responsibility for coming out as well as the importance of coming out. He does not assume that the lesbian or gay parent must shoulder full responsibility for communicating the family structure and its implied meaning to the school. For him, the very act of disclosure is a *shared responsibility* in the sense that he will provide some information, but on a very conscious, deliberate level, he demands that the teacher join the parents in taking risks. Al recognizes the subtle clues that are sent, received, and sent again before the words, "Will you dance with me?" are uttered. This subtle pre-communication communication helps to ease the risk involved for the initiator. Al continues:

> Luca's teacher just found out that I'm not Richard [Al's partner], the father. Richard doesn't go to school. I finally told her when we went to this open school week in October or November that I am the parent, but I'm not the legal parent. I left it up to her to put two and two together. I just didn't say, "We're gay." I said, "Richard is the one who adopted him, but I live with Richard and I'm also Luca's daddy." And she said, "Oh, yes, he calls you Daddy." I think she's intelligent enough to put two and two together. I'm not Richard, but I'm the one who has taken the role of doing this.

Here, pathology is not located inside the parents or the family. Instead, Al locates it squarely within society. We are all part of the social fabric within which we live, and this requires a shift in the placement of responsibility for disclosure. No longer does it rest solely with the parent. And no longer does it mean that we can look at school support in a simple way. It implies that the school staff also needs to take risks *alongside the parents* to find ways where the family situation can be brought out into the open.

Routes of Information

But if the school staff plays a role in the communication process, how does this work? While the flow of information may need to start with the family, the school can set the stage. Some parents and school staff discussed how the simple assertion that diversity is welcome in the school helps to set an important tone. If educators genuinely welcome the possibility of a variety of family structures into the classroom, it can encourage parents to take the next step, perhaps to hint about their family makeup. For example, during curriculum night, or in individual parent–teacher conferences, teachers can communicate a tremendous amount simply by using the words "lesbian" and "gay." One teacher might include in her curriculum night a brief description of her family curriculum, saying that she will include the diversity of the children's own families and hope that there will be a range of families in her classroom this year—single parent, extended family, lesbian- or gay-headed families, and traditional families. Besides welcoming lesbian and gay parents, this announcement also serves notice to all parents that an inclusive curriculum will be practiced in this classroom. For another teacher, this discussion might be more comfortable—and politically safe—in the context of a parent–teacher conference.

Such welcoming also can take the form of more general schoolwide policies. Altering application forms to allow for the possibility of nontraditional family structures is an important beginning. Instead of presenting parents with the assumption that all families include a mother and father, schools can experiment with a variety of ways of opening their forms to the possibility of many types of families. This simple change can set an important initial tone for parents, as the application is often the family's first contact with the school (see sample form, Appendix B).

Schools Set the Stage

Creating spaces for lesbian and gay parents to communicate with the school is another general approach that says, "Differences are welcomed here." Emory, the elementary school principal, describes such an approach.

> I just don't see that [it] should be an issue that's dealt with . . .
> without associating it with other things that are somewhat different. . . . That everybody that we come in contact with is different in some way. . . . Put it in a larger context. I think it allows children to understand that it's a very heterogeneous society—city—that we live in and people are different in many ways.

Part of the context also can be set by the presence of diversity in the school staff. Some parents and school personnel noted the importance of lesbian and gay teachers in helping the school communicate a certain level of acceptance to lesbian and gay parents. Several parents felt that the open inclusion of gay teachers helped them to feel accepted and to make their own family seem less of an oddity. And several school staff members reported that the very presence of openly lesbian and gay teachers on staff was an indispensable asset to a more generally accepting school atmosphere, even if lesbian or gay parents, or their children, never meet these teachers. We have already noted Al's description of the importance of gay teachers in reflecting the wider community. Emory describes the value of a staff that includes gay teachers: "There were a good number of staff members who were gay or lesbian and so there was a certain sensitivity in that school in general."

And Eleanor, a guidance counselor in a Manhattan public school, describes the value of making lesbian and gay people visible in a school.

> I know friends from Massachusetts who were very concerned about education in the schools [who] set up a program where gay people would go into the schools and sort of present themselves so that people could see that they were real and talk about issues. . . . And even to ask of a gay teacher on the staff to help us to be alert and sensitive to what her needs are or what she sees for kids, what she wants for her kids, how comfortable she is.

Perhaps the school Eleanor describes is unusual in encouraging an atmosphere in which lesbian and gay staff members feel comfortable coming out and participating in staff development in important ways. But to the extent that we recognize the value of having teachers represent the cultural backgrounds of the children in the school community, it is not a big leap to extend this concept to sexual orientation. This added visibility of gay people within the school is one aspect of making lesbian and gay life more apparent as part of the community fabric. And if school staff is concerned with opening doors for lesbian and gay parents to disclose their family to them, then becoming more public about their own makeup is a crucial step in that direction.

For school staff, acknowledging both the importance of addressing one's own feelings about homosexuality and the anxiety associated with parental contact around this issue is crucial. Fran addresses what might be a prerequisite to the ability to help parents feel that communication is acceptable in a particular school or classroom.

> What is helpful is that you really should feel that you should approach the parents and that you, as a teacher, need to explore your own feelings about it. Because if you're sitting there feeling, "Oh my God, this is disgusting. What's wrong with these people? They're vile. I can't believe they're doing this and it's so detrimental to the child," then [you] need to address those feelings in [yourself] and really work them through because they are really going to get projected on the family. So I think that you do have to be concerned with the family, but it's also something that's very different for different people. And they have to explore their own feelings about what it means to have a gay family. . . . [There are plenty of people who] think that it's something that exists out there in the world that has nothing to do with them and don't really want to have anything to do with it. . . . I mean, I think it's scary at first to go to the parent, it really is the first time.

This patient exploration of one's own feelings about homosexuality may be closely related to other aspects of one's life. For example, certain religious prohibitions against homosexuality will make this exploration more difficult for educators who practice these faiths. Self-examination also takes different forms in different schools. Some principals have called on guidance counselors to provide workshops so that the issue and the feelings it elicits can be explored. Others might provide staff with relevant reading material. Some might invite lesbian or gay speakers to staff development workshops. And sometimes teachers are left on their own to find ways of discovering what it means to be gay in a heterosexist society. But just as parents must face a range of constraints as they consider their decisions to tell the school about their family makeup, school administrators and teachers face constraints as well. In a more relaxed setting, Lise, the lower school coordinator of a progressive private school in New York City, describes the rationale for open lines of communication.

> And that's why it's so important to have communication about what your home is like, so that we can provide experiences that will best support your child so that he or she feels comfortable. And if our particular structure, for whatever reason, is making the child feel uncomfortable in the beginning . . . please let us know about it, so that we can both figure out what we can do to make this experience more comfortable. . . . Because obviously we celebrate differences and that's part of what we're all about.

Best of all possible worlds aside, the contextual factors in the degree of risk a teacher can take and feels comfortable taking in setting the stage for gay parents to come out are very real and powerful. These factors are not additive; real complexities exist, and it may be more accurate to consider these contextual features along a continuum. Such a continuum would include considering some of the following conditions:

- An administrator who ignores or discourages the inclusion of diverse and controversial issues versus a supportive administrator that encourages diversity.
- A homogeneous community within and/or surrounding the school in which gay people are not seen versus a diverse community that has a visible gay presence.
- A teacher who has never knowingly met or associated with lesbian or gay people, or for whom even saying the words *lesbian* or *gay* is difficult, versus a teacher who is gay or lesbian or has

colleagues or friends who are gay and/or who feels comfortable with them.

All of these elements have tremendous impact on the ability of schools to set a comfortable tone within which parents can take the first step in communicating their family structure. Teachers who communicate, taking these contextual factors into consideration, will let parents know that it is the dance that is important, that they will choose some steps, but are open to the music, the rhythm, and the moves of the parents as well. But the factors we have noted here cannot be diminished. They will affect the level of risk that an administrator or teacher is willing to take in *dancing with* the parent in the process of coming out to the school. And it is a risk.

CHAPTER 5

Finding Gender

Especially in the age group that I have [5-year-olds], there's a very big thing about differentiating boys and girls. What is different, and what do boys do, and what do girls do? And I wonder about that. It's such a strange thing. From the moment you're born, it's the first category you get placed into—boy or girl. If you're in an ethnic group or a minority group . . . then you're not distinctly marked off as, oh, you are Black; oh, you are Jewish; oh, you are White, until later on and you become conscious of the "other" outside of your family. Whereas, with the boy/girl thing, that's immediately apparent. So I guess the children in my class are trying to figure it out.

—Cathy, a kindergarten teacher

The children in Cathy's class are not alone in their quest. Young children face special challenges in first grasping and then finding their individual ways of participating in gender, but this chapter's title refers to the lifelong relationship we have to gender. In much the same way that issues of attachment and separation, for example, continue throughout one's lifetime, so gender-related issues continually resurface for deeper and often different interpretations. We don't *find* our gendered identities and move on to other issues, but rather are continually finding and reconceptualizing our gendered selves in an active and ongoing manner. And whatever we believe as adults about children's gender development, our thinking about their various negotiations is absolutely tied to our own.

This chapter takes us down the long path of early gender knowledge. Its overarching goal is to begin unraveling the complex relationship between early childhood gender development and adult fears about homosexuality. Of the many possible ways to enter this tangled topic, I (Virginia) use our informants' diverse views about young children's developing gender concepts as a forum for the growing and changing understanding that children and adults have about gender, homosexuality, and lesbian/gay parenting. Changing theories about gender are presented to provide some new models for thinking about young children growing up in gay- and lesbian-headed families. A variety of stories and viewpoints about same- and opposite-sex role models are presented for reflection. And specific examples of homophobia and the presumption of heterosexuality are related to demonstrate how children's lived experiences translate into gender learning.

Along the way, our gender path will require us to visit both children and adults, because in spite of the momentous changes that have taken place in the adult gender landscape, there are contradictory forces at work concerning the parallel realm of children. For example, on a public level we can observe a relaxing of certain gender-based norms for adults: Witness the reception granted Dennis Rodman's personal body statements on and off the basketball court, or New York City Mayor Rudolph Giuliani's sporting a dress during a "camp" political appearance. Films like *The Bird Cage* or *In and Out* continue to enjoy national popularity. Regardless of how we may interpret the significance of these isolated events, it seems certain that they could not have occurred even 10 years ago. Nevertheless, they stand apart from the much more conservative societal norms that govern children, and the kind of school and peer experiences that are assumed to influence their gender-related development.

Not only is an equivalent relaxing of gender norms absent in early childhood, it becomes clear that the loosening of adult gender possibilities has in some way led to more restrictive socialization for children. The clearest evidence for this may be seen in a gender identity disorder category (GID) for children that first appeared in the *Diagnostic and Statistical Manual* (DSM) in 1980; the same volume is also the first edition in which adult homosexuality was no longer listed as a disorder (American Psychiatric Association, 1980). These events, coupled with increasing concerns over gender-nonconforming behaviors of boys in particular, raise the spectre of a disturbing situation. Even 15 years ago an attitude prevailed that was less critical of early gender nonconformity in early childhood classrooms *because* it was in young children and the behaviors were seen as less threatening.

As the adult gay-rights movement made significant inroads into changing a predominantly pathological view of homosexuality, research and clinical writings simultaneously linked sex, gender roles, and sexual orientation in ways that profess not to, but in practice too often do, solidify an equation of early gender nonconformity in children, especially boys, with pathology (Green, 1987; Zucker & Green, 1993). The freedoms won for adult expression of one's gendered and sexual self are questionable indeed, if they have been secured on the shoulders of children. The GID category is being contested on a number of grounds, most clearly for mixing a potpourri of attachment disorders and other pathology with extreme gender-nonconformist behaviors. Additionally, diagnostic criteria for childhood GID are paired with the pathology in the parents of the GID children based on only clinical impressions, with little data as backup (Bradley & Zucker, 1997; Coates, Friedman, & Wolfe, 1991).

Like gender itself, our gender findings are complex and provocative. As with issues of disclosure, the middle-class lesbian and gay parents in our study tend to place greater value on gender nonconformity than do their working-class peers. For many middle-class lesbian and gay parents, a central aspect of their personal identities and vision as parents includes a more fluid experience and expression of gender than our current societal norms project. The gender arena is therefore likely to be one in which their goals as parents are at odds with the implicit and explicit gender values expressed in the American school culture. This interpretation was reinforced for us by our interviews with educators. Those educators who expressed concerns about the development of children raised by gay parents based their concerns on their perceptions of how children's development would be affected by having two same-sex parents. Included in this group were a few teachers who might otherwise be described as particularly progressive and bold in conceptualizing curricula to embrace gay families. Because educators' attitudes toward gender are so integral to better communication with gay and lesbian parents and to improved teaching of their children, new directions in theory and practice for teacher education are addressed here and in Chapter 7.

Having a clear grasp of gender development is central to thinking about how all children develop, but it is especially important that misconceptions about it do not distort adult interpretations of children who are growing up in lesbian- and gay-headed families. A working knowledge of developmental theory enables teachers and parents to create a few commonsense hypotheses about the often dramatic and sometimes enigmatic verbal and behavioral statements that children are known to make. In my (Virginia) own work in teacher education and staff development, it has become clear that many otherwise sophisticated professionals often lack even a clear working vocabulary of basic gender terms and that different terms often are used interchangeably. Of course, it doesn't help that various academic disciplines historically have used different language to refer to similar concepts. Increasingly, these disciplines share a common theoretical mission to distinguish biological sex from socially constructed gender roles and to frame gender in a less dichotomized way (Bem, 1993; Kessler & McKenna, 1977; McKenna & Kessler, 1997; Roscoe, 1994; Thorne, 1993). For all the reasons listed above, a short list of gender definitions is provided below.

- *Gender identity.* The personal sense of being male or female.
- *Gender roles.* Social and cultural expectations and attitudes about what constitutes male and female behavior.
- *Gender constancy.* Knowledge that being female or male cannot change as a result of one's behavior or appearance.
- *Gender stability.* The idea that being male or female doesn't change during development.
- *Sexual orientation.* The pattern of both psychosocial behavior and emotional-erotic attraction to others—e.g., the gender of one's love object, often established in childhood. The etiology of homosexual (same-sex) attractions is still in the process of being understood as a measure of interactions between genetic and environmental factors.
- *Identification.* A multi-use term that connotes ways in which one recognizes oneself in another.

OLD HABITS AND THEORY SCRIPTS

If gender issues reside at the heart of lesbian and gay discourse with the predominantly straight world, then theory provides their pulse. As a developmentalist and educator, I have observed how vital a role theories can play in providing clarity for everyday practice. A few significant habits of mind, however, repeatedly act as barriers to that clarity.

As a culture, we tend to treat theory in ways that are simplistic and mechanistic. Many college and graduate texts frame theory in a way that does not promote critical thinking and independent inquiry; on the contrary, readers are encouraged to "learn" theoretical concepts as close-ended facts that define rather than expand understanding. As a consequence, early childhood teachers often emerge from their education and training without any substantial experience in relating theory to their own practice. The climate is familiar: There is never enough time; classes are often packed; and there is not enough room to spread one's theoretical wings, to chart one's own course. Although the field of teacher education has begun to acknowledge that in fact practice often leads theory (Williams, 1996), more often than not lesson plans and issues of classroom management prevail over theory instead of working in tandem with it. Also commonplace is the habit of using a simple cause-and-effect model to understand human behavior. Beginning practitioners are often in a hurry for quick answers or, really, any answer at all. For example, pigeonholing a parent in order to explain a child's behavior seems to work well, and one usually can find a colleague eager to agree with one's perception.

Like branches on a family tree, each of this century's three classical theories of how children come to understand their gendered selves represents a rich and multilayered lineage. One may think of each theorist's contribution as but one of the complex personalities in an ancestral line. And similar to our own family heritage, there are always stories and family myths that are told and retold, creating larger-than-life effects.

In teaching and learning about these theories, however, a form of shorthand methods often are employed to catalogue various theories for easy access. These shorthand methods may be thought of as scripts, not unlike the mental scripts children use to represent the components of complex social tasks (Nelson, 1981, 1986), like what one does at a birthday party, or when it's one's turn to feed the fish. While scripts may provide a necessary "on-the-job" shorthand, a time should come when deeper, more elaborative thinking takes place. Otherwise, a simplified and constricted use of theory can impede a more open investigation of a child's lived experience. Theory can end up serving as a closing off of developmental possibilities rather than an opening. It may be helpful to engage in a personal inventory of our own particular theory scripts to become aware of the times when we go on our own automatic pilots. The three basic theories (see Figure 5.1) are organized in child development texts as originating in

- *Children's early sexual drives*—psychoanalytic theory (Freud and followers)
- *Behaviors of others that are rewarded and observed*—social-learning theory (Mischel, 1966; Sears, Rau, & Alpert, 1965; and followers)
- *Children's ability to understand and categorize themselves as gendered beings*—cognitive-developmental theory (Kohlberg, 1966 and followers)

Yet another pitfall is that in separating out and naming each theory, we can lose common threads that help us weave together complimentary theoretical patterns that ground us in our attempts to understand children. When one goes back to the original thinking behind these theories, one is privy to multifaceted, not linear, concepts that are in-

Figure 5.1. "Theory Script" of Traditional Views of How Males Come to Their Gender Identification

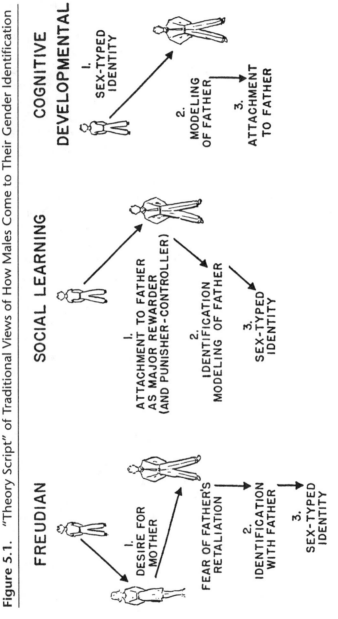

Source: Kohlberg, 1996. Used by permission.

clusive of a range of children's domains of development. A glance at early social-learning theory (Mischel, 1966) shows how this theory was already becoming streamlined and oversimplified so that it was known by only one of its many aspects.

> It is often mistakenly assumed that social-learning theories (SLT) deny the existence of mediating cognitive processes. Men and women, as well as boys and girls, do think. They experience wishes, fears, and hopes; they even dream. . . . Thus, although the existence of mediating processes is acknowledged, [in SLT] they are not attributed the causal powers usually assigned to them in [other] theories. . . . Kohlberg [cognitive-developmental] rightly states that boys and girls label themselves as male and female, and that these judgments of [gender] identity, once firmly established, tend to be irreversible. However, the abundant individual differences found within each sex, and the fact that the behaviors of the sexes overlap to a great degree, suggest that there are many ways to be a boy or girl—and even more ways to be a man or woman. Sex differences in behavior are not, for the most part, universal entities. (p. 62)

Here we have a brief but powerful slice of gender theory that sends us in expansive and integrative directions. We are reminded that in spite of social-learning theory's emphasis on observing behaviors of others, no one is asking us to forget that children *think* about their relationship to gender as well. Mischel's sequence ends with a more basic caveat—that we are human beings first, and that any differences in our gendered behavior should not be overrated. He underscores the "abundant" and overlapping individual differences within each gender, reminding us that gender distinctions are but one small aspect of our humanity. While these points may not be the most essential ones in social-learning theory, it exemplifies a depth of understanding that is lost to simple theory scripts. And so we see that another reason theories become constricted in use is that rich elaborative conversations carried out in books and journals between theorists themselves are rarely in the purview of teachers or parents. Everyday practitioners tend to be exposed to more simplified and rigidified notions of theory.

What does any of this have to do with gender? In the absence of theoretical vitality, thinking about children's gender development goes on automatic pilot. It is the most simplistic versions of theories that have the deepest hold, a reality that requires ongoing conscious work to prevent slippage. When professionals who work with young children and families go on their own theoretical automatic pilots, the result can be constricting.

SHIFTING PARADIGMS

New ideas about gender have emerged because so many of the older classical theories no longer could help us understand our increasingly complex gendered lives. It is widely acknowledged that although attitudes have changed in many sectors of the helping professions (Goode, 1998) the theory practitioners use lags far behind. The needed theoretical changes are but part of larger paradigmatic shifts in many fields. Some of the new approaches in child development question the universality of stage theory, while underscoring the importance of individual differences (Scarr, 1992), variation in developmental paths (Mallory & New, 1994), a contextual view (Emde, 1994) of those paths, and the strong influence children exert over their own development (Sroufe & Fleeson, 1988).

As a whole, classic gender theory, while helpful in certain respects, implies relatively circumscribed categories of behavior and ways of thinking. If many of these theories keep us entrenched and rigid in our perspectives about gender possibilities, what theoretical models are less circumscribed and more fluid? Over the past 15 years it has been a feminist viewpoint, such as can be found in Sandra Bem's (1983) gender schema theory, that has been at the core of a number of new approaches to gender. Bem helps us realize the extent to which we are influenced to categorize objects, events, and feelings into masculine or feminist influence (schemas), and how in doing so we continually remain within the same categories. Her account differs from other developmental approaches. Bem puts the developmental spotlight on the gender polarization of the culture. In order for some behaviors to be "right," or appropriate, others have to be "wrong," or inappropriate. And because our culture is so gender-schematized, both adults and children need to learn and remember that people have a variety of different beliefs. Gender-aschematic children tend to be in the minority and they need to know that their view is just as valid as the majority gender-schematic one.

Feminist influence also informs cultural (postmodern) theorists as seen in the work of Judith Butler (1990, 1995) and Suzanne Kessler (1998). Butler (1990) conceptualizes gender as "a stylized repetition of acts" (p. 140); a kind of performance, albeit a required one. McKenna and Kessler (1997) help us conceptualize how our genders, in fact even our genitals, are a socially constructed illusion and not a fact. These theorists help us understand that the male–female continuum distinguishes power as it determines proper boundaries for behavior. We can better appreciate these ideas of gender as performance when we hear of a woman who has lived her life as a man without anyone knowing, as did the musician Billy Tipton, born Dorothy Tipton. Billy's biographer characterizes her life this way: "*She* was the actor, *he* was the role" (Smith, 1998b).

Anthropologists have opened our horizons by introducing us to cultures around the world and throughout history in which the gender divide is less narrow (Herdt, 1996). One example from indigenous Native American cultures is the berdache, a "two-spirit people" for whom sexuality and gender is not a distinct category in their community, culture, and spirituality (Roscoe, 1994; Schultz, 1993; Wilson, 1996). In our culture, nonconforming sexual orientation becomes a crucial (sometimes, *the*) defining characteristic. The berdache are not seen as "nonconforming." The respect and integrity of a "two-spirit person" is so different from being "gay," that it is even difficult to conceptualize. Indigenous Native American cultures emphasize interconnectedness rather than the polarities we know so well (e.g., female/male, past/present, and spiritual/material). These interconnections are a deeply spiritual force that prevents the world from falling apart. Learning about those cultural constructions of gender that differ from our own highly dichotomized one helps expand our understanding of the range of gender in the human experience.

Finally, much of the innovative thinking on gender currently is housed within the psychoanalytic arena, thinking that is also predominantly feminist in outlook (Benjamin, 1991; Chodorow, 1992; Dimen, 1995; Goldner, 1991; Harris, 1991). Freudian theory was the obvious prime force in cementing gender polarities in our collective unconscious. Muriel Dimen (1995) refers to this phase in our theoretical development using the anthropological term *folk science*. She writes that "although Freud's work tended to be scholarly and revolutionary, still the main thrust of his findings in this area was to codify unexamined popular assumptions about women and implicitly, men" (p. 303). That Oedipal theory has undergone major revisions by theoreticians and practitioners since the 1960s is a fact we seldom contemplate nor are their effects very wide-reaching in our everyday lives. In the sections that follow, relatively flexible and fluid theories will be elaborated as helpful tools to have when contemplating gender issues.

THE LONG PATH WE TAKE

From a developmental perspective, we still have much to learn about the very beginning of gender understanding. Although gender studies is now acknowledged as an important area for psychological inquiry, huge gaps remain in our understanding about the various ways in which young children think about their current as well as their future gendered selves. Certainly the field is in its infancy, for we are continuously learning and reorganizing our new understandings.

Girl or Boy? And How Do You Know?

A study of 2-year-olds verified just how tenuous early gender knowledge is and how easily our adult viewpoint may be superimposed on young children. In a study by deMarneffe (1997), 2-year-olds understood what genitals they had and how that did or did not match up with genitally correct dolls that were presented to them. The children selected and preferred dolls with genitals that resembled their own. In addition, some children knew that they were either a girl or a boy. Neither of these findings are surprising. What is striking, however, is that the knowledge of their gender and the knowledge of their genitals was not necessarily related. From this clear demonstration, we see that for young children, genital identification and gender identity are initially separate.

This finding refutes Freud's assertion that children's first perception of genital difference primes gender's jets, causing children to mentally represent themselves as a boy or girl and then move into Oedipal conflicts. Moreover, simply because adults assume the sex–gender link, does not mean that young children automatically can do so. And even when they are able, this ability does not erase occasional fleeting desires to be both genders—be mommy and daddy—and have it all (Lieberman, 1993). Thus the relatively new emphasis in some circles on naming one's genitals as early as age 2 (deMarneffe, 1997) may only belie the lack of depth that these statements represent. Young children are, of necessity, primarily absorbed in the developmental task of a bodily and sensory experience of the world. It is over the long period of early childhood that they gain enough distance to be able to connect the experiences that they have begun to name and classify. The stage is slowly set over the first few years of life with the complex human ability to represent experience symbolically, an ability that grows through a child's interaction, first and foremost, through the family and committed others.

We know that to determine the gender of others, 3- to 5-year-olds use simple rules and concrete cues, based on what they come to know as being boy- or girl-like (Intons-Peterson, 1988), such as hairstyle, height, voice cues, and so forth. Even 2-year-olds may respond with clear annoyance when asked to engage in the well-worn research task of identifying which of two naked children is a boy and which is a girl. To them, the question itself may seem preposterous. A wonderful example is provided by Coates (1997), who notes one 2.5-year-old's response to this question: "I don't know, they don't have their clothes on."

As children reach the age of about 5, they become clearer about the long-term stability of their gender identity—that is, the likelihood that if they are a girl, they will become a woman (Bem, 1983, 1989)—but once again, children demonstrate these understandings in different ways, based on their individual tendencies in conjunction with their particular experiences. We have very little research concerning who helps make what explicit to them (teaching). We do know, however, that over the course of early childhood, children appreciate that their categorization as one gender or the other cannot be swayed by their physical appearance or their behavior (gender constancy). As Cathy's remarks at the beginning of this chapter illustrate, however, it is still a precarious balance.

Early Attempts: Trying Ideas on for Size

Young children come to understand their gendered selves in the same way they grow into many other concepts. Classifying experience is an important human ability that allows us to participate and communicate with others and to organize and build on the knowledge we collect. It is a primary contention of this book that wide and richly diverse experiences point children toward what Counts (1932/1978) has called "the fullest and most thorough understanding of the world" (p. 9). Diversity in life ultimately promotes clarity and perspective by offering possibilities for children to consider, possibilities from which to construct meaning. So much that we simply take for granted as adults must be constructed slowly and carefully by children. One- to 3-year-olds spend quite a bit of energy attempting to make meaning out of our adult-organized world. Unable to build on categories they simply don't yet have, young children classify experience from what they sense as salient. Often their novel organization of experience makes us laugh because their fresh viewpoint gives us a momentary window into the arbitrary or otherwise ironic basis of adult categories.

Thus each individual child's own idiosyncratic way of categorizing what goes with what can give us some clues of how he or she is making sense of the world. A few months before my son's third birthday, and after his first week in a child-care center, we spent some time going over the names of his new teachers. As we drove home in the car I heard, "Vivian's a teacher," "Amy's a teacher," "Suzi's a teacher." I remember feeling a surge of emotion fueled by one of those first moments when you realize that your child is truly an engaged member of the outside world. Then I realized he had left out one teacher. "What about David?" I asked. With an authoritative air, he replied from his car seat, "David's not a teacher, David's a person!" This story quickly made the rounds at school, and I was good-naturedly teased for raising a sexist child. Although I was sensitive to being criticized in this area, I understood that in correcting me, my son had created his own commonsense categories based on his first school experience, which included a disproportionate number of women teachers. This was a reasonable assumption for him to make given that he had not fully distinguished the categories of teacher and person.

In another story, Leslie, a teacher of toddlers and 2-year-olds tells how Ruthie, a little girl with two mothers, went about the early categorization of gender.

> I noticed that Ruthie went through a thing about a month ago, when we went on [pretend song-game] the Lion Hunt. We put things on, we put on baseball hats . . . and she started adding this beard and mustache, and it was important to her that we put on our beards and then that we shave them off, because we took everything off when we "got back." Apparently, a very good friend of the family, a male friend, has a beard. And I remember as we were talking, instead of saying the father thing, like in other families, she identified men more by their beards. So this man's name was Steve, or something. Every man was not a daddy, but was a "Steve." That was early on, too, at the beginning of the year, and I've heard Ruthie refer to "Steve" whenever she'd see a bearded man. These beards just appeared again in the lion hunts. It's been stopped by Ruthie, and been picked up by other kids.

Beards came to play a central role in Ruthie's construction of "men" as a category. Whenever she saw a man with a beard, she called him "Steve." As her teacher suggests, if Ruthie had a father with a beard, for some period of time she might have gone around calling everyone with a beard "daddy." To varying degrees, young children nest their word usage in their recollections of related circumstances that hold important meaning for them. We notice this aspect of language development in what linguists call over- and under-extensions; calling men "Steve" is a typical example of a young child over-extending a word that is based on her experience.

At first, very young children have only their own family experiences as a lens through which to interpret the world. For children in gay- and lesbian-headed families, integrating other family forms into their reality can begin only once they have access to children from other kinds of families. In an ethnographic study that investigates how very young children of lesbian-headed families are treated in child care, Scott Hirose (1997) was interviewing a lesbian couple about their family's experiences when one of the mothers asked her son how he had come to learn about mommy–daddy families. The little boy mentioned a video he had seen at his center about a child his age learning to use the potty. The child in the video had a mother and father, and this seems to have made a strong impression on him, evidently a stronger impression than the many coming and going mothers and fathers at his child-care center. This child's response helps us remember that exactly when and how children are exposed to different family structures may vary greatly. More important, perhaps, it is not immediately apparent which experiences may prove to be most meaningful to a given child. Below, Fran, an infant-toddler teacher, provides another classic example of categorizing experience as she describes how a "just" 3-year-old boy used his dramatic play to bring his own family constellation to life and try on other family structures for size.

> There were a lot of things when Lonnie would play with the doll people. At the beginning he never really made up the typical nuclear family. He would have two mommies and a little boy, and they did all the things together and that was the way his play went. After a while, he had two mommies and a daddy also, and then after more time, he got rid of one of the mommies and put the daddy there, but sometimes he would put the daddy to the side and the other mommy would come in, and I think he was, in a lot of ways, trying to figure all that out.

For Lonnie and others like him, the issue at hand is most likely not one of *confusion*, but rather of *definition*. Like children's work in categorizing the world with words, young children use play to experiment with different versions of their daily experience. Fran reports that over the course of that year some of the other 3-year-olds began to take turns in their dramatic play. First they would play "mommy–mommy," and then another child would lead the play with "mommy–daddy." Both here and in the previous example (Ruthie's beards in the Lion Hunt), we see how, early on, the sharing of family life becomes a joint construction of meaning in the social world of the classroom.

In a final example of this process, we gain a sense of how children integrate gender and family experiences into their more private developing self. Like Fran, who is quoted above, Cathy is a teacher who knows that such nascent gender concepts form the backdrop against which children place their thoughts and feelings about all parents they observe, including couples composed of two mothers or two fathers. She appreciates that children's comments must be viewed in this context, as evident in the following story she tells about a conversation she had with a 5-year-old girl with two mothers.

> And she told me there's mommy kisses and there's daddy kisses, and there's different kinds of kisses. And all she gets is mommy kisses. She doesn't get daddy kisses. And I said, well, how are daddy kisses different? And she said, men have scratchy chins and stuff from having hair on their face. And I said, do you have uncles or anything? And she said, yeah, I have a bunch of uncles. And I said, don't you get kisses from them? And she said yes. Then I said, then you're getting kisses that are sort of like daddy kisses. And then I asked her if there was anything else. And she was like, "No." I think she's thinking that she's missing out on something, and she doesn't know yet that in a lot of ways she isn't. I don't think she is. She has two very supportive, wonderful parents, and other supportive adults in her life as well.

This vignette holds particular importance. Cathy did not presume that this child was necessarily expressing a loss or sadness, or if she did, she did not allow that presumption to direct her response. Constructing a supportive scaffold, Cathy helps this little girl reach a more sophisticated level of understanding gender difference, and also helps her appreciate what she *does* experience. In a similar vein, when a young child with a mother and father tells a child with two fathers, "I have two daddies too" or, "Why can't I have two mommies?" a teacher of 3-year-olds also can appreciate that he is trying this on for size, and that he does not necessarily wish his mother or father would disappear. A teacher's easy fluidity in navigating this topic makes the difference between a closing off of learning and imparting helpful and creative possibilities for the child to pursue.

At times, children may reveal (directly or indirectly) an emotional need for a parent of the gender their parent/s are not. Developmental, individual, and societal factors make this a distinct possibility at some point in a child's life. All children have emotional needs. Some are more verbal about them, and children experience those needs differently at

various developmental periods as an interaction of their own developing personality and their environment. How parents choose to deal with
these expressions are complex issues that each family ultimately must
work out for itself. A book for children entitled *The Daddy Machine*
(Valentine, 1992) assumes this "need" approach head-on and takes it
to its ultimate extreme in a fanciful story in which children with two
mothers use a machine their parents have left them to play with to
create 64 dads. Reading such a book can give parents a way in which
to explore their children's feelings and thoughts in this realm.

No one would disagree that hearing a child's expression of a perceived need is very important, yet as adults we are handicapped in doing
so, for our conceptions of gender are perhaps too clearly defined. Societal pressures train us to make assumptions about gender knowledge,
yet young children are still actively in the process of constructing these
concepts. For children with gay parents, experience with mainstream
family structures is initially peripheral and expands only as their interaction in the world increases. We therefore suggest that professionals use caution when interpreting children's comments in this area. It
is important to devote considerable thought to what the child may be
expressing, giving the child some time to flesh out his or her own
meaning, while using the time oneself to reflect on a few alternative
meanings. The child may, in fact, be expressing more than one thought
or feeling, or conveying conflicting or ambivalent feelings. And to
complicate it more, what occurs at home and what occurs in school
may look different, and/or actually *be* different, and may need to be
thought about by family and teachers together. Observing, waiting, and
reflecting on children's behaviors and comments are the ingredients
for educators and parents to create good-faith understanding and communicate with integrity. Skipping a few beats, mediating the impulse
to respond immediately, is surely a virtue to be cultivated in any situation involving complex possibilities.

We have begun to explore why the path toward understanding
gender is a long one, and why, like other aspects of development, it
is not always a smooth one. This concept holds truth for all of us—
parents, educators, and anyone else who spends time with children.
As children move out of the more protected world of toddlerhood into
early childhood proper, societally influenced gender-role stereotypes
collude with a new inflexibility of thought. How children conceptualize gender roles exerts a tremendous influence on *what* they learn
(through play preferences), *how* they learn (from whom, when), and
the broader *expectations* they hold of their own, their peers', and adult
behavior (Honig, 1983). In following the path of gender from 2- and

3-year-olds' play, we bump into a more rigid expression of these roles in the preschool arena. As children's ideas about gender roles become more entrenched in custom, often their behaviors do too. Vivian Gussin Paley (1984) refers to these preschool gender behavioral dichotomies as a "stronghold against ambiguity," an overstatement in the service of clarity. We saw from our informants that children with gay and lesbian parents are particularly scrutinized for appropriate gender-role-conforming play, with an unspoken, or even unacknowledged, fear of homosexuality often at the root of this scrutiny. This kind of concern warrants elaboration wherever it occurs, because the fear of homosexuality in early childhood affects many more families than just gay-headed ones.

HOMOPHOBIA: AT SCHOOL AND AT HOME

How do teachers use this developmental information? Let us look at some of the different meanings teachers and lesbian mothers ascribe to children's gender behaviors, both conformist and nonconformist. In the following vignette, Fred, a K/1 teacher, relates a conversation between a few 6-year-old girls and Dan, a boy of the same age with two mothers. They were discussing a birthday party the girls had attended where they all had put on nail polish. Dan said he had done that a few times, and here his teacher shares his reaction.

> So I'm thinking, maybe you get to be a little strident, I don't know. . . . Maybe it's me, because I am not gay, but . . . I'm thinking, "Gee . . . maybe she's [one of Dan's mothers] pushing it, just to show . . . because she was able to go over the edge, to admit it [being gay] to herself. Maybe it's because it [being gay] was in her to begin with, but maybe *she's* making this choice to somebody [Dan] who wouldn't have made it.

Much is communicated in this short statement, both directly and between the lines, and a clash of cultural values is evident between teacher and parent. Using nail polish for a 6-year-old boy, whatever the reason, is connected to the mother's sexual orientation and is interpreted as a form of flaunting. The teacher also suggests the mother is leading the way in terms of modeling an inappropriate choice of sexual orientation for her son, revealing an assumption on Fred's part that Dan is/will be gay. Perhaps the most compelling part of this story lies in the fact that Dan's parents, upon hearing this story, laughed at first and then became quite serious, noting that Dan's experimentation had taken place not at home, but at the home of heterosexual friends. As one of Dan's mothers put it, "We don't even *have* nail polish in our house!" Classic in its provocative qualities, this story is not unique.

Making Predictions

We interviewed other teachers who made references similar to Fred's, reflecting a special concern with attempting to predict a child's future sexual orientation based on particular behaviors or appearances. Hazel, an experienced public school teacher, makes a spontaneous comment about Marcia, the daughter of Shelly and June, who attended the same school Hazel taught in, but was not her student. Hazel believes Marcia no longer looks feminine because her hair is cut short. She says, "Maybe that is my own perception because I know what is going on. . . . If you ask me to predict, I will say that one of these [two] children will be homosexual. I could be wrong, but that is just my opinion." Like Fred, Hazel has made unsolicited predictions about sexual orientation, which she shared in a confidential interview. In this case, she believes that this girl (or her brother) with lesbian mothers is more likely to be gay than other children. Both teachers have a similar tone—they second-guess themselves, say they could be wrong—but the feeling is conveyed nevertheless. One wonders if and how such thoughts may be conveyed, in a less consciously stated form, to the children's families. Although we didn't ask them about this directly, Shelly and June (the parents of these two children) speculate about just such attitudes (see Chapter 3).

The impulse to predict behavior is not reserved for psychologists. Making predictions of all kinds is a popular human pastime of long standing. But predicting sexual orientation is chock-full of complexity, and predicting an adult outcome from childhood behavior can be high-risk behavior indeed. The confluence of individual and gender-related differences, together with a bundle of emerging theories embedded in biological, social constructivist (DeCecco & Elia, 1993), as well as integrative developmental explanations (Bem, 1996), should make for a most humble approach.

And while it is quite evident that the vast majority of lesbian and gay adults were raised in heterosexual families, some new data from a longitudinal study of children raised by lesbians confirm the commonsensical notion that if children raised in lesbian- and gay-headed families *do* experience same-sex attractions in adolescence and beyond, they are likely to be comparatively more open to those attractions (Tasker & Golombok, 1997). Other data from a small but provocative study (Hamer, 1998) found a 33% chance of a daughter of a lesbian being a lesbian herself. If in fact there are differing etiological factors for sexual orientation for the two genders, and given the complex same- and opposite-sex identifications in lesbian- and gay-headed families (also depending on the gender of the child), it makes sense that there could be tendencies toward different outcomes for a given subgroup (e.g., daughters of lesbians). As we move into the twenty-first century, however, there is clearly so much that we still don't understand about the origins of our sexual orientations. Audre Lorde (1984) describes a seasoned view on this issue when she wrote about her adolescent son's growing sexuality as a conscious dynamic between them, saying, "It would be presumptuous of me to discuss [his] sexuality here, except to state my belief that whomever he chooses to explore this area with, his choices will be nonoppressive, joyful, and deeply felt from within, places of growth" (p. 73).

Before this last unreplicated study (Hamer, 1998), research in this area was unequivocal. Children raised by gay and lesbian parents were shown to be no more likely (7–10%) to be gay themselves than children in the heterosexual family population (Bailey, Bobrow, Wolfe, & Mikach, 1995; Patterson, 1992; Schulenberg, 1985). While it is important to mention these data, in some cases it may be more important not to. Even citing the result of such research takes a tack that misses the point, because it still is responding to socially conditioned *fears* of children becoming homosexual. It also does not address the fact that gayness has growing meaning to children of lesbian- and gay-headed families, as do issues of homophobia and heterosexism, especially as children reach school age. Defining who their parents are, and understanding *how* society reacts to them, is clearly a part of children's lives, yet the importance of gayness to these children was not articulated by any of the educators we interviewed. Nor did any observe that a child with lesbian or gay parents who does grow up gay might have a significantly better experience coming out than he or she would having grown up in a heterosexual-headed family. We did not delve into the long-term hopes or fears of the parents we interviewed, but we might project that some would have the courage to be pleased for their children to grow up gay. Perhaps Al, in describing his 3-year-old's use of dramatic play, inadvertently conveys pleasure in the idea. A similar comment from a teacher would be thought to reflect a leap to unsupported conclusions and harbor negative connotations.

Even [3-year-old] Ernesto is going through a stage where he is going to be a homosexual. He walks into his classroom every day, takes off his shoes, puts on the heels in the dress-up corner, puts on a dress, a pocketbook, and stays like that all day. It's actually normal to be like that in that school. Nobody is telling him, "Why don't you play with the cars?" Or, "Why don't you do this?" Or, "Boys don't dress up like that." It's allowed. It's fine.

In practice, the culture has effectively put a squeeze on any parents who might want to support gay development in children (Kirby, 1998; Sedgwick, 1993). This climate shows that untangling the ways in which gender norms and homophobia conspire to inform predictions of children's future sexual orientation requires substantial knowledge as well as personal reflection. In the following section two teachers share their thinking about boys who have been identified by other children as effeminate. We found their ideas to be thoughtful and provocative. They provide quite a different model from the kind of simplistic prediction we have observed more commonly.

Labeling and Its Confusions

What happens when gender-related labeling begins among children themselves, and how does it differ across the developmental spectrum? What responses can be made to effeminate or tomboy behaviors when they are put under the spotlight in the classroom? Sol, a gay male, is a K/1 teacher in our study. He describes some of the developmental changes in children's reactions over the course of his 2 years with the same class, as well as the reasons he chose to act as he did.

Like Hazel, Sol believes that a child, Ralph, in his school may be gay when he grows up. Unlike Hazel, however, he is this child's teacher, which takes many of his responses out of a comparative context with those of Hazel, but not his first comment, in which he buttresses his hunch with more than feelings, saying, "If Bell, Weinberg, and Hammersmith are right, he will be gay, or more likely to be gay." Here Sol is referring to a classic and quite credible study reported in *Sexual Preference* (Bell, Weinberg, & Hammersmith, 1981) that found "childhood gender nonconformity to be more strongly connected to homosexuality than was any other variable in the study," especially for boys (p. 80). A more recent review of studies (Bem, 1996) examining the relationship between childhood behavior and sexual orientation also found gender nonconformity to be the most commonly shared characteristic of boys who later are gay. But Sol also gives Ralph some concrete assistance and support, telling us,

> I sent *Oliver Button Is a Sissy* [de Paola, 1979] home with him, and I read it to the class too. Ralph was called "faggot" by the other kids last year and some of the kids knew it was wrong and one of the girls came and told me. Ralph is much less out about liking to do girl things this year.

This prediction of gayness also differs from Hazel's in that this child was identified as effeminate by his peers and teased about it. Beyond this, Sol took some flack himself and put the same principles to work when the children teased him. As soon as the issue became public, Sol took action.

> There was something else. I don't wear my earrings to work, but nevertheless the holes in my ears are very evident and kids, usually girls, all the time, they just wouldn't give up on it, they would say to me [in a sing-song tempo], "You have a ponytail, you have earrings, that's for girls." And my answer was always this very even-tempered, "Well, I have a pony tail and I have earrings, and I'm a boy, so I guess they're for boys too." And my triumph was when I was watching the kids at the sand table. They were pretending that they were making ice cream. One little girl says, "I'm making a double vanilla fudge." And [Ralph] said, "Well, I'm going to make a double vanilla fudge too," and the little girl said, "No, only girls make double vanilla fudge ice cream." And he said, "Well I'm a boy and I'm making a double vanilla fudge ice cream, so I guess boys do it too."

One can only imagine Sol's feelings at this moment. Ralph's response reveals an exquisite moment that reflects a process in which a child has been listening to, identifies, and internalizes a teacher's message for his own use. In the next sequence we see that Sol is willing to go even further to identify and eliminate homophobia from his classroom. He questions Ralph, who is using the word *faggot* in class. As it turns out, Shanique, Ralph's mother, is a single lesbian mother, and Ralph appears to have picked up the term at home. Before Sol recounted the story below, he reminded the interviewer that the context of this school makes any dialogue with parents difficult. It is uncomfortable for a teacher to ask a parent *any* question without it being received as accusatory, for, as Sol describes it, "parents are too much under the thumb of too many agencies, this school being one of them."

> One piece of advice I'd have for any teacher, of course, is to never tolerate any kind of homophobia in the classroom, or this sort of 6-year-old pre-homophobia that I see. This child [of a lesbian mom] himself has called me *faggot* on two different occasions. I spoke to the mother . . . and I told her how I reacted. And I said, "It's important to me to eliminate homophobia in my classroom in general—it's especially important when I'm dealing with your son, because he's *your* son. Where do you think he's getting this from? Do you think he knows what it means?" And she said, "Gee, I don't know." She was defensive, and then she finally admitted that she refers to his father as "that faggot" when she's angry about his behavior: "Oh, why do you want to see that faggot?"
>
> And then she said, "But you know, Sol, that I don't mean it that way." I think she may have said that because I'm gay myself. I'm not sure and I said: "Well, I know that, but [Ralph] is 6 and he doesn't." I don't know if she stopped using the word; I do know that he stopped using it in the classroom.

This exchange between Shanique and Sol demonstrates one lesbian mother's socialization to homophobia, and the depth of its reach. If ethnographic data represent a "dramatic instance" of another's experience (Leavitt, 1994), then this particular parent–teacher dynamic becomes important for its raw and painful honesty. Shanique's is not a middle-class voice, and, as with our findings about disclosure, we see that often class privilege can help foster a more political and self-conscious advocacy. Sometimes, when a child feels free enough to use out-of-school concepts and language in the classroom, it can help the teacher to better grasp the child's level of understanding. Sol further describes the discussion that ensued after Ralph used the word *faggot* for the third and final time.

> Now there was a third incident soon after this, and it hasn't happened since, when he called another child "faggot" and the kids went, "Whooooo" 'cause they already figured out that I don't allow that word. I turned to him and asked, "What does that mean?" And another child at the table who is very macho looked at me and said, "It means punk." And I said, "What's a punk?" And he said, "It's a homo." At this point he's completely exasperated by my stupidity, but I still ask him, "What's a homo?" And he said, "Some-

one who can't fight." And that was really interesting for me to see the linguistic construct at its beginning and then the content that's poured into it by third grade if not second. Then they know about boys having sex with other boys and that's what "punk" means.

If we think of Sol's story about 6-year-olds exhibiting "pre-homophobia," then following a parallel story of 8-year-olds' responses to classmates' gender-nonconformist behavior takes us into the realm of homophobia proper. But it tells us much more. Gail Bolt (1997) widens the lens to include not only the effeminate behavior of Stephen, the students' responses, and her own, but puts the spotlight on her own understanding of these conflicts that pervade her classroom. She understands that this self-examination is pivotal to figuring out any response to the powerful peer socialization her children exhibit. Her story begins as two girls who have been Stephen's friends since kindergarten inform him that their relationship is over. Why? They don't mince words. "It's time for you to start playing with boys and for us to start playing with girls" (p. 188). Gail Bolt actively sought out a study group composed of other professionals with whom she could examine how cultural norms about gender and sexuality had influenced her own thinking. Articulating an approach we have argued for at numerous junctures in this book, she writes that it was *through taking the time to grapple with my own response* and the responses of others to Stephen that I was able to develop a more powerful way to understand sexism" (p. 190, emphasis added). She became immediately suspect of the very assumption about which Sol was so clear. She asked herself what the real reasons might be for her quick assumption that Stephen *would* be gay. In casting herself into the middle of her children's conflicts, she makes it possible for us to understand more about how gender normativity sharpens its hold as children develop.

Among Sol's 6-year-old girls, "double vanilla fudge sundaes" became a symbol for girl behavior. One can imagine them in shock when confronted by Ralph's bold response. The 8-year-olds in Gail's class are very busy not only "doing" gender, but rating gender performance in a more explicit and self-conscious manner. In one extensive discussion about the children in the class who act more like the other gender than their own, Gail asks them if this is a new topic for them. One child answers: "We talk about it all the time, how Kelly is a boy and Stephen is more like a girl" (p. 193). Gail probes further to discover that Kelly doesn't mind being called a boy and admits to liking boy-type activities. When Gail asks about Stephen's feelings about being labeled as a girl, they say that he gets mad and tells them it's not nice to talk about people. Then a girl adds, "And sometimes he says he is a boy, but boys or girls can do whatever they want" (p. 193).

Here are Ralph's words almost verbatim, reiterated in the older voice of Stephen. The third graders are not just enacting specific gender-typical behaviors, but have begun to analyze, hypothesize, and gossip about gender behaviors in general. Because they own these idealized norms in a more sophisticated way than Sol's 6-year-olds, they are already suspect of the assertion that boys and girls can do whatever they want. They know otherwise. Gail confronts their generalizations by noting that *none of them* conform to these standards exactly and she gives examples of numerous children who like to engage in activities of the "other" gender. The children inform her: "But Ms. Bolt, *mostly* boys like sports" (p. 193). The individual differences are academic. The generalized norms appear to be what count and are already conceived as truths by the children.

Although very aware of the research that would link Stephen's gender-bending behavior with later homosexuality, Gail refuses to do so. She remembers that while Stephen may not like being teased, he probably derives pleasure from his own particular gender performance and has many other qualities and identifications that make up his current identity. She also reflects that how he later constructs meaning from his current life will introduce even more possibilities. She says, "The pleasures and hurts of my students will always be there, to show me the inclusions and exclusions that have been instituted, to remind me that my values and beliefs are always only provisional, always only partly successful" (p. 211). These realizations empower her to use the present in meaningful ways that have immediate results, like preventing children from being cruel to each other and helping them feel safe in their classroom relationships. Sol and Gail are teachers who have moved way beyond theory scripts. They are educated in current research and theory and can hold multiple contradictions in their minds as they reflect on their classroom practice.

We have seen how deeply gender-assigned roles are embedded within our culture and how difficult they are to ferret out. This is true not only for young children who are engaged in establishing gender identities and roles, but for adults as well. A discussion with two teachers of infants and toddlers, Fran and Leslie, demonstrates how the presence of children with lesbian mothers provided an opportunity to question some basic assumptions about parental roles.

Fran: And that was a question that came up for me a lot: Who's like the mother and who's like the father? Well, I don't know.

> In one case, I would have to say that Val is more like the mom,
> and Diane is definitely more like the father who's busy and not
> as accessible and is away more. But I wouldn't say that emo-
> tionally, you know what I mean? And even with Rena and
> Miriam it wasn't as clear at all. But people wanted to do that
> [assign gender roles].

Leslie: I remember one of the things with my staff was overcoming
some stereotypes, and the stereotype with Rena and Miriam
never made much sense to anyone [assistant teachers], that
Rena was the birthmother.

Fran: Because Rena seems more masculine in some ways.

Leslie: One thing I have to say that I've discovered about myself is
that I [now] have a tendency to call the drop-off parent . . .
well, the one who's most consistent. Because that was something I asked myself one day: "Who should I call?" And I
remember thinking this about Rena and Miriam because now I
always call the person who is most involved in the child's life at
the center.

The above is a most poignant example of how gay- and lesbian-
headed families can help a teacher reconceptualize her or his thinking
about parent–teacher interaction in general. This kind of change is
taking place gradually as teachers experience and grapple with family
forms that differ from what has been perceived as the norm.

ROLE MODELS: IN THEORY AND REALITY

The conviction that children need exposure to both genders is a
central concept for all our informants. How that exposure takes place,
and for what reasons, however, appears to be quite open for discussion. Classic psychoanalytic theory argues that boys and girls need a
mother and father to traverse the opposing paths of desire and identity, desiring the opposite-sex parent and identifying with the same-
sex parent, in order to reach the presumed goal of mature adult heterosexuality (Freud, 1905/1965). The theoretical assumption that desire
and identity must be resolved separately and in a particular way is
deeply entrenched in the psyche of anyone who has grown up in our
culture, even if it is explicitly rejected as one's developmental model.
And as new theory questions the presumed normality of heterosexuality (Chodorow, 1992), or asks why desire and identification must be
seen only as opposing forces (Butler, 1995), traditional Freudian theory

continues to overly determine how professionals think about what children need in order to develop.

It became clear early on in our study that individuals assigned different meanings to the term *role model*. Our first task was to find out what the term signified to various informants. Maritza, raising a son in a committed lesbian relationship, offers her view.

> When I think of role model, I think of his teacher, about people who come to his class, people who do things with him every day. I don't think of MTV, we aren't into that. I think about history books. Is that what you mean?

Using Sandra Bem's (1983, 1996) approach, we might say that Maritza's comments appear to be totally unaffected by traditional gender schema. Maritza conceptualizes models first and foremost by the quality of their influence on her son. The category of gender does not even enter her mind, in fact, until the interviewer prompts her to go further in her response. Then Maritza makes it very clear that it is the values she and her partner share about living in the world that supersede issues of gender.

> You mean, does he need other role models? I don't feel that. We feel it is important that he has role models of both sexes . . . people that we feel are good people . . . like the dentist is female. We look for, we feel the same thing about culture. I think it is important that he has his uncles, Andy [his teacher], men who are very sensitive and loving. We wouldn't want him spending time with men who are violent, sexist.

Another lesbian mother conveys a similar view as she answers the question about role models. June reminds us that no family can provide everything to a child; within any family structure certain behaviors/abilities are highlighted and others are less pronounced.

> I think with every family you get some role models and you don't get some others. With heterosexual families, you have a role model of a father who can get out there and make a great deal of money in business, but who never was a role model of taking care of babies. . . . Role models of parents are people of good character who can communicate. We [she and her partner] have a model of a nice marriage. Jeremy might grow up saying I never saw a dad doing *that*. Marcia might say, "I never saw how *that*

could work in a heterosexual relationship, and I really feel deprived of that," yes she might. In one way or another you make up the differences. As time goes by you get a lot of that with their peers and their peers' families. They see a lot of dads in other families, just like they see mothers doing different things in other families. They see their teachers, men and women, and they do not necessarily know if they are mothers or not. You learn from that, too.

This perspective is expressed by gay men as well as lesbians. A single gay father puts it in a slightly different way, but conveys the same general message: that both boys and girls need to see men and women in a variety of activities and roles, not just that they need someone to model specific gender roles for their development.

What's important? That they have a fair view of both ends. That he [his son] sees single straight men, single gay men, married straight men, couples of men, single women, single lesbian women, married women, and lesbian couples. That he knows the range of the possibilities, that at any given time these people are all exactly the same, except for the preference that they've chosen to live out their lives, that show their affection and their love.

Sol is the only self-identified gay teacher in our study. He is White and is not a parent. He further elaborates the concept of "role model," by emphasizing how deeply race and class inhabit the term in the Black community in which he teaches. He frames the term by emphasizing his thoughts about "fatherlessness" in the Black community.

You know there's all this talk in the Black community and the Black educational community about the need for Black male role models. If this community is typical, and I think it is, the number of Black males in children's lives is underestimated. Many of my kids have men in their lives, it may be a father, a second husband, or a grandfather, with the same variety as the women in their lives. All the kids have a woman in their life, at least one, but many have a man too. Racism impacts on all Black people, but there's a special construct for Black males. And so Black male role models are important and I'm pleased when I see Black male teachers in my school and there're not a lot. So I think specific issues of gender role models for children of gay and lesbian parents get lost in a broader community-wide issue.

Once again, Sol reminds us of the importance of context in discussing these issues. Sol lost his own father in childhood (see Chapter 3) and he stresses that while fathers are not to be taken lightly, male energy simply cannot be substituted where it is thought to be missing.

Taking Another Look

The above statements are broadly representative of our interviewees' theoretical conceptions of role models, but at the level of daily life, more complex factors are at work and require a second look. Once we dug below the surface, we discovered that many parents are ambivalent about the availability of a male or female person who is not present in their family configurations. When parents of lesbian- and gay-headed households do discuss a role model as "missing" from their children's lives, they generally attribute their feelings to the culture at large, stating, for example, that other people think it is important. In some cases, role models are portrayed as something that is an acknowledged part of their parental responsibility, but without the passion that is evident around other concerns. As one lesbian mother of a 5-year-old daughter said with a tone of slight resignation, "Whatever needs to be done, we do." Below, Nora and Jacqueline explain that their son has had the experience of a male teacher for 3 consecutive years. The two parents may not be in complete agreement here, but this dialogue expresses Jacqueline's thinking process in exquisite detail as she responds to the interviewer's question asking her to elaborate on how important she sees men to be in Dan's life and why.

> Jacqueline: I don't know the answer to that question. That's the big issue of people in my family.
> Nora: Although interestingly enough, none of her sisters are with their husbands . . . so none of them have any role models of any consistency.
> Jacqueline: If the need were communicated to me from Dan, then it would be something I would pursue. I don't feel it as being real important? [She speaks with the rising intonation of a question.]
> Interviewer: Can you say more about why?
> Jacqueline: I don't know many men who could be . . . [inaudible], much less role models for Dan. [Pauses] That's not altogether true. I have cousins and relatives who could be role models for Dan but who don't necessarily embrace the relationship. [Pauses] But I don't know if I would say that if he didn't have a

> male teacher 3 years in a row. I can't answer that question
> because I don't have any way of basing it otherwise. He spends
> 5 days a week with an extremely nurturing, loving, gifted male
> teacher who adores him and thinks that Dan is just, you know,
> the cat's meow. And I don't think he hurts from that. He
> spends as much time with Fred as with us. . . . I guess I do
> value it.

Jacqueline's statement that role models are not so important conveys some ambivalence. She also vascillates as she appears to be reasoning out the relative worth of each variable she discusses, and as she frames one against the other. Looking at Dan's daily experience provides her with a different window than her "pure" views on the subject. A global role model may not be her top priority, but she understands that this particular relationship is a valued one.

In what follows, Maritza tells us what she thinks is important for her son and relates it to her values for him in general. While she says male role models are not crucial, she also slips in that he has them in his life. She begins and ends by emphasizing the two most important people who serve as models—herself and her partner: his parents.

> We want him to be exposed to as many role models as possible. We
> think it is more important that he is around people who have the
> same kind of morality, ethics, that we have, rather than what sex.
> He has a lot of men in his life who he is close to who are very good
> role models. . . . We are [also] very good role models.

While these apparently shifting views reveal ambivalence, we believe that they seem so only when framed against the larger culture. The scant research on this topic suggests that lesbian mothers want their children to have opportunities for good relationships with either their biological fathers (Kirkpatrick et al., 1981; Lewin, 1993) or other men. More recent data also showed this to be true with a sample of children who mostly had known and unknown sperm donors. These children had great access to grandfathers or other men who were friends of the family (Patterson, Hurt, & Mason, 1998). Yet in Lewin's (1993) qualitative study, some ambivalent feelings also came through concerning the need to provide men in their children's lives. So too in a narrative piece by a lesbian mother, we found a statement that parallels what we heard from our informants. In a chapter entitled "The Myth of the Male Role Model," Cheryl Deaner (1997) writes, "We do not consciously look for men to include in his life, but it just so happens that our lives include men" (p. 66). The kind of attitudes about role models we encountered in our parent informants is reflected with a twist of irony and humor in the popular cartoon series by Alison Bechdel, in which a gay male friend babysits for the young boy of lesbian moms (see Figure 5.2).

In the context of our study, many gay and lesbian parents can feel torn between what they have been *told* is necessary for the healthy development of children and what they believe is right for their children. But considered apart from this background, gay parents are clear that they want their children to have *many role models*, and that variety is the key. This may seem like a subtle point, but we have heard it often enough that it has surfaced as a significant finding. Here we believe lies the essence of the deepest chasm between many gay parents and the educators of their children, for, as we shall observe, most of the educators we spoke with have a quite different emphasis, and have reservations about what it means for children's development to grow up without parents of both genders.

"If There Were a Man Around . . ."

These reservations had a common theme; all the educators who expressed them strongly believed that children in gay-headed households were being deprived of developmentally appropriate role models. Penny is a young but experienced kindergarten teacher who has shown a strongly proactive stance with the gay-headed families of children in her class. When asked about role models, however, she expresses some concern.

Figure 5.2. Role Model Cartoon

From *Hot, Throbbing Dykes to Watch Out For*, Firebrand Books, Ithaca, NY. © 1997 by Alison Bechdel. Used by permission.

I just wonder about long-term. I have a friend in Germany, she is an unmarried mother and is raising a child. And there are no males in this child's life. Her father is dead. She doesn't have contact with her brothers, and there are very few men in her life. The child has no male influence in his life. I think it is something that he has mentioned and it is not good for him. Just a mom. I know that lots of children have grown up when the fathers were away at war or away for work reasons, but I think there were always some males around. Like when Enrico [the principal in her school] said when he was young, his father was away at war but his uncles were around. I think that in that situation long ago when the father was away, there were other people who stepped in and acted as the father.

The words "stepped in and acted as the father" are reminiscent of Sol's comments about feeling anger as a child about the idea that other men could step in and replace the missing role of his father after he died (see Chapter 3). Penny places fatherlessness in the context of other places and times and comes up with the need for a father figure if the father himself is not around. The example that comes to her mind is of a single heterosexual friend. We sense that in using this example, Penny is trying to be "objective," to describe the issue as father-absence rather than lesbian-headed parenting.

Leslie, another child-care teacher who in practice is also very supportive of the gay-headed families of children in her room, reflects a similar worry in describing the physical fears of a "just" 3-year-old boy with two mothers. In describing the child's physical play, she attempts to be specific about a hypothetical deficit.

And I wonder if . . . I remember when Lonnie was first at the center, and his fear of jumping off the red house. I remember thinking, do Denise and Val, do they get rough with him? Where does this fear came from? I mean, he's a tall lanky kid, you know, so I could say that just physically he wasn't ready yet. But this is one of the things I thought, if there were a man around in his life, that this would potentially be different.

In our interview, Leslie had previously expressed concern about how *other* staff made assumptions about children raised by gay parents. We believe she is thinking aloud here in a most private way, which rarely is captured. The first thought reflects an assumption that there are no men in this boy's life. The second idea is a question about what might be different for Lonnie if there were. The questions behind Leslie's thinking are important ones to consider. Even though women are physical, is it different, and if so, how? Doesn't it depend on the particular adult and child? How much is tied to cultural gender role, and how much is truly biology? These larger questions that frame Leslie's specific ones are causing much discussion in the field (Casper, 1998; Pruett, 1998; Silverstein & Auerbach, 1997), as cross-cultural research demonstrates that Swedish fathers (Hwang, 1987) and fathers from other cultures demonstrate less of a tendency toward rough-and-tumble play (Roopnarine, Ahmenduzzaman, Hossain, & Riegraf, 1992), and among the AKA pygmys in Africa, it is the aunts who engage in this typically Western father play (Hewlett, 1991).

Not being this child's primary teacher, Leslie was not even aware of or privy to whether there were men in his life, much less what they might represent to him. What about enduring 2-year-old fears, or the beginning of a child's first all-day, child-care experience? Nevertheless, Leslie's immediate impulse, probably because of the newness to her of the idea of two mothers, was to wonder if more "maleness" would make a difference. As it turned out, the weeks passed, and Lonnie, "a slow to warm up" child, soon began jumping off the red house, and with gusto.

Emory, an experienced public school principal, also makes comments that contrast sharply with those of our parent informants. Asked about children of gay and lesbian parents, and to what extent he thinks they need role models of the opposite sex from their parents, he, like Penny, answers beyond this group. His response differs from Penny's, however, in that he generalizes from what he has observed from all children he has known in his school who are living without fathers.

> That's a hard one to answer. I'm not sure it can be limited to the issue of gay and lesbian parents. I feel that there were kids [at my school] who did not have a male in their lives, whose fathers might have died, who lived with two females. I think that kids who did not have—especially male children who did not have—a male in their lives were very, very close and attached to me and other male teachers in the school. [There was] a lot of hugging, holding hands, and bonding with males in the school. I really don't think it mattered whether there were male children living with two female parents or male children living with their mother because their father had either died or left. So I'm not sure that you can eliminate that other variable. I'm not sure that you can say that it's just because they live with two females, or that they are girls who live with two females and bond with other females in the school. But I

do think the kids sought out that other relationship that they may
not have had at home.

Asked whether he thought this behavior reflected their developing sense
of self, Emory said:

I don't think I can answer that question. I don't know. I just know
clearly there were kids who didn't live with a male . . . boys who
did not live with a male, who would run and give me a hug every
time they saw me. And it was clear after a number of times that
they were looking for some male figure to be able to relate.

Emory is speaking from his own repeated experiences. He seems
to be saying, in effect, "I don't really know *what* I think about this gay
stuff, but I know what I see." He also conceptualizes all children living
without men in the same group. This not only sums up the gist of what
a lot of educators experience and/or believe, but it resonates with a
deficit model of "fatherless." Historically, psychoanalytic theory has
not differentiated between the various causes of a child not growing
up with a father (death, divorce, planned single motherhood, etc.). The
classic theory also assumes that every child without a father in the home
craves a psychological, if not a real, father, and describes children growing up without fathers as exhibiting "father hunger" (Pruett, 1997).
Although the face of the American family has changed, the culture is
still sufficiently habituated to the two-parent, heterosexual family that
it is conceivable that most children do hold a psychological space reserved for "father." How individual children respond to that space
covers a wide spectrum, including the behaviors Emory describes, as
well as a host of others he doesn't, but that are represented throughout this book. Educators need to be wary of political and religious "back
to fathering" movements that glorify and reify fathering beyond its
widely human range, such as those put forth by David Blankenhorn
(1995) through the Institute for American Values and by David Popenoe
(1996).

Father Stephen Moore, a priest in charge of a parochial school, also
presents this point of view but prefaces it with a classic remark, actually saying, "Some of my best friends are homosexuals." He goes on to
share more of his thoughts.

I think kind of a bottom line in my dealing is that with the importance of the traditional family and the presence of the father, with
that being eroded, I don't like to see or participate in things that

would facilitate that erosion. . . . Then we do experience where a parent dies and a child is denied the male presence or the presence of a male father, there is an emotional effect on the child. Children need that presence of the male *and* the female.

This is the most straightforward response we received from the educators and administrators who clearly had questions about a child growing up without a mother or father. It is around these issues, too, that we again see some differences between how educators view lesbian mothers and gay fathers. Society has its strongest messages about boys needing to have male figures available and boys or girls needing a mother figure.

> Fran: It's interesting, I have two gay male friends who are trying to adopt a child, and they got a call about this 7-year-old little girl, and they were considering it. I don't know, but I assumed for some reason that they would have to take a boy. Geez, you know, I thought, well I'll really have to hang around with these guys for a while 'cause this girl she's going to need . . . like, supposing she needs, you know, like a woman to talk to about, you know, her period, or dating boys, or any of that kind of stuff. I really had some concerns about that. Then I thought about it and thought those guys could probably handle that stuff, but I could handle it a lot better [laughter]. I'm sure that I could, because I'm a woman, and I understand those things. So I do think about those things, and in some ways I feel that a woman can handle both sides of the issue. Oh, a woman could be okay for a boy and talk about all those things, and would also be fine for a girl. And maybe that is my stereotypical idea about men, but I guess I have to admit it because I have those ideas.
>
> Interviewer: It's very important to think about it all and try to figure out what your biases are, because we all have them, in one form or another.
>
> Fran: Yes, maybe, in some ways I do. As happy as I am, in some ways, for my friends to be adopting a child, and I think that they'll be great parents, and I wrote a beautiful letter of recommendation for them for the adoption agency, and I do think that there are so many kids out there that need homes, but even if there weren't, I think they'd make lovely parents. For some reason, though, I think two women is a more comfortable thing for me than two men.

This kind of honesty is what we believe can be most helpful to educators. Being unaware of such a bias would be particularly detrimental to any girl with two fathers who might be in this teacher's classroom.

In the case of our parent informants, a parallel example of self-examination centered on a meta-scrutiny about if, how, and/or why the school exerted a specific philosophy by matching the child with a teacher of the opposite gender from the gay or lesbian parents. Maritza, a lesbian mother, ponders, "I wondered why he was in Andy's class. I wondered if the school wondered if he needed a male. Maybe that was more in our mind than their mind. I am sure there must have been other reasons to put him in Andy's class." Here, Maritza lets us in on her thinking with some intimacy. She is not implying that she did not *want* her son in the class in which he was placed; she was very happy with the teacher yet she could not help wondering if her son was matched with a man for that reason above all others. Here we have an example of how even under the best of circumstances and sensitive communication, a lesbian mother cannot erase nagging questions that have to do with the attitudes she has come to expect from society.

"What Do You Want for Kids?"

> And then I also thought, in terms of role models, "What do you want for kids?" You want them to be brought up by people who are somewhat together in terms of having dealt with their issues, they've sorted certain things out, they're nurturing, they care about these children. All of those things. You can have gay and nongay, lesbian and nonlesbian people who have sorted out their issues.

Sasha puts it succinctly and provides an essential answer to her own question and a question all of us would do well to answer for ourselves. H. Rudolph Schaffer (1990), the distinguished British developmentalist, has collected data to answer the specific research question, "Do children need a parent of each sex?" Based on his study, he has observed that "it seems unlikely that imitation of and identification with a same-sex parent play the all-important part once ascribed to them" (p. 104). He cites the example that a boy being raised by a single mother should develop the masculine role simply because she treats him as a male. The quality of maleness is fostered "because someone of influence over the child considers it important" (p. 104).

Ideas about identification also have changed as our gendered selves have been subject to review. If we identify with and react to various people somewhat differently, then we constantly are reconstructing gender identifications throughout life and can think of ourselves as not living in a single gender role, but multiple ones (Schwartz, 1998). Decades before the current gender theorizing was even a paradigmatic flicker, Philip Slater (1961) tried to reframe traditional psychoanalytic theory of identification into a more usable form. Slater expanded on the idea of gender complementarity, or multiple aspects of identification, posing "personal" and "positional" identifications. In so doing, he acknowledged, for example, that a given child may in fact derive his or her sense of nurturance from the caregiving received from the father. In our study, June, a lesbian mother, explains that she derived her drive for out-of-the-home accomplishments from her mother: "You could never have used my mother as a model for parenting, but she was a good role model for how to pursue a career that would give you joy. That she did do well."

When we consider the related issue of gender on parenting effects, the research on heterosexual families points to the fact that children's psychological adjustment depends much more on the warmth and nurturance of parenting behaviors than on the parent's gender (Lamb, 1997). Taken together, with all the research on the solid psychosocial development of children raised by lesbian and gay parents (Kirkpatrick et al., 1981; Patterson, 1992; Patterson & Chan, 1997; Patterson et al., 1998; Tasker & Golombok, 1997), we have an enlarged and enhanced view of children's development in families that focuses on the content rather than the form of the family structure. Audre Lorde put the essence of many parts of our lives into simple, powerful words. On this issue, she also waxed eloquently. Speaking about lesbians raising sons she wrote, "Our sons will not grow into women. Their way is more difficult than that of our daughters, for they must move away from us, without us. Hopefully, our sons have what they have learned from us, and a howness to forge it into their own image" (1984, p. 73).

In Hirose's (1997) ethnographic study he reports on a child he calls M, a 2-year-old boy who tells his two mothers that he wants to be a mommy when he grows up. Anyone with an interpretive axe to grind could gain much mileage here. Is this comment reflective of M's age-appropriate lack of gender stability, or does it express a more generalized lack of differentiation between the sexes? Regardless, isn't M's wish what Slater (1961) would call a personal identification; what Hirose names a "love-filled identification" (p. 13). Such a wish also seems connected to a young child's desire to reach toward the superhero role that parents of young children often fill. Using the theory and research just described, we have a reasonable basis to smile at M's comment as a healthy identification that is productive, not worrisome.

We have emphasized the long path children and adults are on in order to be human beings in our gendered society. In observing the range of behaviors we all choose to express it, it becomes apparent that the developing child and the adults in his or her life hold specific values about culturally defined gender roles. All these factors become intertwined with the gender makeup of a given family. As young children construct these concepts, they need adult support to help them interpret their experiences. Adults can do this only if they themselves are relatively clear about their own gender-related values. Within our study, differing ideas about role models lie at the heart of what gay parents and their children's educators believe children need in order to develop. It is an area where much work remains to be done in child development theory and teacher education, but this is work that we believe will yield the most gratifying results for children and their families. Although this chapter has focused on children's gender "finding" and adult reactions to their search, we have seen that we don't "find" our genders once and for all, but are continually "finding" them as we explore our gendered selves throughout our lives. This is but one avenue in which gay- and lesbian-headed families are leading the way.

CHAPTER 6

Classroom Life

I have one child, Sara, whose mother is a lesbian and who didn't have a partner at the time of her birth. I happened to overhear her friend, Megan, ask her, "Where is your dad, by the way?" It was very frank, and Sara turned and said, "I've never had a dad." Megan asked her, "Well, don't you miss having a dad," and so she said, "I don't know. I've never really had one to miss one. It's just always been this way." Megan stopped and turned around and said, "But, wait a minute, you had to have a dad at one point to be able to be here now, to be able to be born. How did that happen?" Sara turned to Megan and said to her, "Well, this is what happened. My mommy wanted to have a baby very badly, so she went to a doctor and the doctor planted a seed inside of her, and the seed became me, and here I am." Then Megan said, "Well, do you know who your father is? Because there's a man connected to that seed." Sara said, "No, we don't know who he is and we don't need to know who he is." It was as clear as that. As delightful as that.

—Second Grade Public School Teacher

How does the reality of gay families achieve texture and presence in the classroom? Conversations like the one above can and do occur just about anywhere, but, in our experience, they are more likely to take place in classrooms where teachers consciously and carefully nurture an openness and relatedness to children's lives. Moreover, the question becomes not just when and where such conversations may occur, but what happens *after* such an exchange. What are the possible ways to extend all children's thinking about a range of family structures?

A LOOK AT THE CLASSROOM CONTEXT

We know that the conditions in which one teaches always affect what and how one teaches. But the other side of the equation is that teachers also may strongly affect and change the conditions in which they teach. It is this vital dynamic that frames our conversation about the content of classroom life, or, what we know to be curriculum. Many of the teachers we interviewed began to thoughtfully weave the theme of family diversity into the ongoing curriculum in various ways, in interaction with the specific conditions of their teaching world. So while their pre-existing environment limited the level or extent of what they included, it did not prevent determined teachers from finding ways to make lesbian- or gay-headed families a part of their curriculum. The constraints or supports they encountered depended on the kind of school in which they were working; the community in which it resided; whether or not a known child with lesbian or gay parents was a member of the class (Wickens, Schultz, Clay, & Stafford, 1995); and the direction and type of leadership exercised by the administration. And because it is the rare setting that will entirely support the teacher striving to include gay content, real-life classroom teachers most likely will find themselves in a context that offers some combination of support and limitations, including their own readiness to approach this topic.

In what follows we present successful teacher strategies as well as ways to analyze contextual factors that can limit or support teachers' goals of inclusion. Given the significant contributions that many gay parents make, and the strong parent–teacher partnership we espouse, parental concerns about what goes on in the classroom are interwoven throughout the chapter. While some aspects of context seem mundane on the surface, with a closer look they may be seen to affect the teacher and the curriculum in some surprising ways.

School Administration

Although it is not exclusively responsible for the school climate, the school administration is a powerful force in determining classroom life. In our study, administrators set a tone that welcomed or discouraged inclusion in the following ways: through the levels of control they exercised; to the extent that they attempted to help or ignored teachers' efforts in responding to new family forms; and by their willingness or reluctance to create new application forms, emergency cards, and other materials revised to include all families. Some administrators made it clear that teachers' attempts to develop more genuinely diverse curricula would be an integral part of the school's general push toward inclusion, while others explicitly or implicitly forbade them. It is helpful to compare the following two examples of administrators' approaches to lesbian and gay parents:

Father Stephen: It is my judgment more than a feeling that with homosexual people and homosexual groups, there is what seems to me a very obvious effort to establish in the public mind the idea . . . what I view as a continuing and increasingly strong effort to have homosexuality accepted popularly as an equally viable lifestyle. I would not want to be part of such an effort.

Enrico: The only thing I really said to Penny [the teacher who he knew would have a child with lesbian parents in her class] was that she should just be aware of it, that it shouldn't be the focus of any gossip in the school. And that she should . . . be sensitized to the fact that this particular kid has two moms. And Penny has to deal with that, particularly around holidays. . . . I don't personally endorse homosexuality or think that it should be in our culture or our society. . . . I think it should be something we all accept, but not given equal status. For instance, I don't know that in the school, we would teach [or] accept homosexual relationships in some formal way. That doesn't mean that we shouldn't accept them as bona fide. It just means that there is one way that it's not more correct, more a part of the way our society has evolved. Evolution might continue to include both, but at this point in time, I don't see it that way.

While not spanning the entire spectrum of acceptance to disapproval by any means, these two administrators provide an interesting comparison. Father Stephen clearly aligns himself against what he sees as a dangerously increasing encroachment of gay people into the mainstream society. He sees this acceptance as being responsible for the destruction of the moral fiber and the quality of family life in our country. Enrico, somewhat ambivalent about the subject, finally locates the place of responsibility for acceptance or rejection of homosexuality in society. While he does not yet recognize gay relationships as equal to heterosexuality, he does allow that social evolution eventually may change society so that it is more inclusive. Considering these differences, how would a teacher, attempting to develop an inclusive curriculum, find herself supported or constrained by these two administrators? One can approach this question through their views on homosexuality, but this ultimately matters less than the amount and manner of their involvement in working with an individual teacher's curriculum.

An overriding theme expressed by just about all administrators we interviewed (including Father Stephen) is relevant; they all said that, regardless of their own values, they would never do anything to harm a child. Given this common theme, it is interesting to examine several more administrators' descriptions of how this protection of a child with lesbian or gay parents would be enacted in their school.

> *Janet, child-care director on the first parent night:*
> We are proud to have diverse families in our center. Children with special needs, racially mixed families, children with two moms, and children with two dads. I want to welcome you all.

> *Melissa, principal of an independent school:*
> I am sensitive to all families. Divorced families. Families with single parents. Gay and lesbian families. I'm sensitive to all families who have problems.

> *Father Stephen, Monsignor/Principal:*
> I see this kind of family as disruptive to American life. I will not let books about this kind of family be read in my school. But no family or child in this school will be discriminated against.

> *Beverly, guidance counselor:*
> We have a very diverse population here, with all kinds of interesting differences from each other. We have physically disabled children, we have kids from shelters, we have kids whose parents have lots of money who took kids out of private schools to send them here. We have a very wide ethnic mix—Asians, Hispanic, Black, Tunisians, Yugoslavians. It's a very diverse population added to the diversity that we already have. Our teachers and our parents work very hard to preserve that diversity. I don't see that there would be any problem for a child with two mommies. So far as I know, that's been borne out.

Even though the sentiment, "no child will get hurt," was expressed explicitly or implicitly by administrators, clearly there were different levels of acceptance and administrative approaches in this sampling that would encourage—or even allow—teachers to respond differently to nontraditional families. Placing children with gay parents into the category of "children with problems," for instance, sets up a deficit model for seeing and responding to these children on a curricular level. Active welcoming, as Janet's and Beverly's statements both show, sets a very different tone for teachers and parents; it beckons teachers to respond to the diversity of their student body and encourages parents to assert their own family structures.

A range of views are expressed by these educational professionals, a range so wide that we can question the beginning premise—"no child will get hurt"—of one or two of them. Can the active suppression of all material that reflects and legitimizes the lives of an entire group of children go hand-in-hand with a guarantee that no child will be discriminated against? We don't believe so.

It would be a mistake, though, to look at the support or limitations imposed by administrators in a static way. Our experience has shown that they are more fluid. The same principal who offered information and support to kindergarten teacher Penny, gave neither to first-grade teacher Hazel the following year when Jeremy was to begin in her class. The same private school director who discussed the importance of openness and sharing among the staff about specifics of all children's families, did not see to it that the child's teacher the following year knew about his lesbian parents. While some of these inconsistencies may be due to particularities of the system, others may have more to do with the administrator's perception of the teacher: "Is she accepting of this idea?" "Does she need help?" "How accepting is she of my help?" This type of teacher monitoring suggests a reciprocal route of influence between administrator and teacher. The administrator *may* support the teacher in curriculum development, but there is a greater likelihood for reciprocity when the teacher makes it clear that the support will not be turned away.

Still, it is clear that many administrators hold a tight rein over certain classroom practices. Sophia, the kindergarten teacher in Father Stephen's school, was told by him that she could not read a book to her class about a child with two mothers even though the two "mommies" were not labeled as lesbians in the book. In both overt and more subtle ways, administrators exert powerful influences on the tenor of classroom life within the school.

The general philosophical approach of the school itself has a great impact on the degree to which the inclusion of lesbian or gay content is encouraged. Who sets the direction in this regard is a complex question that changes as one traverses across and within public and private school terrain. Public school principal Emory describes the approach of his school.

[Our school's] general theme is that everybody that we come in contact with is different in some way. He's Black, you're White. She's yellow, he's red. He has parents who are not his birth parents. She has only one parent. Her mother and father died. His mother

> died. This child happens to have two male parents. This one has
> two female parents. Put it in a larger context.

This approach to diversity rejects, in some important ways, the call by educators like Diane Ravitch (1992) to emphasize sameness over difference. It instead calls for a recognition of the pluralistic nature of our society. While accepting a body of similarity ("we're all people with feelings, we have need for relationships and intellectual challenge"), it calls for a proud declaration of differences and a simultaneous acceptance of a variety of peoples, practices, families. Emory is saying it is okay to be different, that in fact we're all unique in some ways.

The school context, too, overlaps with other influences. Recall from Chapter 3 the words of Lise, Beverly, Nilda, Enrico, and Emory, as they discussed the importance of past experiences for their present views. But in addition to past experiences, the importance of present situational factors is clear. It is instructive to examine Emory a little more closely. Just as he advocates the inclusion of lesbian- and gay-headed families within a broader multicultural framework, he is deeply affected by the community that surrounds the school. Making an apparent about-face, Emory says:

> I don't think that schools in Queens, Brooklyn, certain areas—I
> would never go to Bay Ridge, Brooklyn, and try to talk to people
> over there about accepting a kid's gay and lesbian parents because
> I don't think their attitudes are as liberal and accepting as they are
> in places like the upper west side.

Still, one also might view this quote as further support for accommodating one's attempt to change the larger community and social context. If we were to read Emory's words in this light, we might suppose that, given the community context, he would find less overt but perhaps equally effective ways to support lesbian and gay parents and teachers who want to implement a more inclusive family curriculum. Regardless, thoughtful consideration and approaches by schools and individual teachers have to precede action. A public school principal (not in our study) gives specific evidence that the concerns, and sometimes objections, of other parents can produce a difficult problem for the educator.

> It dredges up issues for parents, teachers, kids, administrators,
> everybody who's somehow touched by this issue. . . . There are
> parents of kids who are in a class who are adopted, and if another

kid in the same class is adopted you may have two entirely different views on how it should be handled and now you have a teacher having to deal with that issue. Johnny's mother wants the class to know he's adopted and sends a story book to school to talk about adoption. Jimmy's mother says, "I don't want you reading that book because I don't want [my child] to know that he's also adopted." It's parent work, but it's a very difficult situation because you try not, in any case, to violate the rights of anybody. You try to explain to parents that there's a little give-and-take here, that when there are two views that are diametrically opposed, you must find some middle ground. (Personal communication with Steven Schultz, January 23, 1993)

We would add a third view here: the considered position of the teacher. In any true dialogue, the voice of the teacher must be heard. She not only mediates between opposing parental points of view, but includes her own principled and workable position as well.

The various kinds of support offered by school administration and the range of perspectives by the parent body regarding its role and impact in connection with implementing a more inclusive family curriculum do not lend themselves to an easy reconciliation. Perhaps the best way to view these disparate views (and realities) when planning a curriculum of family diversity is to take into consideration all of the other contexts as well: surrounding community (see Chapter 4), teachers' views and experiences (see Chapter 3), administrative or other school support, active support from lesbian or gay parents, and interest and active initiation by the children. By placing the parental piece within this context, teachers can make a more sound (and perhaps a safer) judgment about the manner, extent of, and activity behind their integration of lesbian and gay, and other nontraditional family types, into their curriculum. The degree of emphasis placed on any of these aspects of context will, to some degree, reflect a personal expression of the teacher's political position and most likely will be influenced by the teacher's own base of experience. However, we believe that stretching the given contextual boundaries in a considered direction is most important—at least as important as the actual endpoint. By stretching—pushing at the status quo—teachers do much to change the given social order. This stretching does not accept the role of schooling to be the reproducer of given social roles and current inequities. And this includes all of the contextual areas, including the teacher's own views, the children's level of interest and understanding, and the perspectives of the parent body.

Parents—Gay and Straight

Parents as an aspect of context form a complex, although rarely homogeneous, force in classroom life. They may include lesbian or gay parents who make themselves a more or less visible—and therefore a more or less forceful—influence on the life of the classroom. Of course, this group also involves heterosexual parents, who may be supportive or anxious, or in (sometimes deep) opposition to the inclusion of gay content in the curriculum. Most often, these various constituencies maintain a certain distance from each other. At other times, the juxtaposition of their competing interests highlights complex class and racial differences (see Chapter 1).

Lesbian and Gay Parents. As noted earlier, the opening of communication with lesbian and gay parents can affect in important ways what goes on in the classroom. Learning about what each gay parent may have discussed with his or her child can help direct teachers in their curriculum development. For example, how have gay-headed families dealt with such issues as: "Where is my 'real' mother?" What part does the biological father play in the life of a child with two mothers? What does a child call her two fathers? "How did I come to be without a father?" Often such questions are brought up by other children in the class who are trying to fit a peer's family structure into their own conception of family. Knowing each family's real-life situation can support the teacher in responding to these questions.

Lesbian and gay parents also can play an important role in the classroom by volunteering their time. Parents have contributed materials, given talks about their jobs (when the class was studying parents' occupations), or simply made their presence known by each dropping off or picking up their child, separately or together. Ricky and Maggie described how they made sure to contribute to the classroom during the course of their daughter's nursery school year. They brought in pumpkins at Halloween and some hemp they carried back from a trip to Mexico. Cindy, a preschool teacher in New Jersey, describes how important the simple visibility of two mothers was in her classroom.

Maritza and Sharon both made themselves present and came in to do lots of things with the kids. And I think it is that kind of thing, of being there versus the secret thing, that's helpful. [It helped] the kids to understand and to deal with it because it was different.

Some gay parents are relatively open to having the details of their lives become a part of the curriculum; others are very much opposed to it and regard the inclusion of intimate areas of their lives in the public sphere of the classroom as an embarrassing invasion of their privacy. For example, June described what she considered the inappropriateness of a discussion about alternative insemination, the means by which she and her partner became parents. Some parents would like to see a broader approach to gay content in the classroom, but they are afraid to bring it up themselves for fear of being criticized. Matthew discusses his ambivalence about the extent to which he and James want to assert themselves by bringing in gay-positive materials.

> I think that [an imbalance] comes as soon as we become more active . . . by bringing materials like that book. Not that I think it's pushing, but people could feel pushed by that. So it's all right, you come in in a nonthreatening way, you make a statement, "This is who we are, this is our family, whatever, this is open." We let other people see that. *We* became vulnerable to them, not vice versa. So we set that situation up where people could feel comfortable with us to whatever extent they are able to. *We* did the work and we made ourselves vulnerable. But you start putting books out, and that kind of stuff, then you're not allowing someone else to be comfortable, you're threatening them in a way. And I think it is necessary, but I don't know how to do that. I'd like to have someone else come in to get some ideas of how to incorporate this into the curriculum. It's not my responsibility to figure out what I could do to talk to the history teacher or bring the book in, or that kind of stuff. I'd rather do it through a professional.

Matthew is willing to do his fair share in helping the classroom be more inclusive of gay content, but he would prefer to do it through a third person. He seems to feel the limits of his own efforts as well as the potential issues that may be raised for other parents. Matthew describes himself in the middle of a continuum of parental participation that can find parents who place the responsibility for curricular expansion on the teachers, or see themselves, as gay parents, as curriculum developers (Hirose, 1997). As representatives of a particular group of people, lesbian and gay parents can offer teachers valuable insights into the ways that classroom life teaches subtle lessons to children. Being outside the mainstream often enables one to see from a fresh perspective into the more covert areas of classroom life. But in much the same frame that we described disclosure issues needing to be a shared project, so too the life of the classroom should not be a singular endeavor for teacher *or* parent.

Straight Parents. But what about other parents? Noting the ways that Fred, a kindergarten teacher, and Maritza, a lesbian mother, discuss straight parents is enlightening. Fred says:

> I'm looking at it from the point of view of other parents in the class and being that it is a public school, do they have the right to say, "I don't want that [lesbian and gay content] included"?

Fred is alluding to a "majority rule" approach to parental influence on classroom life: The number of parents there are on either side of the issue determines whether or not it gets included in the curriculum. But what about fairness? What about the construction of a "new social order?" How does change occur? Majority rule is seen as a perspective that *reflects* the present social system, rather than challenges its flaws and helps to build a new one. Maritza says:

> But the most difficult is other parents. I would want more education to go on in the schools about families and alternative family styles. I would want the teachers to be able to address it more up front. Once a year they had meetings and we went in. They would have get-togethers, picnics, and that issue was never addressed.

Maritza is calling for change through the education of other parents, with school staff taking the lead. She wants the school to take a proactive role in expanding present social views toward ones she sees as more fair, more humanitarian, and less oppressive.

Louise Derman-Sparks (1989) writes that a prerequisite for implementing a curriculum around diversity, especially one that may be controversial in some way, is "parent work." She observes that a successful inclusive curriculum usually should begin with discussions with parents about the goals and methods that will be used to guide the introduction of "controversial" issues into the classroom. The discussions can take the form of parent meetings, newsletters, or other types of teacher–parent contact. In some schools, parent work may operate on a schoolwide level, with active administrative support. In others, it may be restricted to individual classroom teachers. In our own work, we found that some teachers were very concerned about the reactions of other parents to the possibility of including subject matter about same-sex-parent families, while others were so at ease about it that they didn't contact other parents first—and were successful in implementing a broad approach without evoking assertions of opposition by other parents.

Hazel is a first-grade teacher in the same school where Penny, a kindergarten teacher, had enacted an inclusive family curriculum without parent discussion the previous year. Here Hazel expresses the concerns behind her decision not to be explicit about gay-headed families as part of her first-grade curriculum on family, even though she had a child in her class who had two mothers.

> I don't know how the [other] parents would feel about that. I don't know how I would feel if it were my own child. A 5- or 6-year-old kid knows a lot today. And you know you can't shield them. I know school is the place to get the education. [But] I don't know if I am prepared to have the discussion about two women living together as a family unit. . . . Some of the parents would not like it at all.

Even though Hazel may be using the spectre of parents as a rationale for not including an aspect of family curriculum, *her* own feelings are not really made clear. Suggesting, however, that one *can't* shield children from such knowledge brings up the notion that it might be better if one could. In another discussion, Hazel describes young children's awareness, from watching television, of two heterosexual women living together.

> I have known setups where women for economic reasons have shared. . . . You see it on television . . . where they had [shows like] "Kate and Ally." They certainly were not lesbians, going out and having their own social life, sharing, the children, [but they] were living together. There are a lot of setups like that. In fact, there are all kinds of family structures. I even use television as a vehicle. That's one of the things I do in curriculum. I do not allude to children of lesbian families.

Here it becomes important to introduce another perspective. By including gay-headed families in her curriculum, Penny may have been relatively confident that her kindergarten children would not bring up connected issues of sex and reproduction. Some part of Hazel's concerns may be influenced by the difference in sophistication and interests of first-grade children. Penny also enjoyed the active support of the principal of the school, while Hazel received no support from this same administrator the following year. Still, by juxtaposing Penny's and Hazel's curricula, we see that Hazel could have searched for ways to be more inclusive. After all, contextual limits do not remove all responsibility from the teacher. Instead, they challenge teachers to find ways to work through them.

Nevertheless, it is important to be aware of these real-life parameters. For example, one New Hampshire child-care teacher's innocent response to a child's question during dramatic play, without prior parent work, met with deeply troubling consequences. When a 4-year-old girl asked Barbara, her teacher, if girls could marry girls and boys could marry boys, Barbara said that they could, and that they raised families like "mommies and daddies." When this idea found its way to the child's home, her angry mother immediately contacted the school's director and said that had she known her child would be told such a thing, she never would have enrolled her in the program. When the director supported Barbara, a scandal ensued. A number of families removed their children from the center, and several staff members quit their jobs.

The divergent outcomes of young children bringing new knowledge about gay families home to their parents demonstrate how important it is that the points of view of other parents be considered by teachers as they implement inclusive curricula in their classrooms. But "consideration" does not imply a rigid response. Wherever parent–teacher dialogue has been silenced, it needs to be "unsilenced" (Delpit, 1988). This is essential to a more public, communal curricular response to the inclusion of social issues by teachers and parents. The New Hampshire example makes one wonder whether some parent work prior to this teacher's response would have made her reply less charged and better understood by the parents in the community. And as Maritza suggests, ongoing parent education that supports an inclusive curriculum *and* the relationships between gay and straight parents can go a long way by engaging parents in a process of working through fears, prejudice, unfamiliarity, or taboos concerning gay topics.

In the end, regardless of the school's atmosphere, the teacher must determine his or her own stance. When the school administration supports the teacher, of course, this stance can be taken more confidently. But once she takes a stand, it is the teacher's responsibility to "fit" it into the real-life parental (and other) contexts in which she works.

Children's Participation in Curriculum

Carla, an experienced teacher of 2- and 3-year-old children, is only partially joking when she says she wants an 800 number to call when children ask her where 3-year-old Alberto's father is. The children always ask her about Alberto, who has two mothers, when they are together at circle time, never in private. Feeling challenged and put on the spot, Carla has not always known how to respond. It would be different, she says, if the question came up individually. But the sensitivity of the topic, the fact that Alberto is present, and that it is a group situation combine to make her feel unsure of what to say, how to respond. Given the newness of this issue for most of the teachers we interviewed, the amount of creativity, energy, and commitment that many of them put into the development of an inclusive family curriculum is impressive.

Sometimes the newness of this topic surprises even the more prepared teachers. Leslie, who has long considered various ways of including same-sex parents into her work with 2-year-olds, decided to read a book to her group about a child with two mothers. She had in her class a child with two fathers and another child with two mothers. Because this segment had been videotaped, Leslie was able to review herself reading many times. After critically reflecting on her work, she realized, she said, that one of the children had been asking her a direct question: How could this child have two mothers? Rather than responding directly, Leslie gave, throughout, a more general response: "Anyone can be in a family." It was only upon this chance to reflect on her practice, and the good fortune to have it recorded on videotape, that Leslie not only saw that she misunderstood the child's question (and therefore responded in an unsatisfactory way for him), but she also became more acutely aware of how nervous she was about the whole topic and how that anxiety affected her ability to be more effective.

In observing a class of 4-year-olds, we saw Leslie's ideas enacted by Jake, a boy with two mothers. The teacher was reading *Make Way for Ducklings* by Robert McCloskey (1948), a story about a family of ducks looking for a home. The father duck goes off ahead, leaving the mother and her ducklings on their own while he searches. After a week's time the mother takes her brood to meet the father on the other side of the island. At this point in the story the teacher asks, "And who do you think is waiting for the mother and the babies?" Jake burst out with the answer, "The other mother duck!"

Children do influence the curriculum. Unless the classroom has a stifling or extremely regimented atmosphere that says to children, "This topic may not be brought up here!" difficult issues for the teacher will surface. And the younger the children, the less skilled teachers may be at reading the more implicit classroom cues that prohibit topics deemed to be sensitive. Still, a major decision related to child input into the curriculum concerns whether the teacher seeks this type of inclusion or not. Creating a classroom atmosphere that invites children to bring up issues important to them means that teachers sometimes will be caught off-guard. While this may result in feelings of discomfort (Carla's wish for an 800 number, for example), it also presents opportunities for more authentic experiences. From a pedagogical standpoint, constructing such an open environment greatly enhances the possibilities for improved understanding on the part of children. When children's partial understandings and their experiential bases can be brought together with the social contributions of their peers and the teacher, a more complete conception of the issue can result (Rogoff, 1990; Vygotsky, 1934/1962). Sasha gives a touching example of the importance of supporting 3-year-old Jeffrey's ability to make his voice heard.

> Even other parents would sometimes say, like if Jeffrey were picked up by a babysitter, "Oh, Jeffrey's mom." And I'd say, "No, that's not Jeffrey's mom." Now this year he'll say, "That's not my mom. I've got two daddies," where last year he would just sort of shrink a little bit.

Children do not always bring up issues directly to the teacher. Cathy provides the following example of how young children's use of dramatic play is a fertile area for the exploring and understanding of out-of-school roles. Through their play, children can attain a better understanding of their families and how they fit in them, and how their families fit in the world.

> Elly was playing in the dramatic area with a couple of other kids. Another girl [Janie] came over to me really upset. She said, "I wanted to be the mommy and Lizzie said that she's the mommy, and I wanted to be the mommy." And then Elly came over to me and said to both of us, "Well, I told Janie that we could have two mommies and that I could be the mommy and she could be the mommy too." And I said, "Janie, that sounds like a great idea. Why don't you both be mommies?" And then they went, "Okay," and they both went back and they were both mommies, I guess.

Here Cathy supports these two children in their dramatic play, while acknowledging Elly's family structure. Children's inclusion of this topic in their play is noteworthy. As Vygotsky (1978b) explains, in play a child behaves "as though he were a head taller than himself" (p. 102). The unique character of dramatic play provides a milieu for children to engage in activities and roles that they could not yet do for many years in "real life." Children are not adults, but by using dramatic play and props, they are able to engage in the activities of mommies and other powerful people in their lives. In assuming these roles, children can extrapolate a clearer understanding of their own family structure (for the child, for instance, who comes from a gay-headed family) and the families of others (for Janie, for example, who could not conceive of a two-mommy family). And while it is important to remember that these roles and topics of dramatic play are, in the main, introduced by the children themselves, teachers have a powerful, although sometimes subtle, influence—to *enable* children to develop particular play themes in the life of the classroom. Through the materials and time they provide, they offer an open, welcoming social atmosphere and their sensitive listening.

When children get older, they may be clearer and more direct in their attempts to include their own issues in the curriculum. After the first month or so of first grade, Alberto, age 7, asked his teacher if he could have a meeting to discuss his family. He wanted to talk about having two mothers because when he discussed this with his peers more informally, "the other children don't believe me." Linda, the teacher, said that he could have this meeting. Prior to the meeting, however, and through the persistence of Alberto's parents, a conference was held with Linda, one of Alberto's parents, a school administrator, and another member of Alberto's extended family to discuss the goals of Alberto's meeting and the type of support that they would provide him. The support was the lending of official weight to Alberto's discussion topic. Linda introduced the meeting and sat by Alberto during the entire discussion; the school administrator and Alberto's parent sat together near the group and were ready to interject on Alberto's behalf if it were necessary. The lending of official school weight to Alberto's claims proved to be an important way for him to legitimize his family in the eyes of his peers. At the same time, open discussion enabled the other children to try out various understandings of Alberto's family. As children voiced their various interpretations, Alberto as the acknowledged "expert" was able to help clarify and expand on the nature of the family. This kind of stretching of possibilities for 6- and 7-year-old children is particularly important, given the research that shows that children in the middle years tend to be more rigid in their definitions of what a family can be than are both younger children and teenagers (Pederson & Gilby, 1986). Alberto's own living example of his family, coupled with the more overt discussion, can be an important influence on children in elementary school who are becoming clearer about societal rules.

A story Sasha told demonstrates the variety of ways in which children bring this topic into the classroom, and the ramifications for the teacher.

> This is just a very funny anecdote that I might have told you. At this age [3] children will hear Jeffrey say, "I have two dads," but it doesn't have a whole lot of meaning for them in terms of what his family is about. So one day when his babysitter came to pick him up, Daniel said, "Jeffrey, your mom's here." And he said, "That's not my mom. That's my babysitter. I've got two daddies." And the kid he was talking to, Daniel, looked at me, looked at Jeffrey, looked back at me, checking this out. I said, "You know, he does, he has two daddies." And quickly Daniel turned to Jeffrey and said, "I've got two daddies too." And you could see him working it out.
> The next day I was waiting with Steve, another boy. We were waiting for his father, who usually picks him up, and there was another man coming down the hall. And Daniel said to me, "Oh, look, it's Steve's daddy." And it clearly wasn't Steve's daddy. We've seen Steve's daddy every day. And I said, "Do you think that looks like Steve's daddy? That's not Steve's daddy." And he said, "Yeah, that's Steve's other daddy." [Then] he turned to me and said, "I have two brothers." Something about numbers, amounts, quantity.

These examples of children bringing this topic into the classroom are varied. This variety is important because it helps to break down these events so that they can be considered more carefully. One of the variables concerns the specific topic of conversation. Carla, who was Alberto's teacher a few years before Linda (mentioned above), describes very young children coming right to the heart of the matter; they want to know why Alberto doesn't have a father, and Carla feels somewhat threatened to engage in a discussion about this, in part because she is unsure of what these young children can understand. Further, she is not sure whether she *should* be discussing topics as delicate as this with the entire group and with Alberto present at the time. Leslie's vignette highlights the need for teachers to be aware of the real intent behind the questions of very young children. "What do they really want to know?" "How can I respond clearly to their questions or lead them to their own discovery?" The dramatic play examples illustrate both the importance of play for young children to try out on a more conscious level the social relationships they experience or hear about, and an investigation of a teacher's own subtle encouragement or discouragement to bring these topics into the classroom and children's lives.

We believe and know from experience that children grow into complex concepts, yet numerous generations of educators were weaned on the notion of "waiting until the child asks" to determine readiness for topics that were challenging for adults, such as sexuality. Another way of thinking about readiness was put forth by Jerome Bruner (1960) years ago and has become close to lore in some educational circles. He argues that *any* concept can be "taught effectively in some intellectually honest form to just about *any* child at *any* stage of development" (p. 33). Judging from his writings on this issue, he did not mean to imply that a child's level of development is unimportant, but rather that just about any idea can be translated to a level that a child can understand, although the burden is clearly on the adult to develop a successful strategy or conceptualization. And he argues that, in fact, concepts can be developed later on with greater complexity when children have the continuity of these earlier fundamental concepts on which to build.

While the notion that *anything* can be successfully taught to *anyone* will be seen as an extreme position by some, it represents an important point of view that is, ultimately, an optimistic and hopeful one, one that is filled with possibilities for learning.

Teacher's Philosophy

As a person with her own values and experiences, the teacher powerfully affects the children in her classroom, as individuals and as a group. She has an overriding influence on classroom events. Harriet Cuffaro (1995) asks teachers to think about what knowledge is valued in society and with which aspects of knowledge a teacher will choose to engage. As was noted in Chapter 2, teachers (and parents) need to observe children to better understand what they know, and to ask themselves what is important for children to learn. As adults do this, Cuffaro (1991, 1995) asks us to reflect on the principles that guide us as we select the content, materials, and activities of early childhood curricula.

The teachers we spoke with described the various ways they infused the lesbian- or gay-headed family into the life of their classrooms. Some of these teachers thought that they did just enough—and sometimes that was quite little. Others wished they had done more, even though it was our impression that they'd come up with creative and effective means for building their curriculum of diversity. Many teachers spoke of the power of the child to contribute to classroom life. Others described their own search for nontraditional family materials and the ways they altered traditional curricular approaches to include the lives of all the children in their classes. Yet others reflected on aspects of their personal selves and their influence on inclusive teaching.

One of the participants in a workshop in Denver where we presented our preliminary research data said that she was a lesbian and a teacher, and that it was more difficult for her than for heterosexual teachers to integrate the topic of gay parents in her classroom. Almost all the teachers we interviewed reported that simply stating that they want to include issues concerning lesbian or gay people immediately makes them suspect for being lesbians or gay men themselves. In the powerful video, *It's Elementary: Talking About Gay Issues in Schools* (Chasnoff & Cohen, 1996), a heterosexual teacher describes how it is widely known throughout the school that she recently remarried. She acknowledges that this fact gives her a greater privilege to be outspoken and supportive of including gay issues throughout the school. Teachers who *are* gay and who teach in settings where it is unwise to be open about their sexual orientation are likely to intensely experience themselves on one side of this unstated equation. Sol, our only gay teacher-informant, told us that as a gay man he would hesitate to introduce the topic of lesbian or gay parents into his classroom.

> I'm already under attack all the time because I teach whole language reading, because I'm a first-year teacher who's really not doing very well, because layoffs are coming, because teaching in the public schools is not a supportive atmosphere, period. So using the words *gay* and *lesbian* in the classroom would really be the straw that broke the camel's back. And that's really scary. And no amount of awareness or consciousness on my part can change that, and I don't know how to approach that dilemma.

At the same time that we examine the limitations placed on some gay teachers, it is important to acknowledge the strength of being a gay teacher: Sol has a firsthand knowledge of what it is like to be gay in our society. He also happens to be an individual with a participant's understanding of the importance of using education for social change, but clearly gayness is not a prerequisite for that understanding. In thinking back to Sol's swift yet measured intervention when the word *faggot* was used or when a boy with effeminate behaviors was being teased (see Chapter 5), we have a robust image of the values Counts (1932/1978) was referring to when he challenged teachers to see themselves as change agents for a better, fairer society. Teachers, Counts says, have to acknowledge the power they hold in the classroom, and through their direct contact with children, must find ways to exercise this power in the service of building a better world. This understanding is particularly important in our enterprise here, as lesbian and gay parenting is part of a wave toward a newer and broader social view of family. Based on Sol's previous comments, we see that although he may not feel able to use the word *gay* or *lesbian* with his first graders, that does not stop him from having a powerful impact on their "6-year-old prehomophobia." The teacher's sexual orientation is but one of many factors that may influence curricular "readiness," but we've seen that *how* one approaches this self-knowledge is the most important aspect of using one's self in the classroom.

THINKING ABOUT CURRICULUM

If we were to begin with an empty classroom, one component of curriculum may be thought of as the materials and equipment used to fill it. The materials used to fill a classroom space, and the decisions about where to place them, can be important means through which teachers can promote the types of activities they believe have value. Some teachers have a great deal of control over this aspect of their curriculum. They are encouraged to order the materials they wish for the year, are given healthy annual budgets with few directives about their use, and are permitted carte blanche in making decisions about where the materials and equipment should be placed in their classrooms. Other teachers have their materials ordered for them each year by an administrator, the budget may be tiny or nonexistent, rooms may be cramped, and certain materials, such as computers, blocks, or workbooks, may be mandated. As we know, there will almost always be a range between these extremes.

Still, the degree of decision making, and the way teachers exercise this area of control, can be an important means by which teachers either support or limit their development of an inclusive curriculum. Indeed, these factors are sometimes subtle means by which *all* teachers influence the life of their classrooms; the curriculum never comes *only* from the children. As a lesbian mother, June understands this point well and articulates it explicitly.

The problem is that a lot of people presume that they're treating the child from a gay family just like everybody else, and they don't realize all the number of times they are referring to "mommy and daddy families." Then they aren't treating that child like everybody else. They're systematically ignoring that child. . . . It would be like teaching colors to a nursery school class and saying, "This is flesh color," and holding up one of those pink colored crayons when half your class isn't that color.

Mirrors of Identity

There are numerous examples of exclusion of important aspects of children's lives that have direct effects on children's identity development. While race and family structure are by no means equivalent, there are some clear parallels that are instructive. Addressing exclusionary racial practices, Kenneth Clark (1970) demonstrated that the decision to place all White dolls in classrooms for very young children was an important factor in the lack of self-esteem expressed by African American children as young as 3 years of age. Certainly this was not the only realm where these children encountered a dearth of images related to their own race, nor did this early work consider the effects of strong, supportive Black families and communities on their children's developing sense of self (Spencer & Markstrom-Adams, 1990). Nevertheless, it was an event that took place in the official school setting, and while it will hardly eliminate racism, to include non-White dolls is an act that explicitly recognizes and addresses the wider society's racism. The teacher who is allowed relatively wide control over material ordering will be able to use dolls of all colors in her classroom.

The teacher who has only White dolls ordered by an administrator will have to stretch to find other ways of combating the effects of racism in her classroom—for example, through initiating meetings, individual discussions, reading library books, and employing artwork and stories. James, a gay father, makes a link between issues of developing identity for children in families of color and those in gay- and lesbian-headed families.

> They talk about mommies and daddies on TV, Sesame Street, and everything. I think it's just part of that process of developing who you are. Just as I think, growing up as a Black child in this society, I asked my parents why was I born this way, because we lived in an integrated neighborhood. But [I] still felt ostracized.

This is a crucial link to make, coming from someone who is African American and a gay man. We have stated these identities to be different; however, through play, conversation, and observation of drop-off and pickup times, all children learn about children and adults who are different from themselves. To not include all those possibilities of families in an explicit way in various parts of the fabric of classroom life is to make children from gay and lesbian families feel invisible at best and "ostracized" at worst.

Using Space and Scheduling Time

Children need space and time for exploration and interaction. For teachers, however, too often time and space are the most precious resources. As Harriet Cuffaro (1995) points out, time becomes a "commodity to be spent effectively and efficiently, something to be filled rather than experienced" (p. 40). Thinking about ways to provide time for children can be a more helpful way to shape their learning days than concentrating on "scheduling."

While most teachers have limited flexibility to truly experiment with scheduling, finding ways to create longer periods of time when young children can freely choose dramatic play, allows them to develop their own family roles and to compare their family configurations with those of their peers. The more time is segmented into discrete subject areas, the more difficult it will be to weave an inclusive family curriculum into these many areas of classroom life. When children are shuttled from one small group or subject area to another, it limits their freedom to connect their own and other family experiences in the context of the classroom. Still, even in classrooms with such highly segmented schedules, teachers can find ways of overcoming that aspect of context and focus on building a diverse approach to families, although it will take concerted planning and creative thinking to help young children to pull together highly discrete activities.

The teacher's allocation of space and arrangement of classroom areas can affect the ways in which gay families are brought into classroom life. The presence of a dramatic play area, to imaginatively create a context for play, furnished with open-ended materials that stimulate children, for instance, generously invites children to act out a variety of family forms. The variety of families can come from their own experiences or from peripheral experiences through classroom discussion and peer talk. A very small block area with no accessories leaves children with fewer opportunities to reconstruct their experiences through the narration of scenes built from the blocks. Penny, a public school kindergarten teacher, describes an incident in her classroom that was facilitated by a block area. There, Jeremy, a child with two mothers, was building with another boy. They both constructed houses out of their blocks. Jeremy narrated his story, which included a family with two mothers. The other child corrected him, saying that it was impossible to have a family without a father; a father is needed to make a baby. Then Jeremy (as in Sara's story, described at the outset of this chapter) told his friend that a father was *not* needed. He had no father; in order to make a baby, the mother would have to go to the doctor to get a seed. In her classroom, Penny provides ample space for building, a rich supply of blocks, and a range of wooden people and vehicles for the children's use. In so doing, she provides the materials and setting for dramatic play to have detail and possibilities for expansion and elaboration.

Meeting with any new situation in one's class *can* influence teachers to question some basic aspects of their curriculum. Through more experience with the unexpected, teachers can see their own curriculum more clearly in relation to their entire program as it affects all of the children in their class. This basic self-questioning reflects an approach to teaching that is observant of the children, their experiences, and their family lives, and that seeks to find ways to positively value them.

Literature and Language

One of the most common ways in which teachers attempted to infuse gay-headed families into their units was through the use of picture books. As discussed earlier, this sometimes meant creative use of available children's literature, since books that specifically include children with gay parents were almost nonexistent before the mid-1980s.

Given the relative newness of this topic in children's books, many of the books that contain gay parent themes are—as we might expect—very pointed and often contain rather impoverished story lines. Still, many gay parents are appreciative that there is some literature that depicts their lives and favor its use in schools, while wishing for more imaginative and expressive kinds of books. Sharon, for example, a lesbian mother, wishes for mystery stories where incidentally the detective is from a family of two moms. But more than one teacher described these types of books globally as "self-help" books. Theresa, a kindergarten teacher, seems to mix two different rationales for *not* reading them in her class. She cautions against their use, saying, "I think those books are really for children to deal with at home with their parents. I think there are certain books that are really meant for personal issues, and then certain books that you can bring into the classroom." Her second line of reasoning is that books for young children should *not* spell things out so explicitly, but rather should try to use metaphor, or even photo-essays. She believes that it is easier and more effective for children to deal with "controversial" topics from a more distanced vantage point, arguing that children think, "This isn't really happening to me." Taking a point of view held by many early childhood educators, Theresa believes children can be both in the story, yet keep another reality.

Theresa's second rationale is more complex, but her first reason was echoed by other teachers who argued that "personal issues" don't belong in school. Opportunities for "personal issues" to surface means that relationships, feelings, or controversial topics then become more accessible, and these are the very topics that tend to make teachers feel put-on-the-spot. Yet, these very issues can provide a connecting link for young children between the world of experiences with which they are so familiar and the life of the classroom. Teachers do have to make decisions about this: Is their classroom going to involve the personal, or will it be detached from real-life circumstances?

Leslie, displaying a great deal of sensitivity to the first child in her class with two mothers, remembers being apprehensive and questioning whether she should have any books about daddies on her bookshelf at all. The conflict surfaced as she noticed a book she had, called *Things I Do with Daddy*. Leslie wondered about putting it on the shelf for display, which she typically did in other years. After an internal debate she thought, "Well, why *wouldn't* I put it on the shelf?" We were appreciative of this story because Leslie demonstrated a thoughtful process that ultimately led her to alter her curriculum in other ways to support this child. If she had given in to her first impulse to remove the book to "protect" one child, ultimately she would have limited the very diversity she sought. What about the breadth of families represented in the books used in the classroom? Sasha, a teacher of 3-year-olds, described her experience in searching for books in 1990, a time when only a few children's books portrayed children with gay parents. Although years later there are more books to choose from, her point is still relevant today.

> When, for instance, we read *The Runaway Bunny* [Wise-Brown, 1942], I sometimes talk about it as the father bunny instead of the mother bunny. And always kids will say, "Why are you saying 'father bunny'?" And I'll say, "Because some people's fathers take care of them." That opened a real interesting discussion this year where I heard a child say, "Yeah, my daddy doesn't live with me, and sometimes I go to his house." And another child who has really been working this through sort of sat there with her mouth wide open, and said, "My dad lives in Puerto Rico." So it really freed everybody from wherever they were coming.

Sasha describes one way to stretch the given context. Regardless of how many books a teacher may be able to find on fathers, she demonstrates how to use available resources in a flexible way to meet—or more nearly meet—her original goals in her book search. At the time of this writing, there are many more specific books that can fit a range of circumstances, such as *Saturday Is Pattyday* (Newman, 1993), a picture book about a young girl whose lesbian mothers have split up. But we wouldn't want this kind of specificity to limit adults' ability to respond to and adapt more basic materials in the classroom. Thinking about how we use language is one of the most challenging aspects of teaching and parenting. Without becoming too censoring, it is important to take the time to think about our adult words with children; not just what *we* mean, but what and how children appear to understand. In the following comment, Sharon describes some other ways to offer explanations.

> In day care, the teacher asked if we had any books, but it doesn't have to be books. There are times it could come up during the day where [other family forms] could be acknowledged [as] a normal kind of life. Like when the teacher was talking about two animals, she was explaining that this is the male, the "daddy," and the other is the "mother." Well, that is how it is in most of society. There is another way. "One is female, one is male." Not "one is male like your father, one is the female like your mother."

And sometimes the best books about family are homemade ones, made either by the children themselves, with parents, and/or by teachers. Whether such books are made at home or at school, children take particular pride in them because they provide the details of *the children's* lives for constant and repeated review and sharing.

A Curriculum of Diversity

Books were not the only way through which teachers tried to emphasize the range of family structures in their classrooms. Cathy discussed one of her goals and some of her methods in implementing a family curriculum in her class where there was a lot of diversity; where, in fact, children from two-parent "typical" families were in the minority. She felt strongly that the child with two mothers should not be made to feel "different."

> In my planning, I was really trying for inclusion of as many different types of families as I could, and I carefully chose literature that

reflected a lot of different styles of families. I didn't like to hand out things that were labeled, "This is where you fill in the mother, the father, the grandmother." I always tried to leave it more open-ended. I felt like the family study was so rich a curriculum. [Now] we're studying bread, and we're going to be studying homes and houses. So I probably will get a bit into family when we do that. What makes a house a home?

Cathy discusses a general approach to inclusiveness in her study of family, which gets translated into taking certain commonly used activities, such as the family tree, and altering them slightly so that they can proudly reflect any child's family. As well, she discusses how family is not left behind once the official unit is over. Diversity can be built into just about any theme. Cathy, for example, responded to another real-life issue by planning and implementing a highly successful study of people who are homeless as a part of her unit on homes.

Many teachers of young children saw a natural place for the integration of an inclusive look at family in the wider framework of diversity. Three-, 4-, and 5-year-olds are bursting with the immediate experience of their family as they participate in creating a new classroom community. One clear piece of educational philosophy was articulated by Lise, an educational coordinator in a progressive private school in New York.

Families are an enormous part of the curriculum. Making a bridge between home and school; bringing the home, as much as possible, the *culture* of the home into the classroom. That's part of our social studies with young children.

The conceptual understanding of similarities and differences was another idea that teachers repeatedly gave as an underlying aspect of their family curriculum. But Jacqueline, a lesbian parent, discusses how a curriculum of inclusion should not rest solely on the family experience of the children in any one particular classroom.

Education in general needs to be one of inclusion. And it doesn't even need to be that the teachers know that they have a child with gay and lesbian parents in their class. It should be part of the curriculum anyway. I think it's part of teachers being open-minded and kind of nonjudgmental and accepting of people out there. We're all the same in some ways and in some ways different.

While we agree that sameness and difference is a crucial concept for young children to appreciate, it is important that we, as educators and parents, consider carefully when, where, and how to emphasize similiarity and difference. As the cartoon in Figure 6.1 pinpoints, society does not help families celebrate their specific configurations, and holiday preparation is an area where educators can help make a better "fit." Carla, for instance, discusses the way she helped to include Alberto during their Father's Day card-making activity.

> You have to always be on the lookout for what kinds of families you have when it's around the holiday times, especialy Mother's Day, Father's Day. I finally just absolutely learned how to be direct, addressed the parents, and said, "What do you want me to do?"

Figure 6.1. Mother's Day Cartoon

"Do you have any cards for two mommies?"

> That was how you could learn because there aren't any guidelines and every family is so different. . . . For Mother's Day it was lucky for Alberto to be able to make two projects. [We told the other children], "Well, he has two mothers so he can make two." And then, of course, when Father's Day came around, you couldn't say, "Well you can't make any." We said, "Who would you like to make something for Father's Day? What father do you know who might . . ."

Carla emphasizes the similarity of all children in this holiday theme, while simultaneously acknowledging a difference. She stretches the traditional meaning of Father's Day for young children to move beyond one's own father so that Alberto might be included in the activity. In a sense, she is implicitly acknowledging the difference in his family, while pulling it into a common classroom framework. It might be questioned, however, whether in fact this approach doesn't reinforce a deficit model. An even clearer alternative would be for the teacher to simply ask if there is anyone the child would like to make a card for, leaving out gender. In the video, *It's Elementary* (Chasnoff & Cohen, 1996), a teacher stretches Gay Pride Day so it can fit a wider group of children. She asks a child from a heterosexual-headed family if he might call the gay man he knows to wish him a happy Gay Pride.

If we are to use "a curriculum of diversity" as a framework in which to place children with lesbian or gay parents, or other gay content as well, it instructs us to look at this content area in a particular sort of way. It helps us to know that a diversity of families is yet another "strand that the teacher inserts in her process of weaving her curricular cloth," as veteran teacher Rob Caramella describes it (personal communication with Steven Schultz, 1993). He is talking about an integrative process that cannot be satisfied through a one-shot meeting or through the inclusion of gay parenting in, say, the book area alone, or (in classrooms of older children) in a separate unit on homosexuality.

Penny's thoughtful comments resonate throughout this book, so it makes sense for us to put the work of this young but experienced public school kindergarten teacher under the spotlight. It is true that Penny received a great deal of support from her school principal and Jeremy's parents, June and Shelly, and that her school was situated in a neighborhood in Manhattan that is more than tolerant of lesbians and gay men. It also should be recognized, however, that a lesbian-headed family was completely new to Penny. The only way she was able to do such a comprehensive job of infusing lesbian- and gay-headed families into the curriculum was because she asked many questions and sought help with materials and ways of stretching them. Penny used class discussions, art, and writing times to integrate *all* of the families reflected in the children in her class. As well, she encouraged less formal areas of her room to be used as vehicles to bring in and expand on the children's family lives. Her clear and comprehensive communication with Jeremy's parents gave her two strong resources in this area.

Because of this continual communication between all concerned parties, Penny was able to find the resources she needed within her own school. When she worried that children might ask questions that she would not know how to answer, Penny discussed this with a school psychologist who said, "Let the kid say what the kid knows." She also discussed it with June, who told her to defer to Jeremy if she didn't know where to go with a question, because, June explained, "he knows how to explain things on a child's level." As Jeremy's mother, June knew he was capable of this because his birth had been explained to him and she also had heard him talking about it to other children.

This approach, of asking Jeremy's help, was tested in school more than once (see Using Space and Scheduling Time earlier in this chapter). Penny described some of the other ways in which she intentionally integrated Jeremy's family into the larger curriculum. Her atmosphere of acceptance ("If the teacher shows it as acceptable, then the children will treat it as acceptable") extended to the children's writing. Jeremy wrote about his family, including his extended family, grandparents and cousins. In his family book, page 1 was about one mom, and page 2 was about the other mom. Of course, other children also brought in photographs of their families. Reflecting approaches taken by several other teachers in our study, Penny displayed these photographs around the room, encouraging the children to cherish their own families and to recognize others. Penny also involved all of the parents in helping to construct a "family book" for each of the children in the class.

> This year I had the parents write a little essay on what the child was like. At first they said they felt they had homework, but now they enjoy it. [They said] it was nice to sit down with your partner and remember things. Some of them wrote four pages and apologized for not making it shorter. This is part of the family curriculum.

Children also culminated their "official" family curriculum by painting a mural of their families, which was displayed in the hallway outside of their classroom.

Penny's approach is presented as but one model, not *the* model. Clearly, much of what she did, and was able to do, was contingent on a number of contextual factors—parents and parent body, administrative support, and surrounding community tolerance. As well, this was *Penny's* style of weaving into the classroom life the topic of diverse families. Some of this must have been shaped by her own background, her approach to teaching and curriculum development, and, not insignificantly, by the children in her class, including Jeremy. Not every 5-year-old could be handed the responsibility of explaining their family to the group, particularly a family about which members of the group might be skeptical.

But Penny's work is still significant. It offers us a way of looking at one teacher's approach in this area. As individuals, we—parents and educators—can lift, argue with, transform, or use as a catalyst, any of her approaches. We can appreciate that a curriculum of diversity, which involves gay-headed families, is possible if it can be in some way integrated into the more general life of the classroom. We can see how a combination of teacher-inspired projects, child-initiated actions, administrative support, and parent contributions can be teased apart in such a way that it reflects the individual teacher's contexts. It allows us to consider the "what ifs," a way that teachers and parents can fashion a whole approach in their own classrooms.

Creating an inclusive or anti-bias curriculum is challenging, and it all is relatively new. But there are increasing numbers of resources for teachers as they begin to experiment with including a range of topics (including lesbian and gay parents) into their early childhood curriculum. There are more and more forums (see Appendix A) in which to gather support. The aura of newness encourages experimentation by early childhood teachers. It asks: Given your principles of curriculum development, your goals in working with young children, and the community and school in which you work, the parent body, your administrative support, and your own present comfort and conviction about this topic, how will *you* fashion a curriculum of inclusion that fundamentally affects the life of your classroom?

CHAPTER 7

Beyond Gossip and Silence: Next Steps

I hate a song that makes you think that you are not any good. I hate a song that makes you think that you are just born to lose. Bound to lose. No good to anybody. No good for nothing. Because you are too old or too young or too fat or too slim or too ugly or too this or too that. Songs that run you down or poke fun at you on account of your hard luck or hard traveling. I am out to fight those songs with my very last breath of air and my last drop of blood. I am out to sing songs that will prove to you that this is your world and that if it has hit you pretty hard and knocked you for a dozen loops, no matter what color, what size you are, how you are built, I am out to sing the songs that make you take pride in yourself and your work.
            —*Woody Guthrie,* Born to Win

Whether through song, or other means, all children need to know that this is their world, as do their parents. What are the responsibilities of educators—teachers *and* administrators—to respond to both explicitly communicated and more subtly discovered information about any family, but through the lens of this book, lesbian and gay ones in particular? How do different contexts mediate our actions? What parts of our own behavior, beliefs, and expectations must all of us question in order to be aware enough to bring change to the classroom? What wider, beyond-the-classroom knowledge and activities are connected to the lives of children, parents, and a curriculum of inclusion? What are the responsibilities of lesbian and gay parents and other advocates for inclusion in these arenas? These questions are the *result* of our work. We do not claim to hand out the answers to them in this last chapter (as if discrete answers to these questions even exist). But we can show how one's own experiences—and the combined experiences of many others—can build upon this work to enable parents and educators to formulate their own answers.

GUIDELINES FOR ACTION

Given the many obstacles that parents and educators describe in this book, we believe that a proactive stance is required. We can move in progressive, incremental steps toward the reshaping of the social world—through careful reflection on our own experiences, developed ideas and values, and an eye to the many contexts that surround our lives and our work—if we accept the notion that a teacher or parent can have a particular point of view and that this view can become a part of classroom practice. This process requires the perception of the educator and parent together. Thinking and talking among ourselves is important. Reading and listening to the experiences of others is requisite. But unless we take action—raising our voices, moving into the larger world in our practice—we stay insulated and eventually may forfeit our goals. We believe that research is valuable to the extent to which it enables action, and it is in this spirit that we introduce some guidelines. We direct them not only to educators and parents, but to everyone who aspires to a society that can thrive on genuine diversity instead of being needlessly constrained by it. Some readers may want simply to try out the strategies we note here. Others may want to use them as a base upon which to build other strategies that are more personally relevant to them. However they are perceived, we offer them mindful that they can succeed only if they are tailored to fit the particular context of every change process. *These guidelines and strategies may be simply taken in for reflection, acted upon by individuals, or used in educational forums (college classes, staff development, focus groups, study groups, etc.).*

Feelings and Comfort Level

If you are an educator, consider your own feelings about lesbian and gay parents. In what ways do your feelings about them help to shape your attitude toward children, beyond simply positive or negative feelings (e.g., protectiveness, uncertainty)? What are your feelings about sharing particular aspects of *your life* in a classroom setting, and with teachers and administrators? What were your own early care and educational experiences like, and how do they affect your view of education? What other experiences have helped to shape your current ideas and values?

Just as it is impossible for any adult enculturated in our society to be free of all racist attitudes, the same truth applies to the development of heterosexist attitudes. Anti-gay feelings have been so pervasive in the culture that they tend to become internalized in gay people as well as heterosexuals, sometimes as a tangled complexity of self-feelings and demeaning attitudes toward other gay people (Friere, 1986). We propose the following process: to examine and recognize our own feelings, attempt to trace their origins, and work consciously at changing those attitudes that we find are harmful to others. The first step in this process requires discovering these feelings—many of which are hidden from us.

• Especially if you are not gay, take a ride on public transportation carrying reading material that is obviously gay-related. Note how openly you display, or how carefully you conceal, the title of the reading. Note how you respond to the glances others direct at you, either frankly or covertly. How safe do you feel? Afterward, write down your reflected feelings from this experience.

• Especially if you are not an educator, take a walk into a school. Note the feelings and associations that arise regarding your own memories of being a student. How were you treated? Did you respect, enjoy, feel affirmed by the teachers and administrators, or did you fear or feel intimidated by them? Were you a "troublemaker"? Were you quiet and "law-abiding"? Did you have an accepted place among your peers, or were you more of an outsider? What were the attitudes of your parents toward education and school personnel? In what ways do you imagine this affected you and your education? Consider and try to note how these feelings affect your current readiness to approach and communicate with school staff.

• Knowing yourself usually can be enhanced through your reflection in the eyes of others. If you are a teacher or administrator, try to gather a small group of other educators to discuss (more generally) anti-bias approaches and (more specifically) the inclusion of lesbian/gay content in your classrooms. Ask yourselves questions about the inclusion or exclusion of this material by questioning what might seem to be "normal" curricular practices; do they assume a heterosexual world? Later, reflect on what you learned about your colleagues' attitudes toward gay people and also whether you know more about your own feelings after the group meeting.

• If you are a parent, talk with other parents about your goals and objectives for your children in school. How might these goals be influenced by your personal contact with your child's teacher or other school personnel? What kinds of information do *you* possess that might help these educators to better meet these goals? How can you tell whether your goals are consistent with the teacher's goals? To what extent must they be? Often, talking with other parents can be a helpful way to clarify your goals as well as to identify the avenues that might be available to communicate them to the school staff.

- For educators and parents: Consciously stretch your own borders of tolerance. If gay people fit comfortably within them, consider your feelings about others who may not. How do you feel about adults who crossdress? What visceral feelings emerge about androgyny, bisexuality, or transsexualism? What about adults engaging in other cross-gender behavior and activity in public? Be honest and ask yourself *why* they cause you discomfort. Is the discomfort associated with fear? With other deep-seated feelings? An incongruity with what you have come to see as "normal"? In what ways has your conscious awareness of these feelings helped you to question them, and to see the behaviors in a somewhat different way? Has knowing someone personally changed your feelings in any way?

- Consider how the following have affected your understanding of human diversity: your family of origin, neighborhood, religion, elementary school, membership in clubs and groups, political convictions, junior and senior high school, employment, college, travel, books. In what ways have these experiences constrained and/or expanded the borders of your appreciation for diversity in terms of people's appearance, behaviors, or expressed feelings? How do your experiences with each of these areas build upon and/or conflict with each other? If you have a group forum, have each person bring an object, or tell a simple story from their own life. It can be as simple as a family tradition, or something that happened with other kids in your neighborhood when you were growing up. These stories can help form bonds within the group and give each person a point of reference from which to move forward.

Examining the Context

Examine the context in which you teach, or in which you as a parent live. Consider where the boundaries of the cultures of the school and the community can be stretched, and where you have to live within them.

We all live and socialize within a complex system of contexts. Contexts are overlapping; not only are we always dealing with more than one at a time, but they also can affect each other as they interact. Two of the most powerful contexts are school and community. It is, therefore, vital to know them. What are the "givens" of the school culture, and how do they affect how far teachers, administrators, and other school staff will—or can—go in responding to new family forms in their classrooms or schools? What aspects of various contextual factors do lesbian and gay parents have to consider as they weigh their decisions to come out to the school, how to come out to the school, and how far to come out?

The most crucial work of parents and educators is that of stretching given boundaries toward achieving the fair, equitable, and humane treatment of all people. Knowing the present boundaries of the school and community is an obvious crucial first step toward moving beyond them. But the process of gaining this knowledge should not be overlooked as a way to help parents and teachers keep a perspective on the immediate changes they are able to bring about, the end-goals as well as where they began. Certain school and community settings are already much more progressive in achieving levels of diversity of one kind or another. These settings may provide more support for further change, but even here, the challenge is to work to maintain the level of inclusiveness and to expand beyond it. Those settings that are more restrictive, and sometimes downright oppressive, still can be moved along a *relatively* equal distance through the actions of parents and educators, even though the absolute level of change may be lower than in more tolerant schools and communities. The following are some strategies to consider:

- Educators and parents can make note of the following: Do you know any gay or lesbian school staff members, and any gay or lesbian parents? Are they well accepted as serious, integral parts of the school, or do you hear derogatory jokes or other comments made about gay people in meetings, teachers' room, informal parent chats, and other casual conversations? Do you respond to these comments? How does it feel to respond or to keep quiet? Are there certain times when speaking up is easier than others? In trying to increase your response to these situations, consider how you figure out when to respond. What is unsafe about countering a parent or colleague's comment, and what might you do to increase the subjective and objective conditions of safety? What shapes can a response take?
- Do you know, or how can you research, what the administrator's, the teachers', and the parent body positions are on bringing diversity into the school/classroom curricula, and on the inclusion of gay people and gay-headed families in particular? In what ways are these positions communicated within the school? How forcefully and in what ways do administrators attempt to have these positions enacted in school practice? Are the words *gay* and *lesbian* visible or audible in your school environment? Where might they be inserted, not in

a manner that is too dissonant with the school culture, but still in a way that can stretch "the givens" a bit?

- Gay or lesbian parents can make note of the following: Do you know any other gay people in your neighborhood? Are there any lesbian or gay businesses? Have you seen anti-gay graffiti around and, if so, how long does it stay visible without being covered or removed? How obvious are you as a gay parent—are you single, do your children "pull you out" in the community? How do you feel when someone in your neighborhood asks you where your child's mother or father is, or why your child doesn't resemble you? Is there an organization of lesbian and gay parents in your area? Considering these factors can help you to gauge the "culture" of your community, both from objective conditions in the community and your own subjective responses to them. What are the ways in which you can begin to enlarge the givens and receive/give support in your community without placing yourself in social jeopardy?

- Find a friendly teacher, administrator, or parent with whom to discuss your ideas for inclusion. Parents who may not be able to come out to the school, or to the parent body, may feel comfortable discussing their family with a particular member of the school staff. Coming out to the school is frequently a process that may begin with secrecy, move to hints, and eventually arrive at full communication. Likewise, educators who feel isolated may be able to find a parent, member of the school staff, or educator in another school with whom to discuss their ideas.

- Parents and educators can try to begin some type of parent work that explores various family forms in addition to the traditional nuclear family. This work may take the form of a newsletter, or a teacher or parent may be able to begin it by making a simple comment at a parent meeting or during curriculum night. Teachers may take the opportunity to approach the subject with individual parents during parent–teacher conferences.

Finding Channels for Communication

Lesbian or gay parents and educators must begin, and continue, to communicate with each other. In this book, we have argued that disclosure and communication must be a joint endeavor. For parents, the challenge involves disclosing their family structure. For educators, the challenge is to create a climate that is conducive to parental disclosure. This climate may involve such areas as assumptions about sexual orientation (remember the assumptions made about single lesbian and gay parents); displaying evidence in the classroom that helps parents to know that all kinds of families are a part of the classroom climate; and other actions that open communication with parents and community and strive to sustain it. Comfort level is important. Reflect on your own level of comfort. Then consider some of the following strategies in relation to that comfort level:

- For teachers and administrators: What are you doing currently to help include all family structures within the areas of contact you have with the community (parents, prospective parents)? Take a look, specifically, at your school's application form, after-school and emergency forms, the parent handbook, any brochures you have about the school, developmental history forms, and any bulletin boards that might be visible in hallways or in your own classroom. What kinds of families are reflected in these materials? What materials can you revise so that they are more inclusive of a range of families? Which materials, specifically, can you first address in representing same-gender parents? These steps can be taken slowly and in the spirit of progression. In some schools, it is necessary to move slowly toward the goal of achieving a visible presence of lesbian and gay people and parents.
- For parents (assuming you want to be "out" to some degree): What hints have you given to any member of the school staff about the nature of your family? Coming out is also a progressive process and one that doesn't necessarily end when it has been done once. Try to list all the various hints you have given to any member of the school staff about the nature of your family or of your own sexual orientation. List as well the steps toward coming out that you consider problematic, and discuss with your partner or a friend why they are dangerous, unwise, or frightening. Consider carefully when and what further (or first) steps you can take along this coming-out process. What support will you need? Can you get a sense of what point of openness will eventually be comfortable for you? How much of this process is your responsibility?

Sexual Orientation and Development

Just as race, culture, and gender are being seen as important contributors to the development of children, it is also important to examine the ways that sexual orientation may alter or contribute to our notions of development. Many teachers subscribe to the view that it is imperative for children to have powerful role models of both genders within their immediate families in order for them to develop proper gender-role identities. Most of the lesbian and gay parents in this study regarded exposure to different genders and gender roles (and sometimes different sexual orientations) as a crucial aspect of their child's development. They preferred exposure to diversity in society at large, not exposure that is self-consciously replicated by "finding" someone to fill such a role. These strategies are offered for your reflection.

- Consider carefully your own ideas about the importance of role models. Try to see if you can figure out where these ideas came from: Were they influenced by a child psychology course? From some reading in the area of child development? From a less specific, more ambiguous source? Try to answer the question: "On what do I base my thinking about the power that gender models play in the development of children," and what *else* might influence gender-role development?
- For teachers: What assumptions do you make about the adults in the lives of children who have lesbian or gay parents? What theory scripts can you identify as key to your daily work? For example, many people find it hard to imagine that a child with two mothers has close relationships with men. Others have difficulty coming to terms with the reality that some children do not have men in their lives. Consider what other ideas are connected with these assumptions: Does having a close uncle mean that the child experiences rough-and-tumble play? Does a child with two fathers engage in twice the amount of rough play as a child with two mothers, or receive half as much nurturing? To what extent does gender define your perceptions?
- For parents: Can you trace various qualities that you feel you received from one or both of your parents? If your own family valued gender-typical roles, from where did your yearning for a wider range of possibilities emanate? What are your feelings about your own child developing relationships with the opposite gender from your own (and your partner's)? What is important to you, and why?

Enacting Ideas for Classroom Life

For educators: What, specifically, can you do in your own classroom to affect the kinds of experiences that children will have? Consider that within the broad sense of curriculum, your role as educator gives you an important base from which to affect classroom life, and note the ways in which you can enrich it for every child. All children enjoy a more productive, motivated, and happy student career when classroom life reflects and validates their own backgrounds. This is true of children from various cultures and races as well as sexual orientation, gender, and family background. Given this, it is crucial that teachers attempt to make sure that their classrooms contain a broad enough view of family that children from all kinds of family backgrounds feel welcome and included. Because our society as a whole is far from having accomplished these goals, this will mean recreating rather than reflecting the social order. Some strategies follow:

- Conduct a children's literature search. Which books seem on target in terms of age and maturity level? Which appear "self-help" in nature? What books do you feel comfortable reading? How can you use some of the classic children's literature in a creative way to include more diverse family configurations?
- What are the "natural ways" of welcoming lesbian and gay parents into the life of your classroom? Try the following experiment: Change the gender of parents in stories you tell children. Display pictures of same-gender-parent families in your dramatic play area or in other areas of the room. Use more generic terms than "mother and father," such as "parent," when talking about children's families. Furnish your block area with several sets of people accessories so that children are able to represent a variety of family configurations in their block play.
- What are the steps you can take toward the goal of saying "lesbian" or "gay" to a child or children in your classroom? Consider the nature of the reluctance you may feel about using these words: Is it based on developmental considerations (e.g., the children are not old enough to hear these words)? Are the considerations moral, religious, cultural? Are they social? (What if the principal walks into the room at that moment, or another teacher or a parent?) Using the words simply because you think it is the correct thing to do will not be helpful for yourself or the children for children are sensitive to adult intent. As you consider this, try to come up with a term that *is* comfortable for you to use. If you have children in your class with gay parents, discuss this with them. "Two mommies" may be easier for some teachers to say to young children, but "lesbian" and "gay" are the accurate terms.
- Try to consider the likelihood of children's asking questions or making comments when they know that a classmates has two daddies or mommies. Will they bring these questions to you quietly or in a group setting? What do you have to learn or know about your own comfort zone *before* this occurs? How much can you discuss in the presence of a child with gay parents? You might even go over certain scenarios

on paper, or in your head: "Jenny might ask _____, I can respond in this way." As you consider your responses, don't fall into the trap of thinking of yourself as the one with all the answers in the room. What does Jenny think? What do the other children think? What have lesbian and gay parents told their own and other children?

- Consider your own response to children who ask lesbian or gay parents in your classroom about themselves. Is your first impulse to shush them? Do you feel that these parents are being put on the spot, or being compelled to answer embarrassing questions? Then consider again. What does shushing children who ask these questions express—subtly—about lesbians and gay people? Consider the source of the children's questions: Are they curious about their awareness of difference, or are they expressing bias? How can you support parents in these situations and at the same time enrich your own curriculum?

- You may not have a child with lesbian or gay parents in your classroom. Don't you still have an obligation to discuss, mention, or in some way include this family configuration in your study of family? What are the benefits of doing so? What are the difficulties? Consider some of the small ways in which you might insert this and other diverse family structures into classroom play or discussion. What opportunities offer themselves to you to help children question the status quo? Unless you are primed for them, these opportunities can slip by without your notice. This may be especially true if you do not have a child in your class who has the family configuration you want to support. What are some ways of bringing in some aspect of *your* life to raise issues that may not exist in a direct manner in the classroom?

For children growing up with gay parents, the simple acknowledgment of their lives is crucial, but it is not enough. Young adults raised by lesbians during the past 2 decades report feeling isolated, intensely aware that their families were not acknowledged in school, and that they knew few, if any, other children living in similar families (Center Kids, 1992). This isolation is far less extensive today, at least for many families living in larger cities, where network and support groups now exist to alleviate it. But open discussion and support of the lives of these children inside and particularly outside the gay community are still relatively uncommon. And it is not only parents and teachers who need to address this issue. It should be reflected in the larger arena of the school where the work of administrators can encourage frank discussions that can support gay parenting by grappling with such questions as: How can the administration help both teachers and parents? What kinds of parent meetings can support the work of teachers in building a more inclusive curriculum? What administrative changes are necessary? If there are a few lesbian- and/or gay-headed families in a grade, should the children be placed in the same class for their mutual support through the creation of a critical mass?

It is not only the subject of gay *parenting* that is absent from both curriculum and parent work in schools. All school personnel—teachers, administrators, guidance counselors, assistants—and teacher educators must begin to feel more comfortable saying and hearing the words *lesbian* and *gay*. Both teachers and parents could be helped to discuss gay family constellations if the fact that lesbian and gay people *exist* is a more readily available concept. For example, older children might hear these words in discussions of the work of James Baldwin. Teachers must feel reassured that the use of these words will not "turn" older children gay, and be confident that there is nothing inherent in them that make them "inappropriate" to use with young children. Aside from having no basis in fact, the argument that lesbian and gay people should not be talked about because it might promote a gay sexual orientation in children is itself biased because it assumes that it is not a good thing to be gay.

Evaluating Teacher Education

If rigid gender theory scripts lie codified deep within our collective minds, then colleges and graduate schools in the helping professions have a unique opportunity and responsibility to help their students gain entry into those scripts for examination, reflection, and rebuilding. Teacher preparation programs also must include lesbian and gay issues in coursework and supervised student teaching, as teacher educators work with teachers-to-be on how to think about and work with any population that is different from themselves. If teachers engage in open discussions in their coursework about the needs of lesbian and gay parents, or begin contact with lesbian and gay people and the ways that society constrains lives, they may feel more comfortable when they meet a gay parent in their classroom for the first time.

Child psychology and development courses must begin moving beyond the traditional theories of gender identity development and include new research and theory. Students need to be exposed to a wider range of theories (including classical ones). As potential educators study theories of gender identification, it is important for them to apply these theories to practice as they consider many different family configurations. Through ongoing sifting between theory and practice, future professionals ultimately can feel free enough with theory to play around with it and claim it for their own.

Teacher educators can do much to encourage their students to become clearer about their own values and deep-seated beliefs about homosexuality, and in the process to take an honest look at where theory and values intersect. By including the lives of lesbians and gay people in development courses, and by integrating anthropology and sociology disciplines within them, instructors can begin to ask students the tough questions about what children need for healthy gender development, and indeed to ask what healthy gender development means. Must it by definition produce the outcome of a heterosexual orientation? If the answer is no, then in what ways can we expand our thinking about the variety of routes children can take toward adulthood? Some of this vital self-reflection may be done on one's own, in conjunction with reading and seeking out other resources. Other courses also can integrate matters of sexual orientation into their curricula. Curriculum and methods courses and social foundations courses offer particularly natural settings for including gay and lesbian people and parents, which can be used as but one area for professionals to questions their assumptions.

TRUST REVISITED

This book began by defining and exploring the importance of trust in any family–school connection. We then presented selected stories educators told about their first experiences across a range of differences, including their first encounter with a gay person. Regardless of school policies, professionals bring these earlier experiences with them, as they have been shaped and reshaped along life's path. We believe that neither a most sensitive curriculum nor an enlightened superintendent's policy alone can create the kind of inclusive shift advocated here. A serious and clear effort is required by *all* parties. Parents need to reflect on how they wish to approach educational institutions and to make efforts to be direct. Schools can begin the process by making the words *gay* and *lesbian* more visible for parents, teachers, and the community. When these words become more ordinary parts of our vocabularies, there will be less of a tendency for teachers and parents to use euphemisms like "nontraditional family" or "alternative families" to the exclusion of the words *lesbian*, *gay*, or *transgendered*. Naming *is* important. When the differences of gay-headed families can be acknowledged without the simultaneous placement of negative connotations, then trust has an environment in which it may grow. It is only then that gay families can begin to be treated like "any other family." Finally, teachers will affect children regardless of whether they act consciously in this regard; the very act of *not* acting serves to powerfully support the status quo (Schultz, 1988).

While we have offered some specific guidelines for parents and educators to broaden and deepen dialogue, we recognize that most readers may find them wanting. After all, each family and each school is different, sometimes in fundamental ways. All need to fashion their own specific styles in approaching the risks inherent in parental disclosure and what follows. The guidelines we present are conceptual parameters aimed at opening the issues and helping others begin and sustain communication. Our conviction is that often the varied, authentic, and too-often-silenced voices of all parents and their concerns truly can affect understanding and promote action. So it is that a teacher in a child-care center advises other teachers to "explore their own feelings about what it means to have a gay family." She says there are plenty of people who

> think that it's something that exists out there in the world that has nothing to do with them and don't really want to have anything to do with it. . . . They need to address those feelings in themselves and really work through them because they are really going to get projected on the family.

We agree. Prior experiences and present values are crucial. But so are our ongoing experiences. Leslie, one of the teachers we interviewed early on in our research, spoke to us after we presented some of our findings at a conference she attended: "I guess I was a little upset to hear some of the things I said. I know I said it, but that was 3 years ago. I've changed." Her words are heartening to us; change is what we intend to nourish and support by the processes described here.

Whenever and wherever possible, we hope lesbian and gay parents will be inspired to move beyond their fears and talk to their children's teachers about their family configurations and their sexual orientation. This is an extra burden being asked of gay parents (no one is asking heterosexual parents to discuss their sexual orientation with teachers), and the stresses and dangers are real, as they are testaments of an unjust society that encourages discrimination against people based on race, gender, class, and sexual orientation. We don't want to romanticize this or ignore the nature of the painfully slow process now under way toward the acceptance of gay and lesbian people in our society. We call on teachers and administrators to meet parents in this effort, to recognize their struggle, and to consciously act in the spirit of inclusion. Change is hard, and more difficult when an oppressed group is the one seeking to initiate it. Still, without their real involvement, the eventual results of change will not reflect their needs. But significant change cannot be built by the schools alone. Social change must occur in league with teachers, parents, and community. Clear and nonbiased conceptualizations of family, gender, and culture will require the actions of teachers, parents, administrators, and activists—indeed, all members of society who understand the rich rewards of genuine diversity and the perils of failing to acknowledge them.

Selected Resources

American Psychological Association (APA).
Contact: APA Committee on Lesbian and Gay Concerns
750 First Street, NE
Washington, DC 20002-4242
(202) 336-6037

Children of Lesbians and Gays Everywhere (COLAGE).
Contact: COLAGE
2300 Market Street, #165
San Francisco, CA 94114
(415) 861-5437
e-mail: colage@colage.org
web: www.colage.org

Family Pride Coalition. (Formerly Gay and Lesbian Parents Coalition International).
Provides support and information services for lesbian- and gay-headed families
through its worldwide chapters and newsletter.
Contact: Family Pride Coalition
P.O. Box 34337
San Diego, CA 92163
(619) 296-0199
e-mail: admin@familypride.org
web: www.familypride.org

Gay, Lesbian and Straight Educators Network (GLSEN). A national organization
working to assure that every member of every school community is valued and
respected regardless of sexual orientation.
Contact: GLSEN
122 West 26th St., Suite 1100
New York, NY 10001
(212) 727-0135
e-mail: glsen@glsen.org

Lambda Legal Defense and Education Fund.
Contact: 120 Wall Street, Suite 1500
                New York, NY 10005-3904
                (212) 809-8585
                e-mail: LLDEG@aol.com

National Association for the Education of Young Children (NAEYC). Committee on Lesbian and Gay Issues.
Contact: The Link
                1001 Hayes Ave
                Oak Park, IL 60302
                e-mail: mawgieb@aol.com

National Center for Lesbian Rights (NCLR). NCLR is a public interest law center dedicated to protecting and expanding the legal and civil rights of lesbians and family-related issues of lesbians and gay men.
Contact: NCLR
                870 Market Street, Suite 870
                San Francisco, CA 94103
                (415) 392-8442

National Education Association (NEA).
Contact: 1201 16th St., NW
                Washington, DC 20036
                (202) 822-7710

Teaching Tolerance. A project of the Southern Poverty Law Center created to provide teachers with resources and ideas to help promote harmony in the classroom.
Contact: Teaching Tolerance
                400 Washington Avenue
                Montgomery, AL 36104

Parents, Families and Friends of Lesbians and Gays (PFLAG). Devoted to promoting the health and well-being of gay, lesbian, and bisexual persons and their families and friends through support, education, and advocacy.
Contact: PFLAG
                1101-14th St. NW, Suite 1030
                Washington, DC 20005
                (202) 638-4200
                e-mail: info@pflag.org
                web: www.pflag.org

Journals and Magazines

Alternative Family Magazine. A national parenting magazine for gay, lesbian, bisexual, transgender parents and their children. Published by the Gay and Lesbian

Alliance Against Defamation (GLAAD). A one-year subscription for U.S. residents is $24.00.

Contact: *Alternative Family Magazine*
P.O. Box 7179
Van Nuys, CA 91409
(818) 909-3792

Family Talk. Published by Center Kids. New York, NY: Lesbian and Gay Community Services Center.

Contact: Kids Talk / Center Kids
c/o The Center
Little West 12th St.
New York, NY 10014
(212) 620-7310
web: www.gaycenter.org

In The Family. A quarterly national magazine for lesbian, gay, bisexual, and straight-ally therapists and related professionals. A one-year subscription for U.S. residents is $22.00.

Contact: *In The Family*
P.O. Box 5387
Takoma Park, MD 20913
(301) 270-4771

Gay Parenting Magazine. A resource for lesbians and gay men who are or wish to be parents. *Cost*: Free in newsprint or on-line.

Contact: *Gay Parenting Magazine*
P.O. Box 750852
Forest Hills, NY 11375-0952
web: www.gayparentmagazine.com

Audio-Visual Resources

"Choosing Children." An award-winning film about women who decide to become parents after coming out as lesbians.

Contact: Women's Educational Media
Box 441266
Somerville, MA 02144
(617) 776-6759

"Both of My Moms Names are Judy." Children from diverse families talk about what it is like to be part of lesbian- and gay-headed families.

Contact: Family Pride Coalition (see above)

"It's Elementary: Talking About Gay Issues in Schools." Award-winning educational video designed to prevent homophobia among elementary and middle school children. "It's Elementary" is designed for adult audiences and up-coming videos will be available for children's viewing in classroom settings. Training materials also available.

Contact: Women's Educational Media
2180 Bryant Street, #203
San Francisco, CA 94110
(415) 641-4616
e-mail: WEMDHC@aol.com

"Love Makes a Family: Living in Lesbian and Gay Families." A photo-text exhibit that brings gay-positive images and voices to any school or community space across the country. Easy to arrange an exhibit that allows for rich curricular possibilities for children and adults alike.

Contact: Peggy Gillespie—for community exhibits
(413) 256-0502
Pam Brown—for school exhibits
(413) 256-0049

On-Line Resources

Gay and Lesbian Characters and Themes in Children's Books Online Annotated Bibliography (Betts, W.E., 1998).
Contact: www.armory.com/~web/gaybooks.htm

Current information about curriculum and local school-related challenges nation-wide.
Contact: www.youth.org/loco/PERSONProject/

Bibliography on Gay and Lesbian Issues in Education by Tracy Phariss.
Contact: glstnco@aol.com

Sample Policy Statement and School Form

SAMPLE POLICY STATEMENT ON FAMILIES AND THE SCHOOL

The Open School understands the essential role of families in the community of our school, and the community at large. In today's world, families come in many wonderfully diverse forms. We welcome all of our families: single-parent families, two-parent families of both the same and opposite sex, extended families, parents who live with their children, and those who do not. Each of you can contribute to our school and significantly enhance your child's school experience in the process.

We want to help you find a comfortable way to share information with us about how your family is organized (including accurate names, addresses, and phone numbers), significant issues in your family's life, and any obstacles you might feel to fully joining our community. Most frequently this information sharing happens between parents and teachers at parent–teacher conferences, but you might find that a different format works better for you. Please know that we welcome any kind of communication with you, in whatever form is most comfortable. We encourage you to attend events in our school such as the curriculum nights, special events, potlucks, plays, and class trips. We also hope you will become actively involved in the PTA and serve on joint parent/staff committees.

—Cecilia Jones, Principal, The Open School

EARLY CHILDHOOD SAMPLE APPLICATION/SCHOOL INFO FORM: FAMILY RELATED EXCERPTS

The Open School
Anywhere, U.S.A.
Main Office: (123) 456-7890
After-School Program: x 1011

Child's Name _____ Sibling _____ Age _____

Date of Bitrh _____ Sibling _____ Age _____

Child's Home Address/es _____ Sibling _____ Age _____

_____

Parent or Guardian _____ Parent or Guardian _____

Home Address _____ Home Address _____

_____

Home Phone _____ Home Phone _____

Work Phone _____ Work Phone _____

Occupation _____ Occupation _____

186

Are there any other members of your household? If so, what is their relationship to your child?

Languages spoken in the home? _____

How will your child get to and from school most days?: *Walk?* *Bus?* *Picked Up?*

Please list people who may be picking your child up:

Name _____ Relationship _____ Phone _____

Name _____ Relationship _____ Phone _____

Name _____ Relationship _____ Phone _____

Emergency number in case these people cannot be reached _____

Child's Health Care Provider/Clinic _____ Phone _____

Is there anything else you would like to tell us about your child/family that you think would help us in working with you and your family?

_____

_____

187

References

American Psychiatric Association. (1980). *Diagnostic and statistical manual of mental disorders* (3rd ed.). Washington, DC: Author.

Arendell, T. (Ed.). (1997). *Contemporary parenting: Challenges and issues.* Thousand Oaks, CA: Sage.

Arnup, K. (Ed.). (1995). *Lesbian parenting: Living with pride and prejudice.* Charlottown, Canada: Gynergy Books.

A team of individuals; almost 10, N.J. quintuplets vie to star on own. (1993, July 26). *The New York Times*, pp. B1, B4.

Badgett, L. (1994, October). *Civil rights and civilized research: Constructing a sexual orientation policy based on the evidence.* Paper presented at the meeting of the Association for Public Policy Analysis and Management Research, Chicago.

Badgett, L. (1997). Beyond biased samples: Challenging the myths on the economic status of lesbians and gay men. In A. Gluckman & B. Reed (Eds.), *Homo Economics: Capitalism, community and lesbian and gay life* (pp. 65–71). New York: Routledge.

Bailey, M. J., Bobrow, D., Wolfe, M., & Mikach, S. (1995). Sexual orientation of adult sons of gay fathers. *Developmental Psychology, 31*(1), 124–129.

Balaban, N. (1985). *Starting school: From separation to independence.* New York: Teachers College Press.

Banks, J. A. (1993). Multicultural education: Historical development, dimensions and practice. *Review of Research in Education, 19*, 3–50.

Barbanel, J. (1993, January 8). Poll finds support for broad teaching on social agenda. *The New York Times*, p. B3.

Barret, R. L., & Robinson, B. E. (1990). *Gay fathers.* Lexington, MA: Lexington Books.

Bedard, P. (1997, August 21). Provincetown preschoolers to learn ABC's of being gay. *The Washington Times*, p. A1.

Bell, A., Weinberg, M., & Hammersmith, S. (1981). *Sexual preference.* Bloomington: Indiana University Press.

Bem, D. J. (1996). Exotic becomes erotic: A developmental theory of sexual orientation. *Psychological Review, 103*(2), 320–335.

Bem, S. (1983). Gender schema theory and its implications for child development: Raising gender-aschematic children in a gender-schematic society. *Signs: Journal of Women and Culture, 8*(41), 598–616.

Bem, S. (1989). Genital knowledge and gender constancy in preschool children. *Child Development, 60,* 649–662.

Bem, S. (1993). *The lenses of gender: Transforming the debate on sexual inequality.* New Haven, CT: Yale University Press.

Benjamin, J. (1991). *Bonds of love: Psychoanalysis, feminism and the problem of domination.* New York: Pantheon Books.

Benkov, L. (1994). *Gay and lesbian parents: Revolution in the family.* New York: Crown Press.

Bernstein, A. C. (1988). Unraveling the tangles: Children's understanding of stepfamily kinship. In W. R. Beer (Ed.), *Relative strangers: Studies of stepfamily processes* (pp. 83–111). Totowa, NJ: Rowman and Littlefield.

Bernstein, A. C. (1994). *Flight of the stork: What children think (and when) about sex and family building.* Indianapolis, IN: Perspectives Press.

Betts, W. E. (1998). *Gay and lesbian characters and themes in children's books: An annotated bibliography* [On-line]. Available www.armory.com/~web/gay-books.html

Blankenhorn, D. (1995). *Fatherless America: Confronting our most urgent social problem.* New York: Basic Books.

Blumenfeld, W. J., & Raymond, D. (1988). *Looking at gay and lesbian life.* Boston: Beacon Press.

Bolt, G. (1997). Sexist and heterosexist responses to gender bending. In J. Tobin (Ed.), *Making a place for pleasure in early childhood education* (pp. 188–213). New Haven, CT: Yale University Press.

Borke, H. (1975). Piaget's mountain revisited: Changes in the egocentric landscape. *Developmental Psychology, 11,* 240–243.

Bosche, S. (1983). *Jenny lives with Eric and Martin.* London: Gay Men's Press.

Boswell, J. (1980). *Christianity, social tolerance, and homosexuality: Gay people in western Europe from the beginning of the Christian era to the fourteenth century.* Chicago: University of Chicago Press.

Bowman, B., & Stott, F. (1994). Understanding development in a cultural context: The challenge for teachers. In B. L. Mallory & R. S. New (Eds.), *Diversity and developmentally appropriate practices* (pp. 119–133). New York: Teachers College Press.

Bradley, S. J., & Zucker, K. J. (1997). Gender identity disorder: A review of the past 10 years. *Journal of the American Academy of Child and Adolescent Psychiatry, 36*(7), 872–880.

Brazelton, T. B. (1973). Neonatal behavioral assessment scale. *Clinics in Developmental Medicine, 50.* Spastics International Medical Publications. London: Heinemann Medical Books.

Bredekamp, S. (1987). *Developmentally appropriate practice in early childhood programs serving children from birth through age 8.* Washington, DC: National Association for the Education of Young Children.

Bredekamp, S., & Copple, C. (1997). *Developmentally appropriate practice in early childhood programs serving children from birth through age 8* (2nd ed.). Washington, DC: National Association for the Education of Young Children.

Brickley, M., Gelnaw, A., Marsh, H., & Ryan, D. (1998). *Opening doors: Lesbian and gay parents in the schools.* San Diego, CA: Gay and Lesbian Parents Coalition International, Educational Advisory Committee.

Brodzinsky, D. M., Schechter, D., & Brodzinsky, A. B. (1986). Children's knowledge of adoption: Developmental changes and implications for development. In R. D. Ashmore & D. M. Brodzinsky (Eds.), *Thinking about the family: View of parents and children* (pp. 205–232). Hillsdale, NJ: Erlbaum.

Bruner, J. S. (1960). *The process of education.* Cambridge, MA: Harvard University Press.

Bruner, J. S. (1992, December). *Six principles for organizing research.* Edmund Gordon/Jerome Bruner Seminar, Bank Street College of Education, New York.

Butler, J. (1990). *Gender trouble.* New York: Routledge.

Butler, J. (1995). Melancholy gender-refused identification. *Psychoanalytic Dialogues, 5*(2), 165–180.

Cain, R. (1991). Disclosure and secrecy among gay men in the United States and Canada: A shift in views. *Journal of the History of Sexuality, 2*(1), 25–45.

Camara, K. A. (1979). *Children's construction of social knowledge: Concepts of family and the experience of parental divorce* (Doctoral dissertation, Stanford University). (University Microfilms No. 80-01884)

Carey, W. B., & McDevitt, S. C. (1995). *Coping with children's temperament: A guide for professionals.* New York: Basic.

Carlson, D. (1997). Gayness, multicultural education and community. In M. Seller & L. Weis (Eds.), *Beyond black and white: New faces and voices in U.S. schools* (pp. 233–255). Albany: State University of New York Press.

Case, R. (1991). *The mind's staircase: Exploring the conceptual underpinnings of children's thought and knowledge.* Hillsdale, NJ: Erlbaum.

Casper, V. (1996, January). Making familiar unfamiliar and unfamiliar familiar. *Zero to Three, 16*(3), 14–20.

Casper, V. (1998, December/January). Letter to the editor. *Zero to Three, 18*(3), 38–39.

Casper, V., Cuffaro, H., Schultz, S., Silin, J., & Wickens, E. (1996, Summer). Toward a most thorough understanding of the world: Sexual orientation in early childhood education. *Harvard Educational Review, 66*(2), 271–293.

Casper, V., & Schultz, S. (1994). Lesbian and gay male parents meet educators: Initiating conversations. In R. C. Savin-Williams & K. M. Cohen (Eds.), *Understanding diversity among lesbians, gay males, and bisexuals: Clinical developmental and social issues* (pp. 305–330). Fort Worth, TX: Harcourt Brace.

Casper, V., Schultz, S., & Wickens, E. (1992, Fall). Breaking the silences: Lesbian and gay parents and the schools. *Teachers College Record, 94*(1).

Center Kids. (1992, January). *Empowering our children: How do we prepare our kids to live and cope in the wider world?* Symposium conducted by Center Kids, Inc. at the Lesbian and Gay Community Center, New York.

Chamberlain et al. v. *Surrey School District #36.* (1998). (Vancouver Registry, British Columbia, Canada), aff'd, No. A972046.

Chan, R. W., Raboy, B., & Patterson, C. J. (1998). Psychosocial adjustment among children conceived via donor insemination by lesbian and heterosexual mothers. *Child Development, 69*(2), 443–457.

Chapman, S. (1992). *The power of children's literature: A rationale for using books on gay- and lesbian-headed families and an annotated bibliography.* Unpublished master's thesis, Bank Street College of Education, New York.

Chasnoff, D., & Cohen, H. S. (Producers & Directors). (1996). *It's elementary: Talking about gay issues in schools* [Film/video]. (Available from Women's Educational Media, 2180 Bryant Street, Suite 203, San Francisco, California, 94110)

Chodorow, N. J. (1992). Heterosexuality as a compromise formation. *Psychoanalysis and Contemporary Thought, 15*(3), 267–304.

Clark, K. B. (1970). *Prejudice and your child* (2nd ed.). Boston: Beacon Press.

Clausen, J. (1999). *Apples and oranges: My journey through sexual identity.* New York: Houghton-Mifflin.

Clay, J. (1990). Working with lesbian and gay parents and their children. *Young Children, 45,* 31–35.

Coates, S. (1997). Is it time to jettison the concept of developmental lines? Commentary on deMarneffe's paper "bodies and words." *Gender and Psychoanalysis, 2*(1), 35–53.

Coates, S., Friedman, R., & Wolfe, S. (1991). The etiology of boyhood gender identity disorder: A model for integrating temperament, development, and psychodynamics. *Psychoanalytic Dialogues, 1,* 481–523.

Cohen, K. M., & Savin-Williams, R. C. (1996). Developmental perspectives on coming out to self and others. In R. C. Savin-Williams & K. M. Cohen (Eds.), *The lives of lesbians, gays, and bisexuals: Children to adults* (pp. 305–330). Fort Worth, TX: Harcourt Brace.

Corbett, S. (1993). A complicated bias. *Young Children, 48,* 29–31.

Counts, G. S. (1978). *Dare the school build a new social order?* Carbondale: University of Southern Illinois Press. (Original work published 1932)

Cuffaro, H. K. (1991). A view of materials as the texts of the early childhood curriculum. In B. Spodek & O. N. Saracho (Eds.), *Issues in early childhood curriculum* (pp. 64–85). New York: Teachers College Press.

Cuffaro, H. K. (1995). *Experimenting with the world: John Dewey and the early childhood classroom.* New York: Teachers College Press.

D'Augelli, A., & Patterson, C. (Eds.). (1995). *Lesbian, gay and bisexual identities over the lifespan: Psychological perspectives.* New York: Oxford University Press.

Deaner, C. (1997). The myth of the male role model. In J. Wells (Ed.), *Lesbians raising sons* (pp. 65–68). Los Angeles: Alyson Books.

DeCecco, J. P., & Elia, J. P. (Eds.). (1993). *If you seduce a straight person, can you make them gay? Issues in biological essentialism versus social constructionism in gay and lesbian identities.* New York: Harrington Park Press.

Delpit, L. (1988). The silenced dialogue: Power and pedagogy in educating other people's children. *Harvard Educational Review, 38*(3), 280–298.

Delpit, L. (1995). *Other people's children.* New York: New Press.

deMarneffe, D. (1997). Bodies and words: A study of young children's genital and gender knowledge. *Gender and Psychoanalysis, 2*(1), 3–33.

de Paola, T. (1979). *Oliver Button is a sissy.* New York: Harcourt Brace Jovanovich.

Derman-Sparks, L. (1989). *Anti-bias curriculum: Tools for empowering young children.* Washington DC: National Association for the Education of Young Children.

Dewey, J. T. (1938). *Experience and education.* New York: Macmillan.

Dewey, J. T. (1956). *The school and society.* Chicago: University of Chicago Press. (Original work published 1900)

Dimen, M. (1995). The third step: Freud, the feminists, and postmodernism. *The American Journal of Psychoanalysis, 55*(4), 303–319.

Donaldson, M. (1978). *Children's minds.* New York: Norton.

Egan, T. (1992, August 16). Oregon measure asks state to repress homosexuality. *The New York Times,* pp. A1, A34.

Elkind, D. (1981). *The hurried child: Growing up too fast, too soon.* Reading, MA: Addison-Wesley.

Emde, R. N. (1994). Individuality, context and the search for meaning. *Child Development, 65*(3), 719–737.

Erikson, E. (1950). *Childhood and society.* New York: Norton.

Ettelbrick, P. (1993). Since when is marriage a path to liberation? In W. B. Rubenstein (Ed.), *Lesbians, gay men and the law* (pp. 401–405). New York: New Press.

Fagot, B., & Leinbach, M. D. (1987). Socialization of sex role within the family. In D. B. Carter (Ed.), *Current conceptions of sex roles and sex typing* (pp. 89–99). New York: Praeger.

Fernandez, J. (1993). *Tales out of school: Joseph Fernandez's crusade to rescue American education.* Boston: Little, Brown.

Flaks, D. K., Ficher, I., Masterpasqua, F., & Joseph, G. (1995). Lesbians choosing motherhood: A comparative study of lesbian and heterosexual parents and their children. *Developmental Psychology, 31*(1), 105–114.

Flavell, J. H. (1985). *Cognitive development* (2nd ed.). Englewood Cliffs, NJ: Prentice-Hall.

Freud, S. (1965). *Three essays on the theory of sexuality.* New York: Avon Books. (Original work published 1905)

Friere, P. (1986). *Pedagogy of the oppressed* (M. B. Ramos, Trans.). New York: Seabury Press.

Gabarino, T. (1992). *Children in danger.* San Francisco: Jossey-Bass.

Galst, L. (1998, June 2). Blood breaks a family. *Village Voice,* pp. 43–44, 47.

Gash, H., & Morgan, M. (1993). School-based modifications of children's gender-related beliefs. *Journal of Applied Developmental Psychology, 14,* 277–287.

Geertz, C. (1973). *The interpretation of culture.* New York: Basic Books.

Gilby, R. H., & Pederson, D. R. (1982). The development of the child's concept of the family. *Canadian Journal of Behavioral Science, 14*(2), 110–121.

Goffman, E. (1963). *Stigma: Notes on the management of a spoiled identity.* New York: Touchstone Press.

Goldberg, C. (1998, May 31). Acceptance of gay men and lesbians is growing, study says. *The New York Times*, p. 21, national section.

Goldenson, R. M. (1984). *Longman dictionary of psychology and psychiatry*. New York: Longman.

Goldner, V. (1991). Toward a critical relational theory of gender. *Psychoanalytic Dialogues, 1*, 249–272.

Goldstick, P. (1993). *Children of the rainbow: The controversy and ideas for implementing an anti-bias curriculum*. Unpublished masters thesis, Bank Street College of Education, New York.

Golombok, S., Spencer, A., & Rutter, M. (1983). Children in lesbian and single-parent households: Psychosexual and psychiatric appraisal. *Journal of Psychology and Psychiatry, 24*, 551–572.

Goode, E. (1998, December 12). On gay issues, psychoanalysis treats itself. *The New York Times*, pp. B7, B16.

Gottfried, A. E., & Gottfried, A. W. (Eds.). (1994). *Redefining families: Implications for children's development*. New York: Plenum Press.

Green, R. (1987). *The "sissy-boy syndrome" and the development of homosexuality*. New Haven, CT: Yale University Press.

Greene, B. (Ed.). (1997). *Ethnic and cultural diversity among lesbians and gay men: Psychological perspectives on lesbian and gay issues* (Vol. 3). Thousand Oaks, CA: Sage.

Greene, M. (1995). *Releasing the imagination: Essays on education, the arts and social change*. San Francisco: Jossey-Bass.

Guthrie, W. (1965). *Born to win* (R. Shelton, Ed.). New York: Macmillan.

Hamer, D. (1998). *Living with our genes: Why they matter more than you think*. New York: Doubleday.

Harris, A. (1991). Gender as contradiction. *Psychoanalytic Dialogues, 1*, 197–224.

Hart, L. S., & Goldin-Meadow, S. (1984). The child as non-egocentric art critic. *Child Development, 55*, 2122–2129.

Heath, S. B. (1983). *Ways with words*. Cambridge: Cambridge University Press.

Herdt, G. (1992). *Gay culture in America*. Boston: Beacon Press.

Herdt, G. (Ed.). (1996). *Third sex, third gender: Beyond sexual dimorphism in culture and history*. New York: Zone Books.

Herdt, G., & Boxer, A. (1993). *Children of horizons: How gay and lesbian teens are leading a new way out of the closet* (2nd ed.). Boston: Beacon Press.

Herek, G. (1984). Beyond "homophobia": A social psychological perspective on attitudes toward lesbians and gay men. *Journal of Homosexuality, 10*(1/2), 1–18.

Hewlett, B. S. (1991). *Intimate fathers: The nature and context of Aka pygmy paternal infant care*. Ann Arbor: University of Michigan Press.

Hewlett, S. A., & West, C. (1998). *The war against parents: What we can do for America's beleaguered moms and dads*. New York: Houghton Mifflin.

Hirose, S. (1997). *From the voices of lesbian parents: What daycares can do to support children of lesbians*. Unpublished manuscript. Bank Street College of Education Minigrant Project.

Hoeffer, B. (1981). Children's acquisition of sex-role behavior in lesbian-mother families. *American Journal of Orthopsychiatry, 51*(31), 536–543.

Honig, A. (1983, September). Sex role socialization in early childhood. *Young Children, 38,* 57–70.

Hornstein, F. (1996). *The experiences of lesbian and gay parents with children in school.* Unpublished manuscript. School of Social Welfare, University of California at Berkeley.

Hwang, C. P. (1987). The changing role of Swedish fathers. In M. Lamb (Ed.), *The father's role: Cross-cultural perspectives* (pp. 115–138). Hillsdale, NJ: Erlbaum.

Intons-Peterson, M. J. (1988). *Children's conception of gender.* Norwood, NJ: Ablex.

Jackson, P. (1992). *Untaught lessons.* New York: Teachers College Press.

Jacobs, S. (1992, September 28). More gay men hearing the call of fatherhood. *Boston Globe,* pp. 1, 5.

John-Steiner, V. (1998, March 16). Faculty Seminar on Collaborative Processes, Bank Street College of Education.

Karen, R. (1994). *Becoming attached: Unfolding the mystery of the infant–mother bond and its impact on later life.* New York: Time Warner.

Kessler, S. (1998). *Lessons from the intersexed.* New Brunswick, NJ: Rutgers University Press.

Kessler, S., & McKenna, W. (1977). *Gender: An ethnomethodological approach.* New York: Wiley Interscience.

Kirby, D. (1998, June 7). The second generation: The children are gay. So are their parents. What do they face? *The New York Times,* Section 14, pp. 1, 12–13.

Kirkpatrick, M., Smith, C., & Roy, R. (1981). Lesbian mothers and their children: A comparative study. *American Journal of Orthopsychiatry, 51*(3), 545–551.

Koerner, M. E., & Hulsebosch, P. (1996, November–December). Preparing teachers to work with children of gay and lesbian parents. *Journal of Teacher Education, 47*(5), 1–9.

Kohlberg, L. (1966). Cognitive-developmental analysis of children's sex-role concepts and attitudes. In E. E. Maccoby (Ed.), *The development of sex differences* (pp. 82–173). Stanford: Stanford University Press.

Kozol, J. (1995). *Amazing grace: The lives of children and the conscience of a nation.* New York: Crown.

Lamb, M. E. (1997). Fathers and child development: An introductory overview and guide. In M. E. Lamb (Ed.), *The role of the father in child development* (3rd ed.; pp. 1–18). New York: Wiley.

Lave, J., & Wenger, E. (1991). *Situated learning: Legitimate peripheral participation.* New York: Cambridge University Press.

Leavitt, R. (1994). *Power and emotion in infant-toddler day care.* Albany: State University of New York Press.

Lee, P., & Wolinsky, A. (1973). Male teachers of young children: A preliminary empirical study. *Young Children, 28,* 342–352.

Lesbian parents' school visit sparks a clash of culture in Boise suburb. (1993, February 10). *Education Week,* pp. 1, 17–18.

LeVine, R. A. (1974). Parental goals: A cross-cultural view. *Teachers College Record*, *76*(2), 226–239.

Lewin, E. (1993). *Lesbian mothers: Accounts of gender in American culture.* Ithaca, NY: Cornell University Press.

Lewin, E. (1998). *Recognizing ourselves: Ceremonies of lesbian and gay commitment.* New York: Columbia University Press.

Lewin, E., & Leap, W. L. (Eds.). (1996). *Out in the field: Reflections of gay anthropologists.* Urbana: University of Illinois Press.

Lieberman, A. F. (1993). *The emotional life of the toddler.* New York: Free Press.

Lightfoot, S. L. (1978). *Worlds apart: Relationships between families and schools.* New York: Basic Books.

Lipkin, A. (in press). *Homosexuality and schools: Staff curriculum and student development.* Boulder, CO: Westview Press.

Lorde, A. (1984). Man child: A black lesbian feminist's response. In *Sister outsider* (pp. 72–80). Freedom, CA: Crossing Press.

Lubeck, S. (1985). *Sandbox society: Early education in black and white America: A comparative ethnography.* London: Falmer Press.

Lubeck, S. (1994). The politics of developmentally appropriate practice. In B. Mallory & R. New (Eds.), *Diversity and developmentally appropriate practice: Challenges for early childhood education* (pp. 17–43). New York: Teachers College Press.

Lukenbill, G. (1995). *Untold millions.* New York: Harper Business.

Main, M. (1991). Metacognitive knowledge, metacognitive monitoring, and singular (coherent) vs. multiple (incoherent) models of attachment: Findings and directions for future research. In C. M. Parkes, J. Stevenson-Hinde, & P. Marris (Eds.), *Attachment across the life cycle* (pp. 127–159). London: Routledge.

Mallory, B., & New, R. (1994). *Diversity and developmentally appropriate practice: Challenges for early childhood education.* New York: Teachers College Press.

Martin, A. (1993). *Lesbian and gay parenting handbook.* New York: HarperCollins.

Mazur, E. (1993). Developmental differences in children's understanding of marriage, divorce and remarriage. *Journal of Applied Developmental Psychology*, *14*(2), 191–212.

McCarthy, C. (1988). Rethinking liberal and radical perspectives on racial inequality in schooling: Making the case for synchrony. *Harvard Educational Review*, *58*, 265–279.

McCloskey, R. (1948). *Make way for ducklings.* New York: Viking Press.

McGoldrick, M. (1989a). The joining of families through marriage: The new couple. In B. Carter & M. McGoldrick (Eds.), *The changing family life cycle: A framework for family therapy* (2nd ed.; pp. 209–233). New York: Gardner Press.

McGoldrick, M. (1989b). Ethnicity and the family life cycle: A framework for family therapy. In B. Carter & M. McGoldrick (Eds.), *The changing family life cycle: A framework for family therapy* (2nd ed.; pp. 69–90). New York: Gardner Press.

McKenna, W., & Kessler, S. (1997, November). *Gender after 20 years: Social construction and social justice.* Invited paper presented at conference in honor of Eva Lundgren, Uppsala, Sweden.

Meers, E. M. (1998, April 14). The model boy scout. *The Advocate*, pp. 46, 50, 51.

Melmed, M. (1997, July). Parents speak. Zero to Three's findings from research on parents' views of early childhood development. *Young Children*, pp. 46–49.

Michaels, G. Y., & Goldberg, A. (1988). *Transition to parenthood: Current theory and research*. Cambridge: Cambridge University Press.

Miller, P. (1982). *Amy, Wendy and Beth: Learning language in south Baltimore*. Austin TX: University of Texas Press.

Minow, M. (1991). *Making all the difference*. Cambridge, MA: Harvard University Press.

Minow, M. (1997). *Not only for myself: Identity, politics and the law*. New York: New Press.

Mischel, W. (1966). A social-learning view of sex differences in behavior. In E. E. Maccoby (Ed.), *The development of sex differences* (pp. 56–81). Stanford: Stanford University Press.

Mitchell, V. (1998). The birds, the bees . . . and the sperm banks: How lesbian mothers talk with their children about sex and reproduction. *American Journal of Orthopsychiatry, 68*(3), 400–409.

Moore, N. V. (1977). *Cognitive level, intactness of family, and sex in relation to the child's development of the concept of family*. Dissertation Abstracts International, 37, 44117B–4118B. University Microfilms No. 77-3960.

Morin, S. F. (1977). Heterosexual bias in psychological research on lesbianism and male homosexuality. *American Psychologist, 32*, 629–637.

Myers, S. L. (1992, December 2). Queens school board suspended in fight on gay-life curriculum. *The New York Times*, pp. A1, B4.

Nabozyne v. *Podlesny*, 92 F.3rd 446 (7th Cir. 1996).

National Association for the Education of Young Children. (1993). *Briefing paper on children of gay and lesbian parents: Governing Board of the National Association for the Education of Young Children*. Washington, DC: Author.

Nelson, K. (1981). Social cognition in a script framework. In J. H. Flavell & L. Ross (Eds.), *Social cognitive development* (pp. 97–118). Cambridge, MA: Cambridge University Press.

Nelson, K. (1986). *Event knowledge: Structure and function in development*. Hillsdale, NJ: Erlbaum.

Newman, J. L., Roberts, L. R., & Syre, C. R. (1993). Concepts of family among children and adolescents: Effect of cognitive level, gender and family structure. *Developmental Psychology, 29*(6), 951–962.

Newman, L. (1993). *Saturday is Pattyday*. Norwich, VT: New Victoria Press.

Newman, L., & Souza, D. (1989). *Heather has two mommies*. Northampton, MA: In Other Words Press.

New York City Board of Education. (1991). *Children of the rainbow: First grade*. New York: Board of Education of the City of New York.

New York City Board of Education. (1992). *Children of the rainbow: First grade* (2nd ed.). New York: Author.

Novick, K. (1986). Talking with toddlers. *Psychoanalytic Study of the Child, 41*, 277–286.

Paley, V. (1984). *Boys and girls: Superheroes in the dollhouse.* Chicago: University of Chicago Press.

Patterson, C. J. (1992). Children of lesbian and gay parents. *Child Development, 63*(5), 1025–1042.

Patterson, C. J. (1995a). Lesbian mothers, gay fathers, and their children. In A. R. D'Augelli & C. J. Patterson (Eds.), *Lesbian, gay and bisexual identities over the lifespan* (pp. 262–290). New York: Oxford University Press.

Patterson, C. J. (1995b). Families of the lesbian baby boom: Parents' division of labor and children's adjustment. *Developmental Psychology, 31*(1), 115–123.

Patterson, C. J., & Chan, R. W. (1997). Gay fathers. In M. E. Lamb (Ed.), *The role of the father in child development* (3rd ed.; pp. 245–260). New York: Wiley.

Patterson, C. J., Hurt, S., & Mason, C. D. (1998). Families of the lesbian baby boom: Children's contact with grandparents and other adults. *American Journal of Orthopsychiatry, 68*(3), 390–399.

Pederson, D. R., & Gilby, R. L. (1986). Children's concepts of the family. In R. Ashmore & D. Brodzinsky (Eds.), *Thinking about the family* (pp. 181–204). Hillsdale, NJ: Erlbaum.

Penn, Schoen & Berland Associates. (1997). *Family issues: A report of the Human Rights Campaign.* Washington, DC: Human Rights Campaign Fund.

Piaget, J. (1928). *Judgment and reasoning in the child.* London: Routledge & Kegan Paul. (Original published 1965)

Piaget, J., & Inhelder, B. (1969). *The psychology of the child.* New York: Basic Books.

Pies, C. (1985). *Considering parenthood: A workbook for lesbians.* San Francisco: Spinsters.

Pollack, S., & Vaughn, J. (Eds.). (1987). *Politics of the heart: A lesbian parenting anthology.* Ithaca, NY: Firebrand Books.

Popenoe, D. (1996). *Life without father.* New York: Martin Pressler Press.

Powell, J. A., Wilcher, B. J., Wedemeyer, N. V., & Claypool, P. L. (1981). The young child's developing concept of family. *Home Economics Research Journal, 10*(22), 137–149.

Pruett, K. D. (1992). Latency development in children of primary nurturing fathers: Eight-year follow-up. *Psychoanalytic Study of the Child, 47*, 85–101.

Pruett, K. (1997). How men and children affect each other's development. *Zero to Three, 18*(1), 3–11.

Pruett, K. (1998, December/January). Letter to the editor. *Zero to Three, 18*(3), 38–39.

Rafkin, L. (Ed.). (1990). *Different mothers: Sons and daughters of lesbians talk about their lives.* Pittsburgh: Cleis Press.

Ravitch, D. (1992). Multiculturalism: E pluribus plures. In P. Berman (Ed.), *Debating P. C.: The controversy over political correctness on college campuses.* New York: Dell.

Reissman, C. K. (1987). When gender is not enough. *Gender and Society, 1*(2), 172–207.

Riddle, D. I. (1978). Relating to children: Gays as role models. *Journal of Social Issues, 34*(3), 38–58.

Rogoff, B. (1990). *Apprenticeship in thinking.* New York: Oxford University Press.

Roopnarine, J. P., Ahmenduzzaman, M., Hossain, Z., & Riegraf, N. B. (1992). Parent-infant rough play: It's cultural specificity. *Early Education and Development, 4*, 298–311.

Rosaldo, R. (1989). *Culture and truth: The remaking of social analysis.* Boston: Beacon Press.

Roscoe, W. (1994). How to become a berdache: Toward a unified analysis of gender diversity. In G. Herdt (Ed.), *Third sex, third gender: Beyond sexual dimorphism in culture and history* (pp. 329–372). New York: Zone Books.

Rotello, G. (1997). *Sexual ecology: AIDS and the destiny of gay men.* New York: Dutton.

Ryan, C., & Futterman, D. (1998). *Lesbian and gay youth: Care and counseling.* New York: Columbia University Press.

Savin-Williams, R. C., & Cohen, K. M. (Eds.). (1996). *The lives of lesbians, gays, and bisexuals: Children to adults.* Fort Worth, TX: Harcourt Brace.

Scarr, S. (1992). Developmental theories for the 1990's: Development and individual differences. *Child Development, 63*, 1–19.

Schaffer, H. R. (1990). Do children need a parent of each sex? In *Making decisions about children: Psychological questions and answers.* Cambridge MA: Basil Blackwell.

Schmalz, J. (1993, March 5). Poll finds an even split on homosexuality's cause. *The New York Times,* p. 11.

Schulenberg, J. (1985). *Gay parenting: A complete guide.* New York: Anchor Press.

Schultz, S. B. (1988). *The hidden curriculum: Finding mechanisms of control and resistance in the preschool.* Unpublished doctoral dissertation, Teachers College, New York.

Schultz, S. B. (1993, October). *Re-conceptualizing gender in early childhood curriculum.* Paper presented at the third annual Re-Conceptualizing Early Childhood Conference, Ann Arbor, MI.

Schultz, S. B. (1994). Review of *Untaught Lessons* by Philip W. Jackson. *Teachers College Record, 96*(1), 129–134.

Schwartz, A. (1998). *Sexual subjects: Lesbians, gender, and psychoanalysis.* New York: Routledge.

Scradnick, P. (1998). A home away from home. Discussion at the annual conference at Basic Trust Infant-Toddler Center, New York.

Sears, J. (1991). *Growing up in the South: Race, gender and journeys of the spirit.* New York: Hayworth Press.

Sears, J. (1992). Educators, homosexuality, and homosexual students: Are personal feelings related to professional beliefs? In K. M. Harbeck (Ed.), *Coming out of the classroom closet: Gay and lesbian students, teachers and curricula* (pp. 29–79). New York: Hayworth Press.

Sears, R. R., Rau, L., & Alpert, R. (1965). *Identification and child rearing.* Stanford: Stanford University Press.

Sedgwick, E. K. (1993). How to bring your kids up gay. In M. Warner (Ed.), *Fear of a queer planet: Queer politics and social theory* (pp. 69–81). Minneapolis: University of Minnesota Press.

Seligman, S., & Shanok, R. S. (1995). Subjectivity, complexity and the social world: Erikson's identity concept and contemporary relational theories. *Psychoanalytic Dialogues, 5*(4), 537–565.

Selman, R. L. (1980). *The growth of interpersonal understanding.* New York: Academic Press.

Shanok, R. S. (1991). Parenthood: A process marking identity and intimacy capacities. *Zero to Three, 11*(2), 1–9.

Shapiro, E., & Nager, N. (1998). The developmental-interaction approach to education: Retrospect and prospect. *Bank Street Occasional Papers Series #2.* New York: Bank Street College of Education.

Shatz, M., & Gelman, R. (1973). The development of communication skills: Modifications in the speech of young children as a function of listener. *Monographs of the Society for Research in Child Development, 38*(5, Serial No. 152).

Siegler, R. S. (1991). *Children's thinking* (2nd ed.). Englewood Cliffs, NJ: Prentice-Hall.

Silin, J. (1995). *Sex, death and the education of children: Our passion for ignorance in the age of AIDS.* New York: Teachers College Press.

Silverstein, L., & Auerbach, C. (1997, October/November). Letter to the editor. *Zero to Three, 18*(2), 40, 41.

Singer, B., & Descamps, D. (Eds.). (1994). *Gay and lesbian stats.* New York: New Press.

Slater, P. (1961). Toward a dualistic theory of gender identification. *Merrill Palmer Quarterly, 7*(2), 113–116.

Slater, S., & Mencher, J. (1991). The lesbian family life cycle: A contextual approach. *American Journal of Orthopsychiatry, 61*(3), 372–382.

Sleeter, C. E. (1996). *Multicultural education as social activism.* Albany: State University of New York Press.

Smith, D. (1998a, January 17). "Queer theory" is entering the literary mainstream. *The New York Times,* pp. B9, B11.

Smith, D. (1998b, June 2). One false note in a musician's life. *The New York Times,* pp. E1, 4.

Spencer, M. B., & Markstrom-Adams, C. (1990). Identity processes among racial and ethnic minority children in America. *Child Development, 61*(2), 290–310.

Sroufe, L. A., & Fleeson, J. (1988). The coherence of family relationships. In R. A. Hinde & J. Stevenson-Hinde (Eds.), *Relationships within families: Mutual influences* (pp. 22–27). Oxford: Oxford University Press.

Steckel, A. (1985). *Separation-individuation in children of lesbian and heterosexual couples.* Unpublished doctoral dissertation, Wright Institute, Berkeley.

Stern, D. (1985). *The interpersonal world of the infant.* New York: Basic Books.

Stoddard, T. (1993). Why gay people should seek the right to marry. In W. B. Rubenstein (Ed.), *Lesbians, gay men and the law* (pp. 398–401). New York: New Press.

Sullivan, J. (1997, August 22). Provincetown curriculum aimed at gay, racial bias. *Boston Herald,* pp. 1, 20.

Tasker, F. L., & Golombok, S. (1997). *Growing up in a lesbian family: Effects on child development.* New York: Guilford Press.

Thomas, A., & Chess, S. (1977). *Temperament and development.* New York: Brunner/ Mazel.

Thorne, B. (1993). *Gender play: Girls and boys in school.* New Brunswick, NJ: Rutgers University Press.

Tobin, J. (1997). (Ed.). *Making a place for pleasure in early childhood education.* New Haven, CT: Yale University Press.

Troiden, R. R. (1989). The formation of homosexual identities. *Journal of Homosexuality, 17,* 43–73.

Tronick, E., Morelli, G., & Ivey, P. (1992). The Efe' forager infant and toddler's pattern of social relationships: Multiple and simultaneous. *Developmental Psychology, 28*(4), 568–577.

Turiel, E., & Davidson, P. (1986). Heterogeneity, inconsistency, and asynchrony in the development of cognitive structures. In I. Levin (Ed.), *Stage and structure: Reopening the debate* (pp. 106–143). Norwood, NJ: Ablex.

Vaid, U. (1995). *Virtual equality: The mainstreaming of gay and lesbian liberation.* New York: Anchor Books.

Valentine, J. (1992). *The daddy machine.* Boston: Alyson Press.

Vygotsky, L. S. (1962). *Thought and language.* Cambridge, MA: MIT Press. (Original work published 1934)

Vygotsky, L. S. (1978a). Interaction between learning and development. In M. Cole, V. John-Steiner, S. Scribner, & E. Souberman (Eds.), *Mind in society: The development of higher psychological processes* (pp. 79–91). Cambridge, MA: Harvard University Press. (Original work published 1930–35)

Vygotsky, L. S. (1978b). The role of play in development. In M. Cole, V. John-Steiner, S. Scribner, & E. Souberman (Eds.), *Mind in society: The development of higher psychological processes* (pp. 92–104). Cambridge, MA: Harvard University Press.

Watson, M. W., & Amgott-Kwan, T. (1984). Development of family-role concepts in school-age children. *Developmental Psychology, 20*(5), 953–959.

Wedemeyer, N. V., Bickhard, M. H., & Cooper, R. G. (1989). The development of structural complexity in the child's concept of family: The effect of cognitive stage, sex and intactness of family. *Journal of Genetic Psychology, 150,* 341–357.

Werner, E. E., & Smith, R. S. (1992). *Overcoming the odds: High risk children from birth to adulthood.* Ithaca, NY: Cornell University Press.

Weston, K. (1991). *Families we choose: Lesbian and gay kinship.* New York: Columbia University Press.

Wickens, E. (1993). Penny's question: "I will have a child in my class with two moms—What do you know about this?" *Young Children, 48*(3), 25–28.

Wickens, E., Schultz, S., Clay, J., & Stafford, P. (1995, December). *How to implement a family curriculum inclusive of lesbian and gay parents when lesbian- and gay-headed families are not in the classroom.* Paper presented at the annual meeting of the National Association for the Education of Young Children, Washington, DC.

Wilcox, K. (1982). Ethnography as a methodology and its application to the study of schooling: A review. In G. Spindler (Ed.), *Doing the ethnography of schooling: Educational anthropology and action* (pp. 456–488). New York: Rinehart & Winston.

Willen, L. (1992, January 26). New version drops mention of gays, AIDS. *New York Newsday*, p. 3.

Williams, L. (1996). Does practice lead theory? Teachers' constructs about teaching: Bottom-up perspectives. In J. A. Chafel & S. Reifel (Eds.), *Advances in early education and day care: Vol 8. Theory and practice in early childhood teaching* (pp. 153–184). Greenwich, CT: JAI Press.

Williams, W. (1986). *The spirit and the flesh: Sexual diversity in American Indian culture*. Boston: Beacon Press.

Wilson, A. (1996). How we find ourselves: Identity development and two-spirit people. *Harvard Educational Review, 62*(2), 303–317.

Wise-Brown, M. (1942). *The runaway bunny*. New York: Harper and Row.

Wolfe, A. (1998, February 8). The homosexual exception: A new study that suburban Americans are surprisingly tolerant—of everyone but gay men and lesbians. *The New York Times Magazine*, pp. 46, 47.

Zucker, K. J., & Green, R. (1993). Psychological and familial aspects of gender identity disorder. *Child and Adolescent Psychiatric Clinics of North America, 2*, 513–542.

Index

About the Authors

Virginia Casper is a developmental psychologist and educator. She has experience with typically developing young children and children with special needs in both research and intervention settings. She received her doctorate from Yeshiva University in 1985 and was guest faculty in the psychology department at Sarah Lawrence College. Since 1988, she has been on the graduate faculty at Bank Street College of Education, where she currently directs the Infant and Parent Development and Early Intervention Program. She is also on the faculty of the Jewish Board of Family and Children's Services Institute for Clinical Studies of Infants, Toddlers and Parents. Dr. Casper has published in *Child Development, Harvard Educational Review, Teachers College Record,* and *Zero the Three*.

Steven Schultz (1953–1996) was a member of the graduate faculty at Bank Street College of Education where he taught child development and directed the Pre-Service Program in the Department of Teacher Education. He received his B.A. from Wheelock College and his doctorate from Teachers College. His work has been published in *Young Children, Teachers College Record,* and *Harvard Educational Review*. Steven worked for many years as a teacher of young children and had special interests in the hidden curriculum and issues of equity and power in education.